FILM
SECOND EDITION
BUSINESS

A HANDBOOK FOR FILM PRODUCERS

EDITED BY TOM JEFFREY
Based on the first edition by Damien Parer

GW00568996

AFTRS
Publications

Distributed in Australia and New Zealand
by Allen & Unwin

First published 1989
Second edition published 1995

© 1995 Australian Film Television & Radio School

Australian Film, Television and Radio School
PO Box 126, North Ryde, NSW 2113

Allen & Unwin Australia Pty Ltd
9 Atchison Street, St Leonards, NSW, Australia, 2065
University College London Press
Gower Street, London, WC1E 6BT, UK
Paul and Company Publishing Consortium Inc
141 Old Bedford Road, Concord, MA 01742, USA

Cataloguing-in-Publication entry
Film business: a handbook for producers.
2nd ed.
Bibliography.
Includes index.
ISBN 0 642 22705 5.
1. Motion pictures – Australia – production and direction –
Handbooks, manuals, etc. 2. Motion picture industry – Australia
– Handbooks, manuals, etc. I. Jeffrey, Tom. II Australian Film,
Television and Radio School.
791.430232

Cover design	Julie Watson
	(inspired by Jinks Dulhunty)
Cover photograph	The film crew filming a scene
	from *Sirens* (dir. John Duigan,
	prod. Sue Milliken)
Layout	Julie Watson

Printed in Australia Southwood Press

CONTENTS

POST-PRODUCTION

MARKETING AND DISTRIBUTION

APPENDIXES

FOREWORD

The first edition of this handbook was designed specifically for the producers of motion picture film, that is, productions shot on film and post-produced on film or tape. Since it was published in 1989, there have been significant advances in multimedia and non-linear editing. Producers 'cross-over' far more frequently, originating material on either film or tape. Therefore, in preparing the second edition of *Film Business,* it was considered appropriate, and necessary, to include information relevant to producers of video as well as film. Each of the contributors have kindly reviewed and up-dated the chapters they wrote for the first edition.

New chapters have been written on corporate video, copyright, financial agents, multimedia and non-linear editing. Additional material has been included in the commercials chapter. *Film Business* will continue to be a reference manual for those people who are producing features, mini-series, telemovies, animated films and videos, documentaries, short dramas, commercials, training films and grant films. It can be read in conjunction with the AFC/ AFTRS *Production Budgeting and Film Management* manual, which provides detailed guidance on day-to-day production requirements.

Film Business also serves as a useful reference to people close to or associated with film production, such as advertising executives, union and media associations, lawyers, investors, sponsors and agents, to nominate a few areas.

Whether you're based in Broome or Bondi, Brisbane or Balranald, I would encourage you to keep *Film Business* close at hand. I'm sure you'll find it a very handy book to refer to, as you develop your projects.

I wish you every success as you pursue your endeavours.

Tom M Jeffrey AM
Editor, 2nd edition

ACKNOWLEDGMENTS

Damien Parer did an excellent job compiling and editing the first edition of *Film Business*. The extraordinary success of it is to a very large extent due to his work. Also recognition should be given to those people who contributed chapters to the first edition, and to thank them for the revisions they have made for this edition. The information in their chapters provides a clear description and understanding of the complexities of the business in which we work and ensures the book's excellence as a reference text.

In relation to this second edition, I would like to thank the authors of the new chapters: Bob Turnbull (corporate video), Ian Collie (copyright), Stephen Peach (multimedia legal issues), Ben Cardillo (multimedia), Hal McElroy (financial agents) and Stephen Smith (non-linear post-production).

I would also like to thank John Daniell for the work he did revising the chapter on commercials, and Jennifer Huby of Tress Cocks & Maddox for her information on the Export Development Grants Scheme, which can be found in Damien Parer's chapter on Marketing and Distribution. The constructive advice provided by Antonia Barnard and Gilda Baracchi was very much appreciated.

Finally I could not have completed the task of editing this second edition of *Film Business* without the considerable contribution of time and resources by Samson Productions' staff: Christine Gordon and Melinda Bryant.

THE PRODUCER

WHAT'S A PRODUCER?

DAMIEN PARER

THE NATURE OF THE BEAST

✳   Not many people outside the film business know what a producer does.

✳   People in the business can't imagine why anyone would want to be one.

✳   Sometimes writers and directors want to be called producers so that their work is protected.

✳   Producers need to have skills and dexterity far beyond those of mere mortals. Producers are required to be tactful, witty at lunch, compassionate, charming to actors, clever with money, patient at the fifteenth meeting, mechanically able to fix a photocopier, and able to remember thousands of details and their significance.

✳   And when things go wrong everyone wants their producer.

Producers may just be the least understood figures in the film industry. Part of this is due to terminology. Once a film was simply 'produced by' so-and-so. No more. A casual reading of credits shows that now there are people who 'present' movies. There are 'Executive Producers' and 'Associate Producers'. There are 'Executives in Charge of Production'. Sometimes there are more than all of the above people for any one film.

This proliferation of titles underlines the complex nature of producing. Some producers are money finders, who arrange the financial backing for the film and take some kind of billing and fee for their efforts. Others are packagers. They buy a concept, do a deal with a distributor and move on to the next problem, be it finding the star or obtaining the right to use an important location crucial to the project. In return, they receive money and a credit. And then there is the case of the person brought into the project solely to keep the pre-production and production wheels running smoothly.

These are all elements of the producer's work, but no one element constitutes the complete role of a producer. For the purposes of this handbook, the producer is:

✳   the person whose job it is to get the picture made;

✳   the person who is ultimately responsible for the delivery of the film in the agreed style and at the specified length;

✳   the person in control of budget and personnel;

✳   the person who, more often than not, is the first one on the project and, years later, after the marketing is completed, the last one off.

THE PRODUCER'S RESPONSIBILITIES

* You are responsible to the investors or clients to deliver the project on time, on budget and to a high level of professionalism.

* You also represent those people who have chosen to work with you. You are obliged to fulfil your commitments to them and respect and protect their contribution. With power comes responsibility.

* The authority vested in you is to be used wisely to ensure that no one is placed in a hazardous or dangerous situation. Human life is more important than any film.

* Having accepted the position of producer on the film, you have committed yourself to providing it with your full attention and effort. If you don't like the project, then step aside and let someone else do it, someone who will produce it better than you will.

* Get the best people, trust them, and delegate everything that's possible. You can usually fix little problems later. People respond well to being given the authority to match their responsibilities.

* Practise unlimited stroking and head patting. Human beings respond to being recognised. But if you find that you must replace someone, then do it with dignity.

* Respect the skills of your collaborators. You have the power to change aspects of the production, so make sure that your decisions are best for the film – not just changes to conform to your taste and whims.

* You are one of the few people with an overview of the whole entity. Delegate where possible and maintain your objectivity – it is essential to the success of the film.

* Don't seek out someone to blame when a problem occurs. Creatively seek a solution and move on. Mistakes are opportunities to learn something.

* Get advice from colleagues, lawyers, whomever. You can't know everything and you don't have the right to jeopardise the production because of your ignorance and pride. Do not assume that it'll be 'all right on the night'.

* Keep everyone informed about what's going on, decisions you have taken, changes you have made. Most particularly keep your investors informed about progress. No surprises.

* The finished film is a new entity and you are obliged to ensure that it effectively reaches its intended audience and that it is respected like any other work of art.

* Remember it's what's on the screen finally that really matters. The process of achieving that is not the main event.

* You are responsible for your own welfare. Get enough sleep, recreation and nourishment. It's no use if you collapse half way through the production.

3

A BUSINESS

Producing a film is the business of film making. Until you recognise that it is a business, you will be chasing rainbows. The buck stops at your desk whichever way you look at it. From the investors' point of view, from the clients' point of view, from the crew's point of view, you are ultimately responsible for the product. A competent producer must be business-like from day one. Crossing the t's and dotting the i's may not be the creative position you had in mind, but if you don't perceive the role of the producer in this way, for your own sake at least, please try another job.

THE PRODUCER'S AREA OF INVOLVEMENT

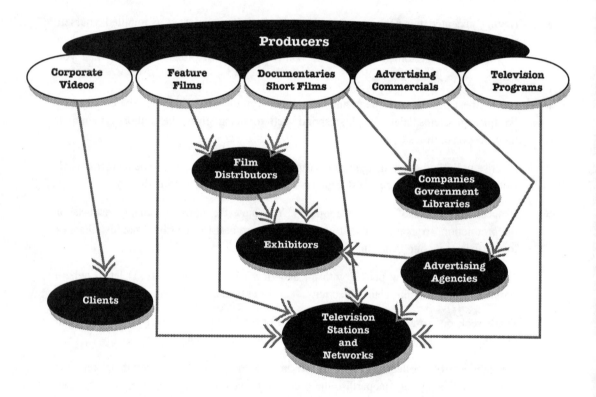

THE PRODUCER'S ROLE IN THE FEATURE FILM

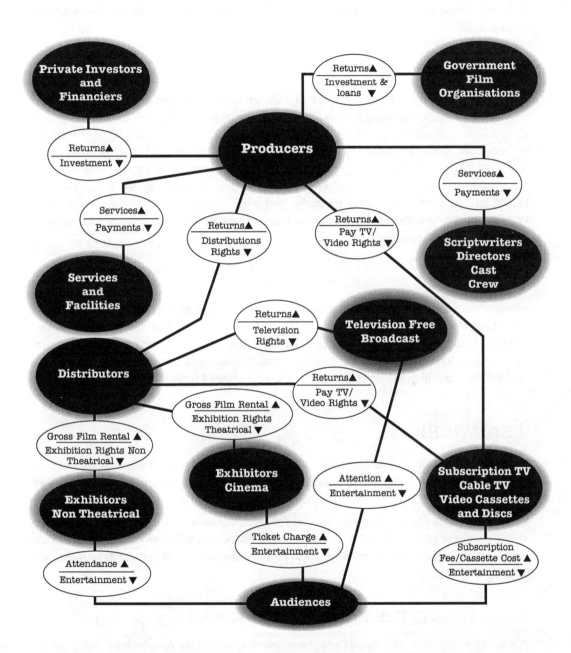

THE PROJECT

The producer must provide the overview. At every stage of the project the desired result should be kept firmly in mind. Indeed, the end is frequently the best place to begin. 'Who is it for?' and 'What effect do you want to have on people who see it?' are the first questions to be asked.

KNOWLEDGE

A working knowledge of every area in the life of a film is essential – not that you will have to do everything (although in low budget productions it sometimes feels this way). As the producer you are the reference point for everyone else. You must know what elements are necessary to the production, given its type, style and budget, and what is unnecessary. You must be able to judge the performance of the people working on the film. Are they being asked to do too much or too little? Are they doing too much or too little? You must be able to assess when to employ specialists and when those tasks can be competently done by those already on the project. All these things can only be done with a good working knowledge of the industry behind you.

PLANNING

Effective planning means effective producing. Deadlines can be met realistically and costs controlled. Planning will keep you on track so that the emphasis of the project is always on your objective. It also helps to expedite the work and keep it on schedule. Planning means writing things down. Don't rely on your memory. Record dates of meetings, telephone calls and any important discussions. Remember that poorly planned films tend to become expensive.

TEAMWORK

The job of a producer can be viewed as a series of relationships which may run concurrently or overlap and usually involve some financial arrangement in return for a service or a legal right.

While producing a film is a business first and foremost, the business itself relies on the abilities of the people employed. Whether or not you get the best possible product depends on the working relationships you develop on each project. The earliest of those relationships will be with the writer.

YOUR RELATIONSHIP WITH THE WRITER

I've never understood why writers are not mobbed at premières or why they don't get fan letters from admirers claiming that they would crawl over broken glass to get at them. Perhaps it is that words on a page seem so remote from the excitement of seeing the story on the screen.

Be a wise producer: don't forget where everything has sprung from. The writer's role in pre-production, rehearsals and post-production is just as important as their contribution at script stage. Make sure you use this excellent resource throughout the production.

A film idea is nothing more than idle conversation until it is put on paper. At this stage you will probably work with a writer to develop the idea to a stage where it becomes possible to use the draft as the linchpin of the presentation you will use in your search for financial backing. Your role as creative motivator starts now. Writers are not an unnaturally sensitive breed. They become sensitive for good reason. Unlike almost any other job, writers must commit to paper everything they think about a project, often in a hurry, and are then held responsible. It is there in black and white. To avoid what could be an almost inevitable collision, tread carefully and thoughtfully during this nurturing period

* If, after discussion, you ask a writer to prepare a full storyline to test the development of the idea, be prepared to pay for it.

* Contracts should be in writing to remove any possibility of misunderstanding about money and conditions which may damage the project.

* Encourage the writer to be represented by an agent. You, the producer, will then be negotiating with a third party and will be able to maintain a better working relationship with the writer.

* Explain your role to the writer.

* Spend time developing a friendly working relationship.

* Instil confidence in your writer. The best creative results come from an environment of mutual trust.

* Indicate to the writer the general parameters of the film. If the budget doesn't allow for overseas locations or specific activities such as recreating historical events, say so early.

* Ask the writer to write to a specific length. Cutting down a script is a painful and wasteful exercise. If the film is to be screened on commercial television, write to the commercial breaks.

* Having agreed on a realistic delivery date, maintain contact but do not pester.

* When the script arrives always send an acknowledgment immediately.

* Do not prolong the writer's agony unnecessarily. Write or call promptly with your first impressions.

* When commenting on the script, be honest without being brutal. Tell the writer what you like about it and what you don't like about it.

* The writer should always be given the opportunity to make the script amendments called for.

✳   Keep the writer informed about the project's development.

✳   Encourage the writer to think about the saleability of the finished film. What does the writer think that an audience will like most about the film? Would particular actors, locations, or music attract more audience? What is the concept of the film? How will it be marketed?

✳   Put the writer and director together and let them discuss the writer's intentions and the director's approach to the script.

✳   The writer should be kept informed of the pre-production, filming and post-production schedules and be involved in script decisions.

✳   Remember the writer has been anxiously waiting longer than anyone else to see the result. Ensure that the writer is given the opportunity to see the finished film before its public showing.

CHOOSING A DIRECTOR

✳   Look at the director's work.

✳   Talk to other producers who have worked with the director.

✳   Have an initial meeting with the director.

✳   Ask the director for his or her response to the script.

✳   If you are considering an alternative director, tell them both to avoid misunderstanding later.

✳   Consult the writer.

✳   Look for some of the following attributes:

    –   understands the theme and emphasis of the script;

    –   can articulate what he or she wants;

    –   is imaginative;

    –   pleasant but firm with cast and crew;

    –   calm in a situation of disorder

    –   energetic;

    –   resourceful;

    –   can relax and enjoy life.

CHOOSING THE OTHER HEADS OF DEPARTMENT

Look for people who are able to perform their tasks well both artistically and managerially – a common problem is that management skills are often lacking. A production designer needs to be able to work to a budget and schedule as well as providing sets, props and wardrobe to a standard. The director of photography on a feature film will be controlling up to fifteen crew. He or she needs to be comfortable with that.

If you can answer 'yes' to most of these questions you are on the way to becoming a successful producer:

1. Are you a story-teller?

2. When you think about a potential project, can you visualise how it should look and sound when it is finished?

3. When you think about a potential project, do you think about its market at the same time?

4. Are you happy to let others take the accolades and praise and content yourself with knowing that you played a major part in the project's success?

5. Do you have a healthy respect for your investors' or clients' money?

6. Do you realise that you will sign for and be responsible for everything?

7. Is your experience strong enough to qualify you as a producer?

8. Are you a self-starter? Can you stick with a project for a long time?

9. Do you work well with other people?

10. Do you enjoy taking risks?

11. Are you a successful negotiator?

12. Can you find compromise solutions in case of disagreement?

13. Do you feel comfortable doing business over the phone or the lunch table?

14. Do you make decisions guided by logic rather than by emotion?

15. Can you work more than eight hours a day when needed?

16. Is your health sound?

POTENTIAL PRODUCER'S POLL

GETTING YOUR ACT TOGETHER

A good start to being perceived as a competent producer is demonstrating the ability to look after your own affairs. Operating smoothly as a business from the start is not just impressive tactics, it is essential for the efficient planning of any project. It may also mean the difference between a profit or loss. So prepare the framework.

You should consider the following points:

* register your business or company name;

* keep books of account, wages book;

* open bank accounts;

* Workers' Compensation Insurance;

* tax stamps or group tax;

* stationery – letterhead, business cards;

* permanent address and phone number;

* answering machine or answering service;

* an office system that allows you easy access to information and files;

* income averaging: some types of income can be spread over more than twelve months;

* income outside Australia;

* provisional tax;

* all allowable deductions against income;

* depreciation on capital items;

* capital gains tax;

* fringe benefits tax;

* join the Screen Producers' Association of Australia.

THE FINANCIAL SET-UP

First on your list are your financial rights, obligations and needs. A trip to the accountant at this early stage is highly recommended.

Matters to consult your accountant about:

* the advantages of leasing your car and office equipment as compared to outright purchase;

* the advantages of trading as a sole trader, partnership, proprietary company or a trading trust;

* the full range of allowable deductions;

* superannuation;

* illness and injury insurance policy;

* Workers' Compensation Insurance;

* bad debts insurance;

* taxation requirements;

* group tax versus tax stamps.

OPERATING AS A BUSINESS

Next on the list is your knowledge of how to operate as a business. If you have been a salaried employee, or have never run a business before, there are certain things you need to know such as how to keep adequate and accurate business records, credit and debt control, planning and cash flow management. In every state in Australia there is a Small Business Advisory Service, set up by government to offer free advice and assistance. These services also sell a wide range of publications.

BUSINESS EXPENSES

The reality of being a producer is that you will, in all likelihood, have at least two projects on the go at the same time. You must be able to identify what are legitimate business expenditures and on which project you have spent them, as much for your own accountant as for future investors. Legitimate business expenses are any expenditures which can be shown to aid the generation of assessable income. Items vary from film to film but the following checklist may be of assistance.

Legitimate business expenditures include:

* office expenses: secretarial services, phone bills, rent;

* project development expenses;

* travel and accommodation costs: location surveys during project development;

* plant and equipment: television, radio, video recorder, camera, sound or lighting equipment, answering machine, filing cabinet, computer, typewriter;

* reference library: publications, books, magazines, records, audio tapes, video tapes;

* budget items: itemised individual expenditures;

* personal costs: salaries and fees; payments to yourself or other employees;

* depreciation of plant and equipment.

Legal Obligations

As a producer you do have certain legal obligations. To avoid problems later, consult a solicitor at this stage to ascertain what your obligations are. If you have decided to operate as a company, you should be aware of your duties and responsibilities as a company director. You should also sign a service agreement between yourself as an individual and your company.

The Arts Law Centre of Australia is an independent non-profit company which provides free legal advice and information to all arts-related practitioners, administrators or organisations. This organisation has a team of lawyers operating throughout the country and can be contacted on (008) 221 457, for the cost of a local call.

Trade Associations

Every profession has its own association which acts as a sounding board for members, agrees on ground rules, and can provide individual assistance. The Screen Producers' Association of Australia (SPAA) functions in this way for producers. By joining SPAA you gain informal access to the experience of fellow producers and are kept informed of industry problems, trends, and the world marketing situation. Regular association meetings and dinners are held. In addition, the Association works at co-ordinating and promoting close working relationships between government departments and all segments of the film and television industries.

Life support system

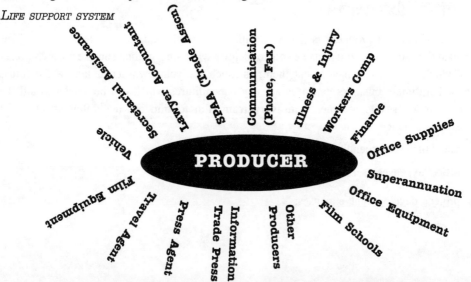

TYPES OF PRODUCTION

Film Categories

Damien Parer

Films can be grouped by genre, principal audience, purpose or any way you see fit. Listed below are some groupings that you may find useful:

Commercial

✳ **Commercial.** A film which advertises or promotes a product. For the cinema it can be up to three minutes long. For television it is usually 30 or 60 seconds in length.

Animated Film

✳ **Animated film.** Any film which principally contains images made without people or documentary footage. A film made with a stop frame camera. The illusion of movement can be made with thousands of two-dimensional drawings or by the use of 3D objects such as clay or plasticine.

Pixillation is the frame-by-frame animation of objects and human beings as distinguished from the animation of hand-drawn images.

An animated film can contain any combination of other elements, e.g. live action.

Sponsored And Documentary Film

✳ **Corporate (sponsored).** A film or video designed to inform or educate an audience about a specific subject, primarily not for broadcast.

✳ **Direct.** A non-fictional representation. Such films (or videos) use actual people and events. They generally examine a social, historical, scientific or environmental aspect of life. They tend to develop in a linear fashion and sometimes use a commentary.

✳ **Presenter or personality.** These programs combine direct documentary with a person in front of camera. The same person usually provides the commentary. The audience is taken on a journey with the presenter.

✳ **Documentary realism, cinema vérité.** The camera records events as they happen. Even though there may be a treatment or script available, the events dictate the film's content. The filmmaker chooses content as it happens.

* **Dramatised documentary, docudrama.** Films are made using actors or non-actors directed to perform in the way a script dictates. These films add a dimension to actuality and intend to instruct or inform the audience.

* **Compilation.** A film which is principally produced from already existing footage. The filmmaker usually incorporates new footage to link the scenes. The film editor's skill becomes the largest component in production.

* **Experimental.** A film using unconventional techniques, generally a reaction against mainstream film making. Some other terms used are avant-garde or underground. The films are non-commercial, often treating a subject matter which is taboo or normally not dealt with in mainstream film making.

* **Non-camera film** (aka direct film). A film made visually without using a camera to record images. This is achieved by exposing film to light under controlled conditions. Film can be scratched or drawn on to achieve effects. Filters and tints can be used. A sound track can be added.

DOCUMENTARY MINI-SERIES

* **Narrative.** Each episode or part makes up a whole story, e.g. *Life on Earth*, *The World At War*.

* **Thematic.** Each part deals with one aspect or angle of an overall theme, e.g. *The Human Face of Indonesia*, *Asian Insight*, *Peach's Australia*.

* **Format.** Each part is a different subject independent of the other parts, but it relates conceptually to the other parts of the mini-series. The format is the unifying element, e.g. *Chequerboard*, *Our World*, *This Fabulous Century*.

Dramatic mini-series can also be unified otherwise than by continuous dramatic line. Anthology mini-series are made up of individual photos and stories unified by a theme, e.g. *Winners*, *Touch the Sun*.

FEATURES

GROUPING BY GENRE

* **Drama.** Anti-hero, western, thriller, action adventure, melodrama, social drama, epic, true story, splatter, super hero, horror, gangster, psychodrama, disaster film, satire, soft-core pornography, science fiction, mystery & suspense, romance, war

* **Comedy.** Comedy-drama, action adventure, comedy-horror, situation comedy, black comedy, farce, satire

15

* **Musicals**

* **Kidult**

* **Art house**

* **Adults only**

ALTERNATIVE WAYS OF GROUPING

* **Principal audience.** Children, family, adult, art house, adults only

* **Country of origin.** For example, Australian films, French films

* **Personality.** For example, Marilyn Monroe's films, Peter Weir's films

* **Special presentation.** 3-D, Dolby Stereo, Sensurround, THX, Smell-Ao, Odoroma, multi-screen (e.g. Cinerama)

OTHER METHODS OF CATEGORISING

* **Subject matter.** Health, sport, wildlife, travel, religion, current affairs

* **Use.** Public relations, archival, motivational, educational, industrial, training, etc.

* **Principal outlet.** Cinema, non-theatre, television, video, point of sale, etc.

* **Screening time.** That is, grouping according to the timeslot available:

  – 30- or 60-minute timeslot for TV series, 90 minutes for mini-series

  – 90-minute timeslot for cinema feature, telemovie, documentary

  – 60-minute timeslot for TV; 1-60 minutes for non-theatre

  – Commercials, etc.

* **Film gauge.** Super 8, 16 mm, 35 mm, 70 mm, IMAX®

* **Obsolete categories.** Some categories have disappeared altogether:

  – X rated or pornographic programs made on film

  – Cinema newsreels

  – Cinema short films (almost extinct)

  – Serials made for the cinema

COMMERCIALS

LAWRIE AND RICHARD McCARTHY
REVISED BY JOHN DANIELL

WHERE DOES IT ALL START?

Advertising courses across America preach to their students that 'in the beginning was the product' and the only reason for advertising is that there is a product to advertise. The advertiser takes this product to an advertising agency which formulates an advertising strategy or a campaign. This campaign will in all probability involve many inter-agency subgroups such as research, marketing and account handling, but essentially it's the agency creative department that creates the image for the product in the marketplace.

The creative director of the agency may get one or two teams working on a product. These teams, made up of an art director and writer, conceive the TV commercial and its associated print and radio campaign. The winning creative submission is then presented to the client by the account executive. In many cases this creative submission occurs before an agency gains an account from an advertiser. The agency may have been one of a number invited by a company with a product to advertise (be it a service or an article) to submit for that company's account.

Selected agencies are generally advanced an amount to expend in this 'sales pitch', although in almost all cases the agency purposely exceeds this budget in an effort to provide the advertiser with the most attractive campaign; this extra expenditure is carried by the agency. Once the account is won by an agency, in most cases it stays with that agency for year, or as long as the agency is successful in promoting the product in the marketplace.

Industry tradition holds that the agency approaches up to three production companies to quote on producing the commercial. The producer and director of the winning production company then rework the idea through the many facets of production design, casting, art direction and finishing to the completion of the commercial.

While this procedure occurs repeatedly throughout the advertising year and involves many agencies, production companies and of course products, there are many opposing principles and forces at work that are changing the way agencies and especially production companies go about their work.

'ENTERTAIN TO SELL'

The feature film or series is seen, on an average, no more than twice by the viewer. In contrast the commercial is seen repeatedly and therefore must be relatively free from error. Continuity must be good, lighting and performance excellent, for the commercial that fails to be crafted by experienced producers and directors will either fail to sell the product or be laughed off the screen. Indeed, 'you have to entertain to sell' is the maxim by which most directors and producers are governed. Because commercials are subject to greater scrutiny by the viewing public, they have become a subject that is either damned or praised each evening by families watching television. While there is an unpleasant, badly produced element (used car ads) that aim to annoy to be remembered, most top directors place incredibly high standards on performance and production techniques, and try to make every second of the 30 or 60 seconds allowed by the station memorable, entertaining and of a high production standard.

Ethics

Morally the writers, producers and directors of commercials should bear in mind that commercials are designed to influence customers to purchase a product or to make use of a facility. Unfortunately, a large proportion of viewers, more often than not unsupervised, are children whose young, inexperienced minds can be influenced detrimentally to their well-being and national culture. The difficulty is to recognise where that common sense line is and not to go over it.

The Unique Difference Is Time

There are really two major elements in a TV commercial that separate it from all other forms of film and television story telling. One is, of course, the product and the other is the restriction and total domination of time.

The product is cause and effect. Drama, comedy, special effects, animation – whatever form the commercial takes – is merely the envelope that surrounds the essential selling message for a cause or a service. Still, it is a rare moment indeed when the actor, scriptwriter and director can move with the freedom that the non-commercial film or TV series allows.

Time is of the essence with most film forms, but in the 30- or 60-second TV commercial the fractional nature of time affects all things dramatically. For example, the simple act of walking from one side of a room to another, while dramatically correct within a story, is a luxury rarely seen in a commercial. Action, whether it be couched in comedy or high drama, must be contained within seconds so that the beginning, middle and end of a story happen within the prescribed time. It would be a rare feature film indeed where an actor is told that his or her line and reaction must occur within, say, seven seconds. In the TV commercial, the whole conversation must be over in 26 seconds to enable the product to be included with a 'super' for the last 3 seconds, if so required.

These dual factors of product and time force the producer and director of the short film into a more disciplined, more precise approach towards film making than is found in the documentary show or feature film. Consequently, the ability of a director to use the product subtly or aggressively separates the top directors from his or her competitors. The ability to fit a complex storyline into 30 or 60 seconds, while at the same time sustaining the dramatic elements present in the longer film form, is a speciality many commercial directors have been able to develop and bring into the feature arena. Britain's Ridley Scott, Alan Parker, Nicholas Rogue, Richard Lester and, most recently, Hugh Hudson, made a fluid transition from commercial production to feature film and continue to make top commercials between feature assignments. In Australia, it's more common to see cameramen cross back and forth between commercials, feature films and TV series. Leading feature directors of photography such as Russell Boyd, Peter James, David Gribble and the late Gary Hansen all began their careers in commercials. In addition, the work of art directors, grips, gaffers, make-up artists and special effects experts have contributed skills that have helped place our commercial film industry at the top of international commercial production. Indeed, the sudden explosion of our feature film industry would not have been possible without the sound foundation of highly skilled commercial film industry-trained professionals.

Unlike most other film producers or directors, commercial people are continually involved in overlapping projects. Unfortunately, we haven't the apparent luxury of weeks or months in pre-production, production or post-production since seconds of screen time require equally compressed pre-production and post-production schedules. Film usage is high and the ratio of exposed stock to televised footage disproportionate. However, repetition and the associated demand for quality are taskmasters few commercial producers can ignore.

THE PROCEDURE

'But I had no idea so much was involved' is the common reaction of most people who watch a commercial production being filmed. The intricacies and technicalities of filming such diverse items as tiny champagne bubbles one day and huge Lotto balls crashing up through a break-away floor the next, has a certain fascination for most film people, whether they are involved in advertising or not. Solving a problem in performance, special effects or story line and making it work, as far as the product and time allow, is a challenge to all involved. Accordingly, filmmakers at every level try to keep informed as to advances made within the commercial industry that benefit all areas of film making. Special effects and video production are two areas most commonly monitored and adapted to the long film.

The basic steps of the concept and development, pre-production, production and post-production are, as indicated earlier, somewhat different from feature and TV drama production.

The basic steps of a commercial from concept to completion, subject to all sorts of variations, are:

1. The concept of the commercial is normally developed by an advertising agency for their client, the advertiser. Occasionally the concept/idea may be jointly developed by advertising agency personnel and an independent writer or commercial filmmaker.

2. From the concept, a script or storyboard is written by the advertising agency either by staff writers/artists or independent contractors. It could, in rare cases, be developed independently as described in step 1, above.

3. The script or storyboard, regardless of how it is developed, is approved by the agency's client, the advertiser, as a specific, separate campaign or as an integral part of an overall campaign for radio, television, newspapers, magazines, etc.

19

4.   The advertising agency then selects one or more production companies (usually three) to quote a fixed price, with contingency costs for wet weather and other exigencies, for the production of the commercial/s. The reason – other than price considerations – the advertising agency selects a particular production company to quote on a particular commercial/s is probably because the agency considers the content and style required for the proposed commercial/s would best suit the style of a director employed or exclusively contracted to the production company.

5.   Part of the quoting procedure may be a full briefing conference at the agency for the production company's producer and director and sometimes such specialists as art director, special effects person, etc. This briefing allows the production company personnel to hear direct from the writer/conceptor of the commercial and the agency producer how they visualise the commercial/s.

Sometimes the advertising agency gives a short written brief and requests the production company's director to submit an illustrated storyboard or detailed script as to how he/she visualises the written brief/script, i.e., the agency is looking for creative ideas from the production company's director. Normally, with complicated or medium to high budget commercials, each production company quote is accompanied by a personalised script or storyboard clearly illustrating how the director plans to translate the agency script or briefing notes into the required commercial/s.

Sometimes (rarely) the advertising agency may develop the concept, script/ storyboard with a freelance director and then seek quotes from production companies for the production of the commercial with the agency-nominated director directing the commercial. The director's fee may be paid by either the production company or the advertising agency.

The production company quote is usually presented in the form of, or similar to, the 'CFPA (Commercial Film Production Association) Production Agreement'. A copy of a standard form of production agreement currently being discussed by CFPA, the Advertising Federation of Australia and Advertising Agency representatives is reproduced at the end of this chapter (where it is discussed in more detail).

6.   The advertising agency recommends to their client a particular production company/director and their quote be accepted for the production of the commercial. The successful production company is then informed that their quote has been accepted and shoot dates, cast, etc. are confirmed between the parties.

Sometimes, but not always, a contract is signed for the production of the commercial by the advertising agency on behalf of their client and the production company.

7.   Usually seven days prior to the commencement of shooting, the advertising agency pays the production company 50 per cent of the production costs, or a contractually agreed sum, the balance being invoiced on completion of the production.

8.   The production company then produces the commercial as per the quote. Any variance, creatively or financially, is approved by the agency production representative (usually

an agency producer) on behalf of their client, or by the agency producer following consultation with the client.

The production techniques used are similar to those used in feature and television drama productions, except that commercials are usually shot in one day – or two to three days at the most – whereas features take six to eight weeks, and a one-hour television drama seven to ten days.

While film or video technicians may work on drama and commercials, it is normal for the heads of department to specialise in one or the other, although many commercials art directors and directors of photography (DOPs) have art-directed or shot features and TV series, etc.

9. The voice over and music track are often supplied by the agency to the production company as either a completed mixed soundtrack or part mixed sound track to which the image is cut or synced to the edited image. Sometimes the sound track is produced and mixed completely by the production company.

10. The post-production of the commercial is usually carried out under the same contract as the production. However, a recent trend from the USA is becoming prevalent in our local industry, that is, to contract with one company to shoot the commercial/s, and with another to carry out the post-production. Although this works well in the USA where the director is not always involved in the post-production, it is creating a few complications locally where the director is usually involved in the post-production right up to completion.

Some larger production companies have their own editing staff and on-line or off-line computerised video editing facilities. Others use the services of freelance editors or subcontract to editing/post-production specialist companies.

11. Completion of the production is usually considered to be on approval of a compiled sound and image film print or video by the agency client. It could also be on approval of silent or doublehead rushes stage at the completion of shooting, with the post-production of the commercial/s being subject to a separate post-production contract with a specialist post-production company.

On completion of the production company's contract, job or brief, it submits a 30-day invoice to the advertising agency for the balance of the production costs plus any agreed extra charges. However the advertising agencies usually stretch payment of the final invoice for up to 90 days or more, regardless of the fact that the commercial in the meantime has already been put to air nationally in Australia.

12. Except where a commercial is compiled partly or wholly from library footage or under specific contractual arrangements to the contrary, it is generally understood that the advertising agency's client, through its agent, owns all material shot for the commercial and has the right to demand delivery to their premises of such footage. This material includes all negatives, workprints, trims and outtakes. The advertising agency has the right to arrange, on behalf of their client, for the production company or another production

company to cut other commercials from that footage, or to edit an alternate version of the original commercial. It is understood that the copyright of the commercial/s, and the film or video footage not used in the commercial, are vested in the client via the advertising agency.

Prior to disposing of any offcut material (negative or positive unused footage or original video footage) the production company requests approval to do so from the advertising agency on behalf of the client.

On payment by the advertising agency, the copyright in the commercial/s passes from the production company to the advertising agency who holds it on behalf of their client. The agency then leases or assigns the commercial to their client.

It should be noted that if at some time in the future the advertiser changes advertising agency, the duplicating masters of all commercials for that client are signed over to the new advertising agency.

13. Animated and part animated commercials follow the same basic production process, with additional time in the storyboard area for the development of the character drawings, animation style, etc.; naturally there is a different, specialised production technique.

FACTS

When you make a commercial it must conform to the Television Program Standards 23 (TPS 23) laid down by the Australian Broadcasting Authority. As a service to television stations, the Federation of Australian Commercial Television Stations – Commercials Acceptance Division (FACTS-CAD) runs a voluntary service which allows advertising agencies to submit commercials for approval under the various regulations and codes, as well as declaring the commercial Australian or foreign under the standards laid down by TPS 23. It is then up to each individual station to control the percentage of foreign commercials screened on their station in accordance with the current regulation, that states:

A licensee *[each commercial TV station]* must ensure that at least 80% of the total advertising (other than the time occupied by exempt advertisements *[eg, advertisements for foreign films]*) broadcast in a year by a licensee, between the hours of 6.00 am and midnight, is occupied by Australian produced advertisements.

QUOTING

In almost all instances, the production company quoting on a job is among its peers, as most agencies are required by their clients to obtain three or more quotes to substantiate the cost of a commercial. The accuracy of these quotes from separate companies can vary enormously. Essentially the rule remains that the better and more accurate the brief from the agency, the more accurate the quote.

Before quoting for the commercial, the producer should be aware of what is being supplied by the advertising agency and/or their client, and of any special requirements or any special terms and conditions of production applicable to the particular job. Some agencies supply a written 'Brief Sheet' which usually takes a form similar to the second page of the proposed CFPA Production Agreement ('Production Specifications and Responsibilities') that is reproduced at the end of this chapter. If a list is not provided, the CFPA page 2 should be used as a checklist to ascertain what the agency/client is providing, so that all the necessary information can be noted, thus enabling the producer to compile an accurate quote.

Once the director has set the creative guidelines, it is then the producer's responsibility to assemble a final quote which will encompass the various areas for costing, including:

* producer's fees   * post-production services
* director's fees   * special effects
* cast's fees   * animation
* crew costs   * location search and hire
* equipment (camera and lighting)   * set design and construction costs
* film stock and processing   * studio hire
* catering   * props and material
* transport   * wardrobe
* accommodation   * animal hire
* insurance   * choreography

Naturally, as with every other area of film making, there are specific requirements within a script which cannot be included in this general listing. In many areas, quotes can differ widely owing to the director's interpretation of a scene and its inherent cost. As with all other areas of film making, costs also vary enormously, depending on a producer's brief to film specialists such as the art director, special effects expert, stuntperson, animation expert, video specialist and the like.

BUDGETING

While commercial budgets, on the whole, are increasing to allow for higher production standards, a common occurrence is that the actual cost of producing the advertising agency's conception bears little resemblance to the client's budgetary allowance.

Agency producers need to be more accurate in preparing their in-agency estimates for clients to avoid potential conflict when a production company actually compiles its budget.

The 'three-quote system', as it has been nicknamed within the industry, is gradually being phased out by some agencies. More clients and agencies in particular, are realising that many areas of creative excellence and cost-saving can be enhanced if they deal specifically with one production company from the outset. The director and producer of the nominated company can invariably assist the agency with innovative ways in which they can bring a creative idea to fruition within a given budget. In many cases, directors are discussing scripts with agencies before the final concepts are presented to a client, enlarging on creative ideas while at the same time avoiding the inclusion of ideas which may prove too costly or impractical.

It is important to mention these areas of involvement within the context of this piece because, unlike other areas of film making, a producer or director in commercials is invariably entangled within the web created by the client/agency/creative/cost argument. If you contemplate a position within this particular part of the film industry, it is important that you have the patience to deal with it, as well as the business acumen to allow it not to interfere with your creative approach to this most rewarding profession.

THE PRODUCTION AGREEMENT

Regardless of whether you are quoting on a $3000 television revision to a commercial, or a $1 million or more megabucks commercial, it is important that both you, your production company, and the advertising agency set down in writing what the deal is, what is being provided by both parties, and the terms and conditions of production detailing such things as upfront payments, etc.

Currently the Commercial Film Production Association (CFPA) and the Advertising Federation of Australia are in the final stages of negotiations of an industry production agreement. The following copy of the three-page agreement is now very close to being agreed upon; but the three pages of 'General Terms and Conditions of Production' (not reproduced in this publication) are still under discussion. This type of production agreement, together with terms and conditions of production, have been in general use in the USA and the UK for several years where the existence of agreements avoids arguments of costly matters like the extra costs involved in a 'weather day', 'location and travel costs', 'insurance', etc.

Until such time as there is an accepted industry standard production agreement, producers/production companies would be advised to tailor the form on pp. 27–29 to suit their particular production company requirements.

The CFPA amalgamated with the Screen Producers' Association of Australia on July 1, 1995.

PRODUCTION AGREEMENT
(Comprising Schedules 1-6 inclusive, Offer for Production,
General Terms and Conditions, and anything else noted as attached.)

SCHEDULE 1. THE PARTIES
(Paragraph A - Offer for Production)

Agency: _____	Production Company: _____
Address: _____	Address: _____
_____	_____
_____	_____
Phone #: _____	Phone #: _____
Fax #: _____	Fax #: _____

SCHEDULE 2. DESCRIPTION OF COMMERCIAL
(Paragraph A - Offer for Production)

Agency Producer: _____   Prod. Co. Producer: _____
Agency Art Dir: _____   Director: _____
Agency Writer: _____
Client: _____
Product: _____
Job: _____

TVC Titles   Duration   Number of . . .
1 _____   Travel days: _____
2 _____   Pre-Light days: _____
3 _____   Studio Shoot days: _____
4 _____   Location Shoot days: _____
5 _____

Agency Brief Date: _____   Proposed Shoot Date/s: _____
Date of This Quote: _____   Proposed Delivery Date: _____
Quote Required by: _____   Proposed On Air Date: _____

FORMAT (mark appropriate box/boxes)

		PRODUCTION COMPANY TO DELIVER TO AGENCY
TV ☐		(mark appropriate box/boxes)
Cinema ☐	Videotape ☐	
35mm Film ☐	Sound Recording ☐	Master Tape or Film ☐
16mm Film ☐	Other (specify) ☐	Fine Cut Double Head ☐
		Other (specify) ☐

SCHEDULE 3. CONSIDERATION - SUMMARY OF ESTIMATED PRODUCTION COSTS
(Paragraph A - Offer for Production)

		Production Costs	Weather Day
1	Pre-Production Crew & Expenses		
2	Shooting Crew		
3	Location & Travel Expenses		
4	Props, Wardrobe, Animals		
5	Studio & Set Construction		
6	Equipment		
7	Film/Video Expenses		
8	Post Production		
9	Insurance & Sundries		
10	**SUBTOTAL: 1 to 9**		
11	Director's/Producer's Fees		
12	**TOTAL: Direct Costs**		
13	Production Fee (markup on items 1 to 9)		
14	Non Mark Up Item		
15	Non Mark Up Item		
16	Non Mark Up Item		
17	**PRODUCTION TOTAL COST**		
18	WEATHER COST ESTIMATE PER DAY		

Date of This Quote:
Product:

SCHEDULE 4. PRODUCTION SPECIFICATIONS & RESPONSIBILITIES
(Paragraph C - Offer for Production)

Responsibility Taken By: (mark appropriate boxes)	Agency ↓	Prod. Co. ↓
PRE PRODUCTION CREW & EXPENSES		
Recce	☐	☐
Storyboards	☐	☐
Casting (incl. video tests)	☐	☐
Phone/fax/couriers	☐	☐
....	☐	☐
....	☐	☐
SHOOTING CREW		
Shooting crew	☐	☐
Art department	☐	☐
....	☐	☐
....	☐	☐
LOCATION & TRAVEL		
Location fees	☐	☐
Location sundries	☐	☐
Location permits	☐	☐
....	☐	☐
Crew - air fares	☐	☐
Crew - accommodation	☐	☐
Crew - per diems	☐	☐
Agency, Client, Artists - air fares	☐	☐
Agency, Client, Artists - accomm'd'n	☐	☐
Agency, Client, Artists - per diems	☐	☐
....	☐	☐
....	☐	☐
PROPS, WARDROBE, ANIMALS		
Props	☐	☐
Wardrobe	☐	☐
Product preparation	☐	☐
Camera-ready packs	☐	☐
Food stylist	☐	☐
Animals, handler, RSPCA	☐	☐
Action vehicles	☐	☐
Special props	☐	☐
....	☐	☐
....	☐	☐
STUDIO & SET CONSTRUCTION		
Studio	☐	☐
Art Direction expenses	☐	☐
....	☐	☐
....	☐	☐
....	☐	☐

Responsibility Taken By: (mark appropriate boxes)	Agency ↓	Prod. Co. ↓
EQUIPMENT		
Camera, lighting, grip	☐	☐
....	☐	☐
....	☐	☐
FILM/VIDEO EXPENSES		
Film stock, develop and/or print	☐	☐
Video stock	☐	☐
....	☐	☐
....	☐	☐
POST PRODUCTION		
Rushes only	☐	☐
Final edit (no opticals)	☐	☐
Final edit (with opticals)	☐	☐
Videotape transfer/master	☐	☐
Artwork/titles	☐	☐
Answer print(s)	☐	☐
Safety copies	☐	☐
V/O recording and mix	☐	☐
Music	☐	☐
Specialist sound mix	☐	☐
Agency cassettes (2)	☐	☐
Animation	☐	☐
Computer enhancement	☐	☐
....	☐	☐
....	☐	☐
INSURANCE		
Negative insurance	☐	☐
Public liability	☐	☐
Artist (accident)	☐	☐
Artist (non appearance)	☐	☐
Travel	☐	☐
Weather	☐	☐
Prop insurance	☐	☐
....	☐	☐
SUNDRIES		
Child welfare	☐	☐
Library research	☐	☐
Library footage: royalties	☐	☐
Still photographer	☐	☐
....	☐	☐
....	☐	☐
....	☐	☐

Date of This Quote:
Product:

SCHEDULE 5. SPECIAL WEATHER CONDITIONS
(Clause 5.4 - General Terms and Conditions of Production)

SCHEDULE 6. SCHEDULE OF SPECIAL CONDITIONS OR REQUIREMENTS
(Paragraph D - Offer for Production)

* NO SPECIAL CONDITIONS APPLY / * SEE ATTACHED

* delete whichever is inapplicable

OFFER FOR PRODUCTION

A. The production company ("Company") whose details are more fully set out in Schedule 1, offers to the advertising agency ("Agency") whose details are more fully set out in Schedule 1, that subject to this Offer and for the consideration being the amount of the Production Total Cost specified in Schedule 3 the Company will produce the advertising or other cinematograph film or videotape and/or sound recording ("the commercial") as described and stipulated in Schedule 2 for television transmission and broadcast or cinema theatre display or use in any other medium anywhere in the world.

B. The commercial shall be produced generally in accordance with the requirements and/or treatment, script, artwork, storyboard or other documentation attached to this Offer and/or supplied by the Agency (prior to the date of this Offer or by a date hereafter agreed to by the Company) or approved by the Agency.

C. The Company and the Agency shall respectively take responsibility for in connection with the production of the commercial such of those items expenses or things appearing in Schedule 4 as are indicated in the boxes appearing opposite those items expenses or things.

D. Upon acceptance by the Agency of this Offer the Company and Agency hereby agree and acknowledge that a legally binding agreement shall have been created and subsists between them upon and subject to the terms, conditions and provisos contained in this Offer, the said documentation (if any) attached, the CFPA General Terms and Conditions of Production ("General Terms and Conditions of Production") attached or any agreed variations or additions to this Offer or the General Terms and Conditions of Production made by the parties in writing as appear in Schedule 6.

E. This Offer may be accepted by the Agency at any time within thirty (30) days from the date of this Offer.

F. In addition to any other mode of acceptance of this Offer, this Offer may be accepted by the supply or communication by the Agency to the Company of the Agency's official order number. For the purposes of this paragraph the expression "Agency's official order number" means the order number specified as such in any schedule or other document attached to this Agreement or any written correspondence or communication from the Agency to the Company in respect of the commercial.

G. References in this Offer or the General Terms and Conditions of Production to a schedule is a reference to the Schedules appearing above and/or attached to this agreement.

DATED this .... day of 199   .

PRODUCTION COMPANY
   (Signed)
                                    ....
                                    For and on behalf of Production Company

                                    ....
                                    Print name of signatory and Position Held

AGENCY
                                    This Offer is hereby accepted by the Agency

   (Signed)
                                    ....
                                    For and on behalf of Agency

                                    ....
                                    Print name of signatory and Position Held

IMPORTANT NOTICE TO PARTIES: It is essential that a copy of the CFPA General Terms and Conditions of Production and any variation to them is attached to this document.

ANIMATION

SANDRA GROSS

USES OF ANIMATION

The initial concept of an animated film grows out of the producer's knowledge of the subject and the particular audience for which it is intended. Once this has been ascertained it is the animator's task to create the desired visual presentation of the idea.

Special animation equipment provides the film producer with an infinite number of techniques and effects; the amount and variety is limited only by the imagination of the people who plan and produce the animated films.

Animation has a wide outlet in terms of use in overall film production:

* in the cinema: animation can be used for full-length animated films, short entertainment films, or animated segments incorporated within a full length feature;

* in television: animation is often used for advertising, for sponsored promotional films, for instructional films for industry, science, technology, and for sales promotion and music clips;

* in instructional and educational films, a complicated process of argument can be presented in its simplest terms. A carefully planned instructional film can add analytical clarity by simplifying a process which is either too complex, too fast, too slow, or too obscure to be seen clearly when photographed in live action;

* animation is used for entertainment, specially designed for children, in the medium of cartoon and puppet films;

* animation is an excellent tool for the experimental work of a producer who would like to express an abstract idea or a philosophical, political or social comment in a medium as free and as flexible, unique and original as the drawn film;

* interactive games and videos, CD and computer systems are emerging for entertainment and eduction, which use animation in all its forms.

FORMS OF ANIMATION

What is common to all normal animation is frame-by-frame generation of image. This is the fundamental distinction from live action filming. It is a form of art in which the artist's idea and the technique used to express it are closely interrelated.

There are unlimited forms of animation. Some conventional styles are: animation of still pictures, electronic video animation, drawing on film, graphic animation, animated cartoon on celluloid, silhouette, puppets, three-dimensional object animation and computer-generated animation and graphics and effects.

The producer can use several of these techniques.

STANDARD STEPS IN TRADITIONAL ANIMATION PRODUCTION

There are similarities and differences between preparation and production of live action and animated films.

∗ **Script.** A script is written much the same way as for live action. Nevertheless, if he or she is not an animator, a writer should work in consultation with an animator-designer-director.

∗ **Storyboard.** The storyboard is the visual presentation of the script in a series of sketches. It is a combined effort of the director and the designer of the film to achieve a clear and comprehensive guideline. It contains the storyline and instructions to animators, and may indicate the soundtrack and dialogue. It should begin to show the style and shape of the film.

∗ **Characters.** The designer or chief animator, in consultation with the director, will carefully design the characters, which will eventually become the 'actors', each with its own character voice and identity. A 'model' for each character is drawn and should show at least three positions: front, profile and back (with some facial expressions).

∗ **Sound.** The sound should be designed at the storyboard stage: dialogue, music and sound effects. The recording of dialogue is the first stage of production. The director must cast actors for various characters, after some voice tests. The dialogue is recorded in the recording studio from a script using the storyboard as a guideline.

∗ **Design and layout.** Based on the storyboard, the layout artist will – like a cinematographer – design, shot by shot, drawings from the point of view of the angle and composition and the exact pictorial appearance of the film.

∗ **Charting and dialogue track.** This comprises an analysis of every film frame in terms of its dialogue, as a guide to animation for lip sync.

∗ **Key animation, in-betweening and backgrounds.** Based on the storyboard, the model sheet and the dialogue chart, the animator works on the key drawings of each scene, leaving the in-betweener to draw the continuation of the movement, the gaps left by the key animator. The background artist prepares the artwork of the background as indicated by the layout artist.

* **Inking and painting.** The animation, drawn on paper, is transferred to celluloid by means of hand tracing or photocopying. The painters paint the characters in the colours which were previously chosen by the designer.

* **Photography.** After a careful check of the cells and backgrounds, the drawings are shot on special camera equipment, each frame shot one at a time. The camera follows the code numbers which are given in the charts prepared by the animator.

As computer technology enters further into video and film production, considerable effort is being aimed at assisting and enhancing stages of animation. Today some studios are replacing inking, painting and photography with computer systems, which will in the future add speed and additional effects to animation. With the increased use of three-dimensional panning, a computer system greatly simplifies the generation of animation that does not use the traditional 'flat', locked-off camera approach.

From this point in the production process, whether the animation is produced conventionally or otherwise, the production is similar to any other live film production, that is, developing, editing, music and sound effects, etc.

BUDGET

In all forms of animation a large portion of the work is done by hand, by highly specialised artists and technicians. Therefore the cost of animated films becomes a highly individual matter for each studio and there is a considerable variation in the scale between studios. In most small studios the producer (who is usually an artist) does everything from planning the animation, drawing the animation, to keeping the company books. As the work of the studio grows it becomes economical to employ a number of artists and technicians in each department to accommodate the additional work.

To arrive at the budget the producer must consider a number of factors: the style of animation, the complexity of the movement, the fixed costs, salaries of staff and contractual employees.

A producer of live action who wants to incorporate animation in a film will be advised to approach an established animation studio.

If a producer wishes to establish a crew for animation outside an established studio, the advice of an experienced production manager, who is familiar with the animation process, is essential.

There are a number of animation studios in Australia. While their sizes vary, all are highly professional with experienced artists and technicians who can achieve all kinds of animation from the highest standard – the most expensive, to the cheapest or the simplest, to suit the requirement of the subject.

Computer animation is hardware intensive and hence expensive at this point, whereas conventional animation is labour intensive, but the advances being made in computer animation systems have meant that the cost is falling quickly while the quality is increasing.

CORPORATE VIDEO

(INCORPORATING 'SPONSORED FILMS' BY DAMIEN PARER)
BOB TURNBULL

DEFINITIONS

'Corporate video' has come to mean almost any program that is designed to inform or educate an audience on a specific subject but that is not primarily for broadcast. They range from in-house productions to externally commissioned programs, teleconferencing and, more recently, interactive multimedia.

The corporate video industry also includes generic programs such as the John Cleese Video Arts series that can be rented or purchased off-the-shelf. While these programs represent the major usage of the medium in Australia they represent only 6 per cent of expenditure on corporate video.[1]

The corporate video invariably fits into one of two categories: internal communication for electronic newsletters and staff training, or external communication for marketing and public relations.

BACKGROUND

Under generic titles such as 'Industrial Documentaries' or 'Sponsored Films', corporate videos have been with us almost since the beginning of the film industry. It was the advent of the domestic VCR as a distribution medium in the early 1980s that led to the dramatic development of a comprehensive corporate video industry.

In the mid-1980s a number of companies and, in particular, the major financial institutions, established their own internal video production units, complete with fairly sophisticated hardware, but by the early 1990s most of these units had been disbanded. These companies found it difficult to justify the cost of upgrading production hardware due to technological advances and so concentrated on their core business.

USES

It was once said that corporate videos are made to either make money or save money. Obviously a training video is designed to save a corporation or institution money by increasing productivity, while the marketing video is designed to assist in making sales. The objectives for the producers of corporate videos are, therefore, closer to the objectives of television commercial producers than feature film or TV producers, in that they are required to modify the thinking, behaviour or purchasing habits of the viewer. What the corporate video producer is making is a management tool.

'Training and education' represents just over 40 per cent of total corporate video product while 'sales promotion and marketing' is the next highest category with just over 20 per cent. [2]

PRACTITIONERS

The recession of the early 1990s, which reduced opportunities in features, television, commercials and documentaries, saw a number of companies and individuals normally reliant on those areas for their income become involved in corporate video production. Many writers, directors, DOPs and actors with excellent screen credits made the transition to corporate production and made the transition to the different disciplines that exist in corporate production.

THE CLIENT

Those clients responsible for commissioning a corporate video are often experts in human resources and marketing; however, their familiarity with the film or video medium, its processes, techniques, capabilities and limitations is often negligible. Only a minority of commissioning clients are able to give a concise brief on the aims and objectives, the target audience and the available budget for the production they have in mind.

This can be a distinct advantage for the producer. The client is generally open to creative concepts rather than holding to a pre-conceived notion of what the genre of the program should be.

THE BRIEF

The typical starting point to develop a manageable brief is to ask the commissioning client an appropriate selection of the following questions:

* **Aim.** Is the video to be used as a sales promotion, for staff communication, product demonstration, or some other purpose?

* **Objectives.** Is the video to assist increased sales, improve brand awareness, raise a company profile or change community thinking on an issue?

* **Audience.** Is your primary audience current clients, prospective clients, executive staff, shareholders or even the community at large?

* **Audience pre-knowledge.** What level of understanding does your audience already have on your chosen topic?

✱ **Video use.** Will the video be presented by somebody, or used as a stand-alone item? Will the audience be in large or small groups?

✱ **Interactive.** Must the audience do something in response?

✱ **Product(s).** Can your product be demonstrated? Is your manufacturing procedure particularly important? Is it a non-demonstrable story you are telling?

✱ **Market position.** Are you market leader in your field? Is it a cluttered market?

✱ **Production requirements.** Will it be necessary to shoot interstate or overseas? Is it important to have a live presenter?

✱ **Existing material.** Do you hold historical footage and have you produced videos before?

✱ **Language.** Are foreign language versions or foreign accents required?

✱ **Approval.** Are the scripts and budgets subject to committee approval? Is there one person nominated to liaise with the producer?

✱ **Identity.** Is the video linked to other advertising or public relations activity?

✱ **Support material.** Are printed training aids required?

✱ **Budget.** Has an allocation been considered or determined?

Some of the briefing questions may seem superfluous; however, it is important to know well in advance of preparing a concept and treatment if, for example, there is a need for a version in Mandarin. A foreign language version can influence the choice between a presenter or voice over. A Mandarin track can take 25 per cent longer to speak than English. Also it is important to know how the video is to be presented. If it is a group discussion starter, then it needs to be designed differently from a video that is to be watched in a stand-alone environment, or by a salesperson and a client.

The more information you can get before you start, the better you can make the end product.

BENEFITS

The title 'corporate video' generally conjures up the idea of private sector companies; however, more and more programs are being made for, and by, the public sector that have nothing to do with sales or economic issues. They are designed to inform the community about social issues. For example, award winning programs have been made about sexual harassment in the work place, AIDS awareness, and the developmentally disabled moving from institutional care to community units.

Increasingly, some companies are using the medium to bring about changes in workplace procedures and to introduce new skills more quickly and economically than is possible with the old classroom methods of teaching.

For example, a major bank wanted to explain to staff what they should do in the event of

33

a hold up. A video was made and shown to all staff. When a hold-up did occur the staff were less traumatised and required far less counselling to overcome post-trauma stress because, as some staff explained, the real event for them was like deja vu.

Another example concerned an Australian manufacturer who was planning a joint venture plant in China. A visiting Chinese delegation was shown a video overview of the company with a Mandarin sound track. The visitors were delighted that westerners had bothered to communicate with them in their own language. This led to very warm negotiations between the two groups.

Today it is necessary for marketing executives visiting overseas to carry their corporate video. It is as important as their business card.

A research document commissioned by the International Television Association of Australia and the Australian Film Commission in 1992, entitled 'A Study of the Corporate Video Market in Australia', provides some excellent data on the industry, its size, the clients and the practitioners.

PITFALLS

Too often in competitive **tendering** situations, commissioning clients ask for creative concepts to be submitted with budgets without ever having given a full brief, or providing an opportunity for the producer to research the target audience. It is as though the corporate producer can pull a script off the shelf, or conjure one up out of thin air that will work effectively for the client without having any access to the data needed to define the audience, or the aim and objectives of the video. Regretfully this can lead to programs that fail to be effective.

CHECKLIST FOR THE CORPORATE VIDEO PRODUCER

> Date, name of organisation, address, phone and fax numbers
> Nominate one person to liaise with the production company
> What is the primary purpose of the proposed video?
> What should the audience think, feel or do after seeing the video?
> What is the video to be about?
> Why is the video needed?
> Who is the video aimed at? Primary/Secondary/Other
> Distribution: primary outlets, other outlets, expected number of prints
> Delivery – When is the video required?
> Will there be any other support material available?
> Technical: stock, length, drama, documentary, animation
> Is there a best time to shoot?
> Budget – What is the client's expectation of cost?
> Research – What can the client provide?
> Other information

BUDGETS

The first question asked by many potential clients is 'How much does a corporate video cost?' There is a benchmark commonly used in the industry to assist the uninitiated – that is, $2500 to $3000 per finished minute. All of the variables that happen in any production – such as travel and talent – then have an effect on those figures, but a budget of $30 000 for a ten-minute program is not unusual.

It should be remembered that audiences expect the corporate video to have the same technical and creative values of normal broadcast standard television programs. Therefore most corporate videos are shot on betacam and finished on betacam or 1", often through a high-end post-production facility.

CONTRACTS

The International Television Association (ITVA) has developed a standard contract suitable to the corporate video industry that spells out terms of payment, costs related to changes to the brief and scripts, copyright and other matters that may arise in production. It is fairly common in the industry that one third of the agreed budget is paid on commissioning, a further third on completion of principal photography and the final payment on delivery of the master.

THE FUTURE

In the early 1980s the rapid use of the domestic VCR as a distribution and exhibition medium gave rise to the enormous growth of the corporate video industry. The VHS cassette will now be superseded quite quickly by the CD-ROM and the PC. These will become the tool for corporate communications in the future. And they are capable of delivering more effective training and marketing messages.

The opportunities for producers in the interactive multimedia environment are boundless. The boffins writing software programs for interactive multimedia will not be the producers of corporate communications. They need today's producers to bring their communication skills to the interactive domain, and they also need those producers in order to convince the market that the increased budgets needed for the production of interactive communication products is still cost effective for their message.

The development of digital non-linear editing in post-production is a tool well suited to the transition from the linear video cassette to the CD-ROM.

NOTES

1. 'A Study of the Corporate Communication Market in Australia.'
2. 'A Study of the Corporate Communication Market in Australia.'

DOCUMENTARIES

DAMIEN PARER

WHAT IS A DOCUMENTARY?

A documentary can probably be described as some of the following:

* actuality – from uncut film from a camera in a fixed position to dramatised documentary with a cast;

* a considered point of view by the filmmakers;

* a slice of life, typical of what really happens, an unrehearsed situation;

* a responsible truthful dissemination of information;

* a filmmaker sharing his or her point of view with an audience.

MAKING IT HAPPEN

You have a great idea for a documentary film. Before you make a move, think about it!

> ### FOOD FOR THOUGHT
>
> * Why should the film be made?
> * Does it have an appeal and for whom?
> * What market would there be for such a film?
> * Does it have a limited life?
> * Would the cost far outweigh the possible returns?
> * What is the perfect length for the film?
> * Do you have the time to give to the project?
> * Do you feel a strong commitment to the project?

Only after you have assessed the project to your own satisfaction should you prepare to start work on it.

THE PRESENTATION

Having committed yourself, your task initially is to raise the money. This requires a presentation which outlines the idea itself, together with a number of relevant pieces of information which will indicate to a source of finance, the type, scope and style of the project, together with your legal right to produce such a project.

With a documentary proposal a written presentation is essential early in the project's life. Try to give as much information as succinctly as you can, together with an overall flavour of the project.

THE WRITTEN PRESENTATION

The following information should be included in the written presentation:

* **Front page:** title of project, copyright, who to contact, etc.

* **Introduction:** selling page, an interest-attractor.

* **Contents:** this makes it easier for the reader to find information.

* **Purpose (or background):** the film's objectives, the aim of the program. This should include a statement describing the fundamental reason for the film, that is, define the problem to be solved, the goal to be achieved or the attitude that the film sets out to challenge, or the information gap it intends to fill.

* **Style:** emphasis of the film. Which of the categories of short film will it be most like? Which level of audience will it suit best?

* **Treatment:** description of the film content. What are we actually going to see?

* **Audience:** who is the principal audience? Who else would be interested in seeing the film?

* **Budget estimate.**

* **Schedule:** when will the film be available to the audience?

* **Marketing:** how will it get to the primary audience? What else will be done to distribute the film?

* **Credits:** details of the crew, cast or presenter involved.

ADDITIONAL ELEMENTS

While not necessary, the following elements are of value and should be included in the written presentation if you have them:

* letters of encouragement, commitment or authorisation;

* financial details, e.g., investment procedure;

* revenue potential – high and low world sales estimates;

* examples of successful similar films;

* authoritative sources for the information in the film;

* illustrations, maps, still photographs, press cuttings;

* locations list;

* video or audio presentation to accompany the written presentation.

THE LIVE PRESENTATION

Often you may have an opportunity to 'pitch' your proposal to an intended financier or buyer. This should be kept to 30 minutes or less. Rehearse your oral presentation and keep it to ten minutes. Allow another ten minutes for questions and a final ten minutes for an informal chat.

PRESENTATION POINTERS

* **Preparation.** If the thought of an oral presentation daunts you, do a course in public speaking and/or personal development.

* **Personal presentation.** 'Open and friendly' means you believe in your project. Your appearance and image are important in your presentation.

* **Enthusiasm.** Everyone likes to meet someone with commitment and zeal, even assessors in government bodies.

* **Delivery.** There is no business like show business. Show slides, play music, use charts and diagrams.

* **Atmosphere.** Relax your audience. Make the occasion comfortable with tea, coffee, drinks, snacks, etc.

* **Audience.** Try to keep the group small. This makes it easier to develop a rapport and to handle questions. Find out as much as possible about your audience in advance so that you can tailor the presentation.

* **Audience response.** Ask yourself what your audience is looking for. If they back the film will it make them look good; is it a risk for them; what are the guarantees that you can achieve the objectives of the film and that you can stay on budget; will the film get any exposure other than the market you are targeting; are there any tax advantages; when is the money required; can they take their spouses or partners on the shoot?

SAMPLE PRESENTATION

Pachyderm Productions

Asia Unlimited

**A Major Television Event
of Thirteen Half-hour Programs**

Writer	**Producer**
Paddy Goldman	**Louis B Selznick**
© Copyright 1995	Address all enquiries to:
	Louis B Selznick
All rights reserved	418 O'Connell St Sydney 2000
	(02) 123 4567

Introduction

Whatever happened to the mysterious Orient? The vital 'extra' that makes Asia such an incomparable draw? We have it.

Things like severed heads, potent magic buried under the patio flagstones. Or Grandma's mummified body propped watchfully on a hill overlooking the house. Or a spirit whose possession of your block of land is so powerful that you must build two houses – one for you and one for the spirit.

These are all everyday matters of life and death in Asia. And if we in the West have grown away from such superstition (or think we have) are we still interested in other people's gods and ghosts? There are thousands of millions of reasons, every one of them a tourist dollar, for knowing that we certainly are.

Contents

2

40

Background

One of the biggest things the East has going for it is tourism from the west. Asia draws millions of tourists every year from the UK and Europe, the United States, Latin America, Australia and New Zealand.

It's a huge market – and a huge audience. Yet where is the television material aimed specially at people who have visited Asia, plan to visit Asia, or would like to visit Asia? There isn't any. We propose to make it.

Westerners don't go to Asia just to look at the view. The attraction of Asia is its dramatic and exciting difference. Of course views are important to most holiday makers – and Asia has the most spectacular scenery in the world. But people are looking for escape from the familiar, for romance, a sense of mild (and safe) adventure, and a few shopping bargains. Some are looking for sexual adventure – and you can't get more adventurous than some of the Asian nightspots.

All this we intend to show, both on and off the beaten track, explaining where necessary, sharing our own expertise and enthusiasm for the region, and very occasionally warning that visitors should stay away from some proffered delights.

All that is enough to make our proposed series a unique offering on television. A world first. But there's more.

Style – it's about enjoyment

The series will contain thirteen half-hour programs.

It will be about enjoyment. The touch will be light – no deep analyses of culture, history and politics.

Mind you, we are not planning a remake of the Oooh-Aaah Fitzpatrick travelogues, with the sun sinking tiresomely in the west right on cue.

We will show audiences the Asia they would love to see, but which tourists in fact rarely do see unless they have really expert personal guides and have done a good deal of research beforehand. We are the guides, and we have done the research.

This series will be up-to-the-minute contemporary, entertaining and accurate. It will also be, occasionally, raunchy and a bit naughty. It will have to be if it is to be honest about what Asia offers the visitor.

And it is going to be honest. We have a reputation worldwide for expertise in the television coverage of Asia, and we plan to guard it jealously.

3

The series

The countries in the series will be (in no particular order, and including a couple of 'spares') : Hong Kong, India, Japan, South Korea, Malaysia, Indonesia, Burma, China, Sri Lanka, the Philippines, Nepal, Singapore, Pakistan, Taiwan, Thailand. Some glimpses :

Blood flows at Easter in the Philippines. The Filipinos' version of Christianity is highly flamboyant. Sick, some would say. In Cebu Island 'flagellants' flog themselves with chains until the skin hangs from their backs. A few young men have themselves crucified (temporarily).

Throughout just about the whole of Asia, Westerners should beware of any place calling itself a 'motel'. Why? Because it's most likely to be a 'short-time' hotel catering for the local whores and their customers. So tourists should stay away. Unless, of course ....

Numerology rules in Hong Kong. There's an obsession with lucky numbers. TV entrepreneur Robert Chua bought a 'lucky' car registration plate for $2000. He also moved house from number 4 (the same word as for 'death' but with a different tone) to number 9 (same word as 'enduring'). He's still alive. Perhaps it works.

Patpong I and Patpong II, the tourist-trap centre of Bangkok's nightlife, had a spectacular and destructive fire referred to, no doubt unfairly, as a 'Chinese stocktaking'. Like the occasional police campaign it interrupted, but did not end, a mind-boggling collection of exhibitions and services. And to see how, and where, some of the girls smoke a cigarette, no wonder the place burned down.

In India astrology is king. Even a nuclear scientist going abroad will make sure he leaves on an auspicious day. Almost all non-Communist Indian politicians believe in astrology and plan their lives by it. The whole of India in fact is a bazaar of superstitions, religious prohibitions and supernatural obsessions of one kind or another.

Did you know, incidentally, that one of the biggest operators in the Patpong nightspot scene is a dry-cleaner from Tasmania?

And while we're in Bangkok, if you want the really kinky 'live exhibitions' we know where to go, far from the usual touristy areas. Trouble is, we haven't worked out yet how to show it while not quite showing it, if you see what we mean.

Throughout Asia Expatriate Europeans are not immune from world influences. Donald Wise of the Far Eastern Economic Review suffered a vague but distressing illness for months. He moved his desk on the advice of a geomancer, and has not been sick since.

4

Geomancer? One who can divine fung shui, the arcane science of the breath of nature which determines whether a building, a doorway, a piece of land, or whatever, is best placed to put main harmony with nature.

Strange? Maybe. Trivial? Not likely. The department which runs Hong Kong's New Territories consults geomancers over town planning, and has spent $45,000 in two years on elaborate Taoist ceremonies to assure good auguries.

The Japanese have a realistic view of the boy-meets-girl business. There's no secret about the 'lovetels' – motel-style places mainly near big cities, specially prepared for assignations. We know a particularly plush one with a suite containing, in addition to the usual remote-control TV for porno films, a circular bed with a matching ceiling mirror which moves up or down on electronic command.

In Tokyo, capital of one of the world's most advanced technological nations divining the future with I Ching sticks. Computers compete. At Sukiyabashi intersection in Ginza, an electronic palm-reading machine offers the future for $1.

After an exhausting tour of the nightlife, some breakfast perhaps? There's a pleasant little cafe we know in a Tokyo suburb, just right for a quiet chicken-and-rice and green tea. Lots of pretty, blonde girls too, a bit weary, apparently, and with laddered stockings. But why have they all got a black stubble? Because they're men. There's a flourishing transvestite scene in Tokyo. A rival for Bugis Street, even.

5

43

Treatment – how it will look

To give an idea of the shape of the programs in the series, let's pick out the seductive and stunningly beautiful country of MALAYSIA. Major sequences in the episode will go something like this:

CAMERON HIGHLANDS

Malay peninsula's rooftop. Stylish, cool resort of the kind the British in India, Burma and Malaya used to call a hill station. An engaging remnant of British influence: improbable Tudor-style buildings, upper-crust Malays in tweed. Some genteel nightlife, golf, several pleasant hotels. Very relaxing and cosy. And deceptive. Jim Thompson, the Thai silk tycoon, was staying in the jungle near his hotel. He has never been seen again. And he was an old Asia hand. (We'll be looking over his mind-blowing house in Bangkok in our Thailand episode.) Enjoy the Cameron Highlands. Go for jungle walks. Carefully. Remember this is the oldest rainforest on earth and it is not tame. Do not leave the path.

THE JUNGLE

You can trek safely in the jungle that covers two thirds of the country, but you need to be pretty fit. Perhaps you'd do better to come with us. There's plant and animal life to stagger the imagination. (And poachers, too. Powdered rhino horn, anyone? Bezoar stones found in monkeys' stomachs? We'll explain all that.) Meet orang asli (original man), the aborigines living in secluded villages. Have a wary look at their blowpipes and poison darts.

It wouldn't be Asia if there weren't spirits of one kind or another in, up or behind every tree. They include pontianak, sad vampire spirits of women who die in childbirth. Or there's orang minyak (oily man) who preys on young girls. He's not the only one. Rural Malay newspapers which solemnly report escapades by frisky spirits have also noted over the years a whole string of sexual assaults on girls by bomohs (Malay medicine men). In one case on the East Coast the victims were three girls, all 15, who said they thought the bomoh was helping them to pass their examinations.

6

EAST COAST

But then, the East Coast is a pretty magic-prone sort of place. Relatively unspoiled. Pretty fishing villages, beautiful beaches. A sort of elegance about the people, the boats, the lifestyle. This is Malay village life as genuine as you would find now, what with the encroachment of blue jeans and Japanese motor bikes and so on. You'll be welcome in this gentle world, but keep a few guidelines in mind. Shoes off to enter the mosque, no bare female shoulders or skimpy shorts. Be polite; never shout. And do not chat up the girls. As everywhere in Asia, smile.

The East Coast is a good place to visit a sultan's court, see the ceremonial regalia, hear the stories about the magical properties of the royal kris, of the drums in a new sultan, and whatnot. If you want to giggle about any of this, do it in your hotel room.

KUALA LUMPUR

A big place, with everything other modern cities have got – stinky traffic, noise, expense ... the full catastrophe. Lovely for tourists, mind you, with some marvellous hotels. We'll tour a few. Very classy pictures. This is where the Chinese Malaysians come into their own, in the cities and in the money. We'll meet a Chinese millionaire, have a look at his lifestyle, go to a Chinese festival of some kind, try to catch the flavour of the 'other world' of old Chinese belief and superstition. We might be lucky, and get invitations to the 'wedding' of two dead children, arranged by the parents of a deal girl so that she won't spend the rest of time as a spinster.

BATU CAVES

The Indians, although they are the smallest of the three major racial and religious groups here, are a hard act to top when it comes to colour and drama. At the festival of Thaipusam, penitents visit the Hindu temple at Batu Caves (not far from KL). Some young men perform spectacular penance with spikes driven through both cheeks and through the tongue, and with large metal frameworks suspended on hooks in the flesh of back and chest. They feel no pain, apparently, and do not bleed.

SARAWAK

We can't visit Malaysia without at least a brief taste of the island which used to be called Borneo. Sea Dyaks, former headhunters, will welcome you to their longhouses on inland rivers. See Kuching, full of relics of the heyday of the Brookes, the White Rajahs of Sarawak. Half an hour isn't long enough, is it?

Audience

The series is designed specifically for a world television audience. The programs will be edited to half-hour commercial television length and sold to world television. Secondary markets are to be found through print and tape sales to the travel industry. We also anticipate that the series will become available to the huge home video market.

Budget estimate

Preliminary budgeting indicates that the series overall will cost $2,340,000 to produce. That is $180,000 per episode.

Schedule

Finalisation of funding .... July 1995

Research, scripting, pre-production.......................... September 1995

Shooting .... May 1996

Post-production .... January 1997

Series available for release .... August 1997

8

Marketing

Marketing of the series will commence after script stage.

In Australia the Producer will seek pre-sales from Australian television networks. Overseas sales agents will be appointed. They will actually sell the series at film markets and through their extensive contacts.

Other sources of revenue

The sale of the series to:

- the travel industry
- the home video market

A coffee-table style book will be published to coincide with the release of the series.

A record of the music used in the series will be released.

9

Credits

Paddy Goldman's credits, in addition to his regular locally based appearances in the ABC's *View From My Desk*, include films shot for the program in Japan, the Philippines, South Africa, Rhodesia, Zambia, Tanzania, England, Italy, Hong Kong and Taiwan.

In 1990-91 he was working on the *Orient Exposed* series.

He has had two books published, The Mysterious Middle East (Angus & Robertson) and Paddy Goldman's World Insight (University of Queensland Press).

Louis B Selznick's credits include, as Production Manager, *Asian Voyage*, the multi-award-winning telefeature *Visions Going*, and two other telefeatures.

As Producer his credits include the television series *The Orient Exposed*, a multi-award-winner completed in 1992; and *Inside Medical Practice*, an in-depth series on doctors.

10

SAMPLE BUDGET ESTIMATE FOR SHORT FILMS

WORK TITLE:	PRODUCTION NO:
SPONSOR:	ESTIMATED RUNNING TIME:
FOOTAGE:	SHOOTING RATIO:
ESTIMATED SHOOTING PERIOD:	

CODE SERVICE	COST
A STORY & SCRIPT	
B PRODUCER & DIRECTOR	
C PRODUCTION UNIT SALARIES	
D HOLIDAY PAY ETC.	
E ARTISTS	
F ORCHESTRA & COMPOSER	
G COSTUMES & WIGS	
H ART DEPT MATERIALS	
I FILM & LAB CHARGES	
J POST-PRODUCTION	
K EQUIPMENT	
L RENTALS & STORAGE	
M TRAVEL & TRANSPORT	
N HOTEL & LIVING EXPENSES	
O INSURANCE	
P PUBLICITY	
Q OFFICE EXPENSES	
R MISCELLANEOUS EXPENSES	
S VIDEO PRODUCTION COSTS	
Y FINANCE & LEGAL	
Z OVERHEADS	
SUB-TOTAL	
CONTINGENCY	
PROFIT MARGIN	
TOTAL	

SAMPLE BUDGET ESTIMATE FOR SHORT FILMS

CODE COST HEADING	DETAILS	COST ESTIMATE	SUB-TOTAL
A STORY & SCRIPT			
Research			
Expenses (Research)			
Writers			
Script Typing & Duplication			
TOTAL A			
B PRODUCER & DIRECTOR			
Producer			
Assistant Producer			
Director			
TOTAL B			
C PRODUCTION UNIT SALARIES			
Production Manager			
Accountant			
Assistant Director			
Cameraman			
Camera Assistant			
Sound Recordist			
Sound Assistant			
Production Assistant			
Continuity			
Electrician			
Gaffer			
Grip			
Make-up			
Make-up Assistant			
Hairdresser			
Wardrobe			
Art Director			
Props			
Editor			
Editor's Assistant			
Technical Adviser			

Sample Budget Estimate For Short Films

Sound Mixer	
Stills Camera	
Casting Director	
TOTAL C	
D HOLIDAY PAY ETC.	
Payroll Tax	
Superannuation	
TOTAL D	
E ARTISTS	
Narrator	
Extras	
TOTAL E	
F ORCHESTRA & COMPOSER	
Music Copyrights	
Composer	
Musical Director	
Musicians	
TOTAL F	
G COSTUMES & WIGS	
Costumes	
Make-up	
TOTAL G	
H ART DEPT MATERIALS	
Construction	
Props	
Action Props	
Livestock	
Stage Rental	
Locations	
Special FX	
TOTAL H	
I FILM & LAB CHARGES	
Original Stock	
Developing	

Sample Budget Estimate For Short Films

Workprint

Magnetic Stock 16 mm/35 mm

Magnetic Stock $^1/_4$"

Dupe Negs

Stock Shots

Sound Neg

Answer Print

Neg Cutting

Opticals

Release Print

Slash Dupe

Safety Printing Material

Shooting/Developing

Process Titles

Video costs including:

- Transfer

- Grade

- Stock

- Video cassettes

- Off-line Edit

- On-line Edit

TOTAL I

J SOUND POST-PRODUCTION

Transfer

Music Recording

Post-sync/Commentary

Recording

Projection Theatres

Dubbing Theatre

Mixing

TOTAL J

K EQUIPMENT

Camera

Lenses

Sample Budget Estimate For Short Films

Crane	
Grips	
Lighting	
Lamps	
Generator	
Gels	
Sound	
Special Effects	
Stills – Materials	
Miscellaneous	
TOTAL K	
L RENTALS & STORAGE	
Editing Room & Equipment	
TOTAL L	
M TRAVEL & TRANSPORT	
Transport	
Freight	
TOTAL M	
N HOTEL & LIVING EXPENSES	
Accommodation	
Travel Allowances	
Catering	
TOTAL N	
O INSURANCE	
Equipment	
Negative	
TOTAL O	
P PUBLICITY	
TOTAL P	
Q OFFICE EXPENSES	
TOTAL Q	
R MISCELLANEOUS EXPENSES	
TOTAL R	

SAMPLE BUDGET ESTIMATE FOR SHORT FILMS

S VIDEO PRODUCTION COSTS
Video Camera(s)
Camera Operator
Technical Director
Vision Switcher
Video Stock
Audio Stock
Transfer Time
Colour Correction
Off-line Editing
On-line Editing
Sound Editing
Dubbing Time
Dubs
TOTAL S
Y FINANCE & LEGAL
Audit
Legal Fees
TOTAL Y
Z OVERHEADS
TOTAL Z

MULTIMEDIA

BEN CARDILLO

WHAT IS MULTIMEDIA?

Over the past four years I've heard dozens, perhaps hundreds, of definitions of multimedia. In my (not so?) humble opinion no one ever managed to get it quite right. Then it occurred to me that multimedia is a little like the holy Trinity – it's actually three things rolled into one.

The term 'interactive multimedia' is used to describe:

* a new technology;

* a new form of cultural expression; and

* a new method for distributing information and entertainment.

All are equally important elements. In multimedia they are indivisible, yet each can be described separately in technical, artistic or commercial terms. It's from this unique combination that the real power of multimedia to change the way we live, work and play is derived.

The existence of various definitions for multimedia often reflects the industry background of the person suggesting the definition. For example, people from information technology or computer backgrounds often define it according to the technology involved e.g., CD-ROM. A person from the telecommunications industry may define it according to method of delivery or cable capacity required, e.g., video-on-demand or 3 megabits per second.

So, what is multimedia?

Multimedia is a **new technology** because it enables media which previously existed in different physical forms, to be stored in a single electronic, digital environment, that is, a database. In the past, words, pictures and graphics existed on paper, music on a vinyl record and moving images on a strip of celluloid or videotape. Now multimedia technology makes it possible to store (and display) all media (words, pictures, graphics, sounds, animations and moving images) in a single system.

It's a new form of cultural expression because a digital database allows random access to any part of itself, in any sequence. This means that information need no longer be organised in an inflexible linear stream as in a film or video. Random access allows the user to have control over the delivery of information, including the rate, complexity and mode. Therefore, every interactive exploration can be a highly individual, unique experience.

Finally, it's a new method of distribution for information and entertainment to mass audiences.

Multimedia is currently distributed on compact disc (CD-ROM), similar to a music CD. In the next few years it will also be available over national and international telecommunications networks (broadband services). These two distribution formats haven't existed before. Consequently, they will provide significant commercial opportunities to a large range of content developers, service providers and telecommunications carriers.

In the last years of the twentieth century we are seeing the evolution of a giant new transnational industry. This new super, mega, global industry is the result of the convergence of many other industries:

* information technology

* telecommunications

* audiovisual arts

  - feature film

  - free-to-air and pay television

  - corporate video

  - advertising

  - video games

  - music

  - radio

  - theatre

* publishing

  - newspapers

  - magazines

  - fiction & non-fiction books

  - reference works (encyclopaedias, dictionaries, etc.)

* heritage and cultural displays

  - museums

  - libraries

  - art galleries

  - visual artists

* education (especially distance education)

56

* training (including competency-based training)

In revenue terms, by the end of the twentieth century, multimedia will be bigger than almost any other service industry in the developed world. This is not so hard to believe. Already in the US the video games industry out-grosses the combined revenue of the feature film and television industries. And it's early days yet. International information networks, especially the Internet,[1] are also growing at a seemingly exponential rate, fuelling commercial expectations that consumer demand will produce spectacular revenues.

Naturally, it is expected that many new interactive titles and services will need to be created to supply this projected global demand. This is one reason why interactive multimedia is so important and why filmmakers should, at minimum, keep abreast of multimedia industry developments.

MULTIMEDIA AND THE FILMMAKER

The growth of multimedia in the past four years or so, from a technical curiosity to a powerful new medium for communications and entertainment, poses real challenges for traditional filmmakers – both artistic and technical challenges.

THE ARTISTIC CHALLENGE

Until now our storytelling techniques and visual language conventions have been constrained by the delivery media we have been using, i.e., film and videotape. The linearity of film and tape has affected the way we construct storytelling sequences. And, while we have invented clever 'work arounds' for these limitations, such as cutting between parallel action, flashbacks and jump cuts, most stories still start at the beginning and end at the end.

With multimedia there are no limits. There can be hundreds of beginnings and possible endings, and an unlimited number of dramatic pathways in between. Now, many filmmakers might argue 'So what? An audience doesn't want to be bothered with having to makes dozens of choices. They just want to lie back and let the experience (created by us brilliant writers, directors and producers) simply wash over them.'

Well, I'm afraid this Couch Potato Theory isn't backed by our experiences in the past 100 years of cinema and television. Remember the Hollywood studio boss who, in 1928, said that 'talkies' were pointless because people were perfectly happy with silent movies? And, if people don't want choice why are there 50 varieties of salad dressing sold in Australia?

In any case multimedia is here to stay. IDC Research, Sydney, estimates that in 1994, 275,000 CD-ROM drives were bought by Australian consumers. By 1998, an additional 5.25 million CD-ROM drives will be sold. It seems our audience has already chosen.

I believe that, just as filmmakers made exciting discoveries in visual language in the first four decades of the cinema (e.g., the close up, jump cut, etc.), there are similar discoveries to be made in multimedia programs.

We still don't have basic conventions for non-linear modes of navigation. For example, universally accepted icons which intuitively describe basic functions such as Forward, Exit and Back to the main menu are yet to be developed. We are still unsure of many aspects of screen design. For the adventurous filmmaker there are many journeys of discovery yet to be made.

Developing a visual language is one area in which a country like Australia, peopled by a creative, resourceful community of artists and technicians, can truly excel. We can do this by developing a wide range of stunning multimedia applications. However, this will not be easy.

THE TECHNICAL CHALLENGE

The development of the cinema in the 100 years since the Lumière brothers opened their first cinema in Paris in 1895 has been marked by slow technical change. For example, there is little difference in the way documentary film was shot and edited in a film cutting room in 1922, when Robert Flaherty shot *Nanook of the North*,[2] and the cutting room of a natural history filmmaker today. Sure, the gauge, colour, quality of the stock and some of the tools may have changed, but the cut and paste process is fundamentally the same.

Another example of the slow rate of technical change in our industry is television. Although the first television broadcasts were made in the 1920s, it wasn't until after the Second World War that television became universally available in the United States.

It was around 30 years after the first television broadcasts that videotape was first used in a studio production (1955) and another eighteen years before it was used on location to record a current affairs documentary (1972).

Work practices and distribution channels have taken decades to evolve. The main benefit of this slow rate of change has been that filmmakers have had time to adapt. In contrast, no such luxuries exist with the development of multimedia technologies. It has taken only sixteen or seventeen years from the time Steve Wozniak, Steve Jobs and friends built the first Apple PCs in their mum's garage, to the Power PCs of today – only sixteen years from a bunch of computer nerds hacking code in Basic to 50 million Windows users worldwide. Welcome to future shock.

Multimedia technologies have been developed by a personal computer industry driven by rapid technical innovation[3] and fast-evolving and very price-sensitive markets. To survive, these computer companies have had to develop competitive marketing strategies and work practices.

Not surprisingly, the film industry, particularly the Australian film and television industry, cosseted by supportive funding institutions, appears positively dinosaur-like by comparison. If we are to play a key role in multimedia production, we must become more flexible and more competitive.

Our general level of computer literacy must improve. We must learn to work with computer industry and telecommunications industry professionals. We must learn their jargon, just as they must learn ours.

Keeping up with developments requires an inquiring mind and a fair bit of hard work. It's a real challenge, made more difficult by the fact that, in Australia, appropriate professional development courses are in short supply.

How Can Filmmakers Profit From Multimedia?

Find Out What's Going On

Filmmakers can begin by joining professional multimedia industry bodies such as the Australasian Interactive Multimedia Industry Association (AIMIA). This will at least put you in contact with a network of multimedia developers and other like-minded filmmakers. Professional organisations such as AIMIA are also useful lobby groups that can pressure state and federal governments and educational institutions to run appropriate professional development courses.

Read as much as you can about what's happening in multimedia. Australia has its own multimedia industry newsletter, *Multi Media Digest*, published by John Sheehan in Sydney [Tel. (02) 871 8413]. *Multi Media Digest* contains valuable local news, technical articles, summaries of local conferences and a useful precis of overseas news, especially from North America.

There are also a number overseas periodicals that are a 'must-read' for serious professionals, including *The Multimedia Monitor*, *New Media* and *Wired*. The computer bookshelves of all the major book retailers are groaning with titles – including a large number on multimedia.

Finally, all newsagents carry a range of locally published computer magazines and newspapers. All carry features and regular articles on various aspects of multimedia and its technologies.

Develop Creative And Business Opportunities

The emerging multimedia industry in Australia is plagued with the same problems that afflict many of our other industries:

∗   lack of market size means it is difficult for multimedia producers to recover their production costs (and make a profit) from the local market;

∗   consequently, producers have to rely on overseas distribution channels for revenue;

∗   in turn, this means producing a product with 'universal appeal', i.e., one that will sell in the US; and

∗   inevitably, there are significant challenges in producing programs that will have mass appeal in North America yet reflect important aspects of our Australian cultural identity.

The importance of guarding our cultural heritage from a foreign (mainly US) invasion has been accepted by government ministers, departments and agencies with a stake in our multimedia future. But it cannot be left entirely to government instrumentalities. The industry itself must move to claim the high ground. This can only be done by producing world-class multimedia applications.

The Australian government has already stated on a number of occasions that it is prepared to 'prime the pump' to stimulate the development and growth of a local multimedia industry.

How it is doing this is described below. However, the government is determined not to allow the development of a highly subsidised industry, similar to the Australian film and television industry, which absorbs nearly half a billion dollars annually[4] in state and federal subsidies and grants. This means that any producer considering a high quality multimedia project should assume that overseas distribution is an indispensable part of the marketing strategy for the project.

TAKE ADVANTAGE OF GOVERNMENT PROGRAMS

In October 1994, the Prime Minister released a major cultural policy statement, *Creative Nation*. The statement contained five complementary initiatives specifically designed to create *'a dynamic Australian multimedia industry providing Australian content for Australian and international consumers'*.

The Government has committed up to $84 million over four years to fund these initiatives. They are:

❋ **Australian Multimedia Enterprise (AME).** AME will be a government-owned proprietary limited company which will invest $45 million over four years in the development and publishing of multimedia titles. At the time of writing, the board of AME has yet to be appointed and guidelines for investment applications by multimedia developers have not been published. However, it is expected that AME will operate in much the same way as the Film Finance Corporation. Investment decisions will be based on the perceived commercial potential of the project being proposed and, therefore, applicants will require investment and other commercial participation (such as distribution guarantees) by third parties in their project.

AME will be administered by the Department of Communication and the Arts.

❋ **Co-operative Multimedia Centres (CMCs).** CMCs will offer *'education, training and professional services, access to state-of-the-art equipment and facilities, access to leading-edge research and development, and assistance with the handling of issues such as intellectual property and evaluation'*.

Six CMCs will be set up over two years. Their fundamental purpose is to assist the emerging Australian multimedia industry by providing education and skills training for people intending to work in multimedia. They will be collaborative enterprises between the education and training sectors and other public and private organisations. The Government will commit $56.6 million over nine years ($20.3 million over the first four years) to the CMC initiative.

Funding for each CMC will be up to $2 million per year. The first CMCs will commence operation in the 1995-96 financial year. An independent, competitive assessment process will be managed by the Higher Education Division of the Department of Employment, Education and Training (DEET) and Purchasing Australia.

❋ **Multimedia Forums.** The Department of Industry, Science and Technology will conduct a series of national multimedia forums ($3.9 million over four years). The forums will allow the multimedia community to discuss major strategic issues relating to the development of the industry. Their aim is to increase dialogue between the creative and software communities and will involve the participation of the *'cultural community including filmmaker, broadcasters and educational institutions'*.

* **Australia on CD Program.** The Department of Communications and the Arts will provide $7.6 million over two years for the production of ten interactive CD-ROMs on *'significant Australian cultural themes'*. Four copies of each CD-ROM will be made available to every primary and secondary school in Australia, as well as to AUSTRADE offices and our overseas missions.

  The purpose of this program is to showcase the quality, richness and diversity of Australian culture through the use of innovative multimedia technologies. Although guidelines for applications to the Australia on CD Program have not been published at the time of writing, it is expected that major cultural institutions, such as the National Museum of Australia, will be involved. The first five CD titles will be commissioned in 1995.

* **Special Assistance to Government Agencies**. The Australian Film Commission and the Australian Children's Television Foundation were allocated special funding ($5.9 million and $750,000 respectively) in the Creative Nation Cultural Policy Statement to assist in the funding of interactive multimedia titles. In addition, the Australian Film, Television and Radio School received $950,000 over four years to set up multimedia training courses for filmmakers and other professionals wishing to learn new skills.

In addition to the initiatives announced in *Creative Nation*:

* AusIndustry, a section of the federal Department of Industry, Science and Technology, has various industry programs that may be of assistance to multimedia producers undertaking projects with a significant R&D component. For example, competitive grants of up to 50 per cent of the cost of R&D and concessional loans are available to qualifying companies.

* through programs such as the National Industry Extension Service (NIES) AusIndustry provides assistance in developing business and marketing strategies and developing export markets. There is an AusIndustry office in every capital city.

THE FORMAT JUNGLE

Filmmakers sometimes find the profusion of different technical standards and delivery formats for multimedia confusing. This isn't helped by the fact that when comparing one format against another, it is often impossible to compare apples with apples. Coping with the format jungle, therefore, isn't easy for beginners.

Here's what you need to know:

* Despite what the hype merchants and Breathless Bennies write in magazines or spout at computer conferences, there is no doubt that the mass consumer market has chosen CD-ROM as the preferred delivery medium for multimedia applications over other formats such as CD-I or 3DO. Penetration of CD-ROM drives into the consumer market exceeds its nearest rival by millions of units. It's a no-contest.

* CD-ROM is not a particularly good medium for delivering multimedia. There are other formats that utilise special graphics chipsets or interleaved data streams to get excellent quality video on the screen, CD-I for example.

* However, the market has spoken. The realities are, if we want to publish a multimedia title and ensure the widest possible audience, we must publish on the CD-ROM format.

Technical advances are working around the limitations of the CD-ROM standard. For example:

* double, triple and quadruple-speed CD-ROM drives are currently delivering fatter data streams and better access times than earlier drives;

* better compression and decompression algorithms are producing better full motion video quality off CD-ROM;

* new authoring tools are making it easier to produce a single CD-ROM that will play on any IBM-compatible or Apple Macintosh computer without sacrificing database size or quality of content;

* Philips, Sony and 3M are currently prototyping a new, high density CD-ROM that will store 3.7 gigabytes of information, five times more than the present standard of 650 megabytes.

Finally, a clever producer will always ensure that whatever is produced for any delivery medium will be engineered in such a way that, at some future time, it can migrate fairly painlessly to other delivery platforms, thereby ensuring a long shelf life and profitable, multiple revenue streams for every title.

The Future

After three or four years of market instability due largely to the rate of technical change and the development of a multiplicity of delivery formats,[5] it seems the multimedia industry has finally settled down to a period of market development and consolidation.

The mass market has chosen CD-ROM as the preferred format and, with CD-ROM drives reaching production figures of tens of millions of units annually (with consequent falls in retail price for consumers), it is hard to see a radical change in delivery platform in the next three or four years. In computer industry terms that is a long time.

By 1997-98, telecommunications companies and service providers will start rolling out a range of interactive and conventional services delivered to homes, schools and businesses by terrestrial cable systems. Though relatively modest at first, these systems will eventually be capable of delivering up to 500 channels of information, retail services and entertainment to every subscriber.

The range of services touted by potential service providers and telecommunications carriers is quite astonishing. They include:

* conventional free-to-air TV

* pay television programs

* movies-on-demand[6]

* interactive games, including live interaction between multiple players

* gambling, of all forms, including TAB-style betting on race fixtures around Australia

* retail banking and all kinds of other financial transactions, e.g. home loan applications

* home shopping, including grocery shopping

* tourism services, booking flights, holidays, etc.

* home-delivered fast food and restaurant services

* video telephone communications

* high speed computer data transmissions

Where does the filmmaker fit into this grand vision? Well someone has to produce the content that will be stored on these systems.

A significant number of multimedia developers from computer industry backgrounds, who previously stated that they were able to develop titles without 'outside' assistance, have now realised that without special skills and experience in creative disciplines, it is quite difficult to produce high quality multimedia. This is particularly so when original video sequences have to be created. Therefore, they are currently seeking experienced creative personnel to join projects as collaborators.

More developers will follow this trend. It is imperative that filmmakers move quickly to acquire the special skills they need to form these collaborative partnerships.

Finally, there's little doubt that a significant portion of our traditional business, including some drama, infotainment television programs and corporate video for example, will migrate to interactive multimedia environments. Initially, this will involve publishing and distributing on CD-ROM. Towards the end of the decade more and more business will migrate from CD-ROM to on-demand telecommunications-based systems. Filmmakers will either move with the business or miss out.

NOTES

1. The Internet is a worldwide network of computer networks. It is estimated that there are about 20 million Internet subscribers accessing information held in more than 17,000 computer networks around the world. And, new subscribers are joining in their millions. The most remarkable feature of the Internet, apart from the fact that no-one owns or controls this worldwide web, is that once logged on, navigation to any part of any database on the Net is relatively effortless, whether the information is physically stored half a kilometre or half a world away. Navigating the Net is often called 'surfing in Cyberspace'.

2. First released in 1923, *Nanook of the North* is still regarded as one of the most remarkable natural history documentaries ever made. Robert Flaherty spent more than a year living with Eskimos in the Arctic circle, recording their fast vanishing way of life. It was the first feature-length documentary and the first documentary with a discernible dramatic narrative.

3. The chips that are the 'heart' of personal computers have been doubling in speed and power every **two** years. Many industry pundits joke that by the time most PC products make it to the market they are already obsolete or near obsolete. Many local PC companies have product cycles of only 3–6 months. Prices also halve every two years. The computer industry calls this phenomenon 'Moore's Law'.

4. This figure is calculated by totalling the amount of money allocated by state and federal governments and agencies to the Australian Broadcasting Corporation for its television service, SBS, Australian Film Commission, Australian Film Finance Corporation, NSWFTO, Film Victoria and other state film agencies. This **excludes** money spent by governments on television advertising and corporate video productions, which also assists the industry by providing significant employment opportunities. It also excludes taxes forgone by the Australian Tax Office through the use of tax incentive schemes.

5. CD-ROM, CD-ROM XA, CD-I, 3DO, DVI, Quicktime, AVI, Indeo, etc.

6. 'Movies-on-demand' or MOD is a term used to describe a technology which allows movies to be stored and accessed on very large computer hard disk arrays. Subscribers will be able to chose a movie from a large catalogue and, after keying in a PIN number and payment details, have the movie played via cable directly into their home when they want, i.e. on demand. The MOD technology is so advanced that thousands of subscribers can all call up the same movie at around the same time. The computer controlling the system will deliver a continuous, coherent data stream to each subscriber, irrespective of when they chose to start watching the movie. Advanced trials of this technology are already being conducted in the US by Time Warner Inc. Australian trials are also due to begin in 1995.

GETTING STARTED

PREPARING A CONCEPT DOCUMENT

(Reprinted with permission from
Writing for Television,
by Ginny Lowndes,
Allen & Unwin Australia, 1988)

GINNY LOWNDES

The pathway to selling a script goes something like this:

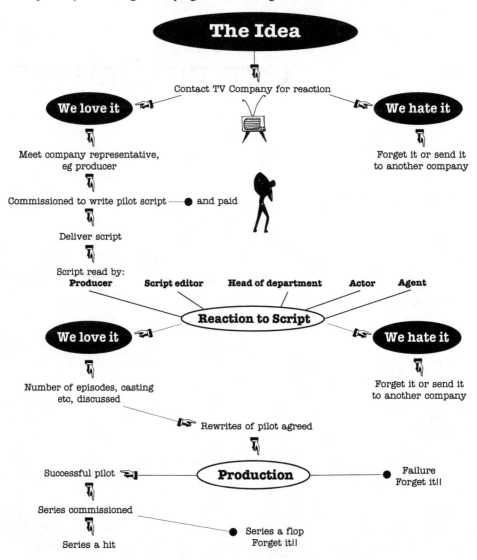

A brilliant presentation will get you through the minefield and hopefully to a hit production. The following outline for a concept document is to give you an idea of what is expected. This concept is not fixed and you can play around with it until you find the best possible way of giving your script a running chance.

THE TITLE PAGE

EXAMPLE –

A Twenty-six Part Series for Television

Define the format

Title

THE EASY EARN

Writer's name

by

GINNY LOWNDES

Subtitle (if any)

- A Laconic Look at the Other Side of the Tracks -

Name & address

Name: **Ginny Lowndes**
Address:
Telephone:

Year & writer's name

© 1982 Ginny Lowndes

Australian Writers Guild Registration No.

ALL RIGHTS BY ALL MEDIA RESERVED

STRICTLY PRIVATE AND CONFIDENTIAL

THE SECOND PAGE

Use the second page for the outline of the idea. Start with the title. Do no forget to put the title and a page number on every page.

As the ability to summarise your idea is imperative, write your outline as if you are describing the plot of a film you saw last night, so that you can give an immediate impression of what the project is all about. In other words, distil your plot to its essence in one to two paragraphs (indented) and centre it on the page.

After this, leave lots of white space.

Next, briefly describe the background to the proposed idea which will give an immediate sense of a concrete yet colourful setting of the time, place and period in which your proposed idea will take place.

Again, you must leave lots of white space, before proceeding to the next step.

Describe, in a couple of lines only, what kind of format you are proposing for your idea, i.e., a teleplay, a series, a mini-series, a telemovie, etc., and how you propose to treat the subject you have chosen, i.e., a commercial half-hour comedy of thirteen episodes, a 72-minute telemovie, etc.

EXAMPLE —

THE EASY EARN

THE EASY EARN is a witty, entertaining, colourful, street-fast series which centres around Mike Barnes, an ex-cop in his late thirties, with a laconic sense of humour and appealing sexy charm, who solves the problems of the 'ordinary man on the street'.

Mike moves through their lives and problems in an easy style, with skills learned in the force. He mixes comfortably with the rich tapestry of inner-city life which has been his home since the day he was born.

Mike is always involuntarily involved in some type of 'crime' adventure, ranging from the petty crime life of the Cross to the wealth and glamour of the jet set, always hoping for and on the lookout for the easy earn.

Somehow, it is nearly always just out of his reach ...

THE EASY EARN is a contemporary drama series set in the inner suburbs of a large city ...

THE EASY EARN is a 26-part series presented in weekly episodes of one hour each ...

THE EASY EARN will centre around Mike Barnes and the lives, loves and humour of our colourful cast of characters, interwoven with the racy street life of Sydney's Kings Cross.

THE SYNOPSIS

To present the dramatic realisation of the idea, write a synopsis (on a fresh page) of the whole idea for your proposed format, in no more than one or two pages. (A synopsis of each episode is prepared if it is a mini-series or a series.)

EXAMPLE –

THE EASY EARN

THE EASY EARN centres around the personal and family dramas of Mike Barnes, coupled with the people of the inner-city streets. It is woven together to form a powerfully dramatic, ironic and humorous, contemporary Australian television series, shot in a fast and realistic style.

Mike Barnes –

- ex-cop
- ex-crim
- ex-husband
- ex-father
- out of prison
- out of work

and still irrepressibly unrepentant of it all.

Mike Barnes – outwardly learning to live with his life gracefully and humorously. Looking for an earn – any earn.

The Royal Commission into the Police Force reckoned Mike was always on the take, and the blind eye Mike had turned to the minor criminal or questionable activities of the inner-city people was usually out of compassion, understanding, generosity and giving the chance of another go after suitable warning.

It became, in the skilled, ambitious, investigative hands of his junior partner, Theo Stevens, bribery and corruption.

Mike knew he'd been set up.

The easy-going, almost larrikin style that marked Mike's seventeen years in the force was against him.

It was over.

So was his marriage to Janet and his relationship with his teenage daughter, Kate.

There was little Mike could do but wear it.

Mike was sentenced to two years in Parramatta Jail, but, as he laconically remarks to the CES clerk, he got off twelve months early for good behaviour.

It doesn't get him a job. There aren't any vacancies for a convicted cop.

69

EXAMPLE –

> Not these days.
>
> It is the 1980s.
>
> Times are tough. The recession bites deeply into the lives of ordinary people. A lot of them are on the street, grimly hanging onto the last bits and pieces of their lives, giving to it a curious kind of dignity.
>
> More and more people crowd into the inner city, looking for work and left fighting for survival.
>
> Too many give up.
>
> The crime rate is exploding.
>
> It becomes a way of life for many people.
>
> An already overworked police force cannot solve the avalanche of crime which confronts them or help the people who demand they do.
>
> Most times the police hope the insurance companies will cover some of the losses. More often than not, that loss is the final straw for the victim.
>
> Money is replaceable – well, sooner or later. Losing something you value which cannot be replaced will find you out in the street, looking for someone to get it back.
>
> Mike Barnes will, for a fee and with charm, laconic grace, irony and humour. A street solver.

THE AREAS OF DRAMA AND CONFLICT

After you have written your synopsis, you next prepare, on a new page, one to two paragraphs which will describe the main areas of drama and conflict that will take place between the protagonist and the plot.

EXAMPLE –

> The areas of drama and conflict will shift through the streets of Sydney and into Mike's life as he uses his life skills to solve the problems of ordinary people, for a fee in money or kind, always taking the people he deals with and their situation seriously, but never himself, etc.

THE EXTENDED BACKGROUND

In one to two (new) pages, expand the background stated on the second page under the heading 'The extended background'. The extended background will give a potential producer a well-realised idea of:

✳ the central character;

✳ where the dramatic setting is;

✳ how the central character lives;

✳ how the central character relates to other people (the major and minor characters) and his/her environment;

At the end of your extended background, write: 'This is the situation at the beginning of the series (mini-series, telemovie, etc.)'.

EXAMPLE —

THE EASY EARN

THE EXTENDED BACKGROUND

Mike Barnes was born towards the end of the Second World War, into an Irish Catholic working-class family.

His father, Marcus, died in the war. His widow, Bridie, worked as a dressmaker and laundress to support Mike and his younger brother, Tim.

Mike grew up in the working-class, rather poor but fiercely proud inner-city suburb of Darlinghurst.

As soon as he was old enough to earn a living at anything, Mike did.

He worked as a runner for an SP bookie, a paper boy, a delivery boy, as anything, so long as he could ease the financial burden on his mother.

Mike also began to run wild, until Clarrie O'Brien, an old-time fighter turned trainer and family friend, took Mike under his wing and taught him the discipline and noble art of boxing.

Mike became good enough to earn a reputation as a fine amateur boxer, which got him into the police force at seventeen.

Bridie, his mother, used the extra money to put Tim through university. Tim seized the opportunity to shift social status, and left the poor suburban background and his family behind. Mike then became the centre; his mother's pride and joy.

Mike met Janet Cleary and fell instantly in love with her. They were both nearly eighteen, and by the time they were nineteen, they had their first child, Kate.

71

Mike, known in the force for his rough and ready attitude to things, working hard, moved up and assumed a reputation for being honest in his own way, with a bit of give and take on both sides.

Mike kept in touch with Clarrie and helped keep the kids off the street by being actively involved in the Police Boys Club, tutoring in boxing. Mike and Clarrie helped encourage and train a young street kid, Jimmy Crotty, to use his skills in the ring and not the school yard. Jimmy was a great source of pride to them both as he rose up in the ranks of the amateur fighters.

Everything ran smoothly for Mike, until a Royal Commission into crime and loud noises from Parliament demanded investigation into inner-city crime and the activities of Dan 'The Man' Davis in particular.

Mike took on 'The Man' and corruption within his own patch.

But Dan had a lot of friends who owed him.

Mike delegated a lot of the routine investigation to Theo Stevens, his junior partner, to gather up evidence without fear or favour.

Theo did.

He came up with a deck stacked against Mike, plus a small-time nightclub owner who swore Mike had been on the take for years.

Soon there were all sorts of people coming out of the woodwork to state their bit, and the inevitability of the whirlpool of accusation and counter-accusation surged around Mike to take him down on bribery and corruption.

Theo took over Mike's job.

In jail, Mike put his knowledge of the law to use and helped people who were on the inside with alternative legal advice.

He regained his self-respect and his sense of humour.

Mike, in an effort to save Janet, his wife, any more hurt, confusion and pain, filed for divorce, deciding once more in his own way, it'd be in her best interests and also his daughter, Kate's.

The old love that is between them is still unresolved. Clarrie O'Brien was Mike's only visitor. He brought Mike's mother, Bridie, with him on occasions when she could bear to come to see her son in prison.

When Mike got out, Clarrie was waiting for him.

He gave Mike a home at his gymnasium.

Mike helped Clarrie out around the gym, especially in training Jimmy, who has worked his way up in the ring to become the contender for the Australian Lightweight Championships.

When we first meet Mike Barnes, he has been out of prison for three days and is looking for a job.

THIS IS THE SITUATION AT THE BEGINNING OF THE SERIES.

THE MAJOR CHARACTERS

On a fresh page, briefly describe the major characters around whom the dramatic action will take place. Begin with your central character, then your major characters under the heading 'The major characters are'.

EXAMPLE –

THE EASY EARN

THE MAJOR CHARACTERS ARE:

MIKE BARNES

Late thirties. A laconic Australian male with a well-developed sense of humour and sexy charm whose good-hearted compassion for the trouble that people manage to get into has only been strengthened by his spell in prison. Mike's always been a sucker for a sob story and he now uses what he knows to help bail people out, and provide himself with a rough-and-ready living.

CLARRIE O'BRIEN

Sixtyish, with an Irish Catholic background. Clarrie got himself out of the fight game with enough money to buy his gym and set himself up as an honest trainer.

He is a wisp of a man with a dry Australian wit, an old-fashioned trainer who believes that too many women will weaken a bloke. Clarrie likes a drink, a bet, an argument and preferably in all-male company. He views most women with suspicion, reverent courtesy or outright distrust.

JIMMY CROTTY

Nineteenish, Jimmy grew up on the back streets of Kings Cross and learned to handle his small size with engaging charm, ease and when that failed, with his fists. After Jimmy had several run-ins with the law as a kid, Mike shifted him and his energy into the Police Boys Club and trained him in boxing. Jimmy is now Clarrie's greatest hope in the Titles.

Jimmy loves girls, good times, fun, daredevil excitement and the prestige of being a contender, all of which has gone humorously to his head. He delights in tormenting Clarrie, and loves being in on whatever Mike is doing.

And so on ...

THE MINOR CHARACTERS

On a fresh page, describe the minor characters who will add to the dramatic action under the heading 'Other characters include:'

EXAMPLE –

THE EASY EARN

OTHER CHARACTERS INCLUDE:

DAN 'THE MAN' DAVIS

Forties. Well preserved, extremely well kept, totally bent, crime king of the inner city who now projects an image of a businessman with standing in the community. As a patron of the arts, and with his well-publicised donations to charity, Dan secretly hopes for respect and a knighthood. He's come a long way for a teenage standover man, who now lets other people run his business interests in nightclubs, strip joints, prostitution, restaurants, race horses and people.

TONY DAVIS

In his early twenties and, as Dan's son, has had the best money could buy. Unfortunately it couldn't buy brains. Tony is good-looking, has a certain charm, and attempts to do things that will please his father. Few do. After Tony's mildly successful touring of an aging rock star, he now feels that he can describe himself and what he does as entrepreneuring. Dan is very proud of his son, the entrepreneur.

And so on ...

THE STORYLINE

On a fresh page, you next prepare a storyline of your idea. A storyline is an extended version of your synopsis, written in narrative form in the historic present tense, and will run from five to eight pages. Space does not permit me to give an example here. It should read like a well-written short story.

SAMPLE OF DIALOGUE

On a fresh page, select one scene from your storyline which will be best illustrate your ability to write dialogue. Prepare it so that it gives a more accurate feeling for the way your characters move, speak and act, so make it your best slice of action, humour and dialogue. Here is the way to lay it out.

EXAMPLE –

WK 2

EP 2

SC _

SCENE 1. STANDARD OPENING

0.35

WK 2

EP 2

SC 2

SCENE 2. O.B. EXT. DARLINGHURST ROAD DAY 1 (6.30 A.M.)

MIKE BARNES

BILL SCOTT (50)

POLICEMAN (50)

OFFENDER (50)

MIKE TURNS INTO DARLINGHURST ROAD WHERE HIS ATTENTION IS DRAWN TO A PADDY WAGON. HE STOPS TO LOOK AT TWO COPS MUSCLE AN OFFENDER INTO THE VAN.

MIKE RECOGNISES THE OLDER COP.

MIKE: Need a hand, Bill?

And so on. The next scene will be prepared on a fresh page.

SELLING YOUR IDEA

On a fresh page, write out a short statement of not more than one to two paragraphs on why you think your idea will be considered for production by a commercial network, and why you think the potential audience will respond to your project.

EXAMPLE –

THE EASY EARN

THE EASY EARN has a rare blend of ingredients and values. It has an identifiable cast of characters and easy access to the classic conflicts between right and wrong, families, and friends which will be played out against the backdrop of one of the most dramatic cities in the world.

THE EASY EARN is a difference series in the cop show vein.

THE EASY EARN combines laconic street humour with classic adventure drama etc.

And so on …

POSSIBLE TIME SLOT

Indicate in which time slot you envisage the project will be best placed. This is to give an idea whether it is suitable for children, family viewing, or adult only.

EXAMPLE –

THE EASY EARN will fit perfectly into the recommended viewing time of 8.30 p.m.

THE CURRICULUM VITAE

So that people will know who you are, what experience you have and if you are able to turn the possibility of your idea into a reality, a writer has a curriculum vitae prepared to send with his/her application.

EXAMPLE −

Curriculum Vitae

Name:

Born:

Education:

Graduate:

Radio Credits:	Project Title. Produced by. Year Produced.
TV Credits:	Project Title. Episode Number. Produced by. Year Produced. Directed by.
TV Concepts:	Project Title. Produced/Not Produced. Year. Subject Matter.
Films:	As above.
Commercials:	As above.
Documentaries:	As above.
Investments:	Project. Year. Investor. Subject. Produced/Not Produced.
Script Editor:	Project/s. Year. Written by. Director. Producer.
Storyliner:	As above.
Producer:	Project Title. Year. Written by. Director.
Director:	Project Title. Year. Written by. Producer.
Books:	Project Title. Published by. Year.
Publications:	Project Title. Produced by. Year.
Records:	Project Title. Produced by. Year.
Theatre:	As above.
Awards:	Project Title. Year. Nature of the award.
Work Experience:	Anything which gives a well-rounded picture of you, your world and your ability to handle diverse subjects.

NOTE

Every year, The Australian Writers Guild issues *The Writers' Directory*, which lists writers for radio, screen, stage and television in Australia. Your name should be in it.

TO RECAP

The preparation of your submission will be, by now, approximately twenty pages in length, neatly typed on A4 paper, with one and a half spacing between lines. Each page will be correctly numbered and have the title of your project inscribed on it.

Your concept now contains:

*   The title page (Step One)

*   An outline of the idea (Step Two)

*   An outline of the background (Step Three)

*   A statement of the idea format (Step Four)

*   A synopsis (Step Five)

*   A statement defining the areas of drama and conflict (Step Six)

*   An extended background (Step Seven)

*   A major character list (Step Eight)

*   A minor character list (Step Nine)

*   A 5-8 page storyline (Step Ten)

*   A sample scene of dialogue (Step Eleven)

*   A statement about marketing potential (Step Twelve)

*   A statement on time slot placement (Step Thirteen)

*   A curriculum vitae (Step Fourteen)

MAKING THE MONEY

DAMIEN PARER

HOW TO GIVE YOUR FILM AN EVEN CHANCE

To give your film an even chance of returning its budget in the marketplace:

* Clearly define the potential world market for the film. Talk to the people who are selling film for a living. They will be hard-edged, but it is better to know the minimum expected returns first so that you can make a business decision about the whole project.

* Calculate an average return for the film in the various markets around the world. Remember, the Australian market alone rarely covers the budget. Subject matter may preclude the film from a particular market. Think carefully about all these aspects.

* Do audience research. Conduct some market surveys about content and characters. Ask exhibitors, distributors and others in the selling role for opinions on the viability of your film proposal.

* Calculate potential income and compare it to the production budget.

DEFINE THE AUDIENCE

Before production you must be able to define the target audience for the film. Whether it is a feature film or a specialised documentary, the success or failure of the project depends upon clarity.

If the definition of the audience is uncertain, then the film will be forever in search of the unknown. Without clarity, how can you brief the following people:

* investors;

* writer and director;

* publicist;

* distributors?

POTENTIAL INCOME FROM FILMS

When assessing the viability of your project consider whether the markets described below may be potential sources of revenue in relation to your target audience:

* **theatrical exhibition**
- Australian
- foreign

* **non-theatrical exhibition** (released on 16 mm or video)
- renters pay a hire fee, e.g. airlines, prisons, clubs
- non-theatrical sales (prints and video)

* **television**
- released or broadcast standard video: 2 inch, 1 inch, or Betacam
- pay per view – current releases
- pay-television – subscriber service
- US network – NBC, CBS, ABC
- commercial broadcasting – free television
- public broadcasting
- syndication

* **video**
- sales
- rental

* **new technologies**
- videodisc
- multimedia

* **merchandising**
- novelisation; book about the film; music from the film; study guides; and other products
- toys, novelty items

* **other income**
- film about the film, recut the film for different market, package it with other films after its initial release
- newspaper or magazine serialisation
- music clips for TV, e.g. MTV
- still photos from film sold to a library
- publish the script
- stock shots from the film, e.g. scenery, wildlife
- NG takes sold as goof material to TV shows

* **rights may be saleable**
- remake

80

- precursor to the story
- sequel to the story
- offshoot series, stage play or radio program
- music publishing rights
- spin-off to a TV series
- film could be re-released after current contracts end

Average production costs: a guide

Feature	high budget	$5 million +
	medium	$3–5 million
	low	$800,000–$3 million
Children's feature	same as feature	
Telemovie		$750,000–$1.8 million
TV mini-series	per hour	$400,000–$1.2 million
TV series	per hour	$100,000–$200,000
Documentaries made for TV	per hour	$70,000–$300,000
Short films	drama	$2500–$3000 per minute
	non-drama	about $2500 per minute

GLOBAL RETURNS FOR AUSTRALIAN FILMS AND TELEVISION PROGRAMS

Below is a guide to the average global returns for Australian films & television programs in Australian dollars. The fees are net, after deducting distribution fees and agent's commission.

Feature film $

Australia & New Zealand	theatrical & non-theatrical	10,000 – 200,000
	broadcast TV	50,000 – 400,000
	video	10,000 – 80,000
US/Canada	theatrical & non-theatrical	50,000 – 1,000,000
	broadcast TV	100,000 – 1,500,000
	video	50,000 – 200,000
	pay TV	50,000 – 500,000
Western Europe (incl. UK)	theatrical & non-theatrical	100,000 – 500,000

Feature film contd.

$

		$	
	broadcast TV	50,000 –	300,000
	video	50,000 –	150,000
Eastern Europe	theatrical & non-theatrical	50,000 –	70,000
	broadcast TV	10,000 –	30,000
Central America & Mexico	broadcast TV	20,000 –	50,000
	video	10,000 –	60,000
South America	broadcast TV	50,000 –	150,000
	video	10,000 –	35,000
Africa	theatrical & non-theatrical	5,000 –	30,000
	broadcast TV	5,000 –	15,000
	video	5,000 –	15,000
Middle East	theatrical & non-theatrical	5,000 –	30,000
	broadcast TV	5,000 –	20,000
	video	2,000 –	10,000
Asia (including Japan)	theatrical & non-theatrical	40,000 –	300,000
	broadcast TV	20,000 –	100,000
	video	15,000 –	30,000

Children's feature

Australia & New Zealand	theatrical & non theatrical	10,000 –	50,000
	broadcast TV	40,000 –	250,000
	video	10,000 –	40,000
US/Canada	theatrical & non-theatrical	30,000 –	200,000
	broadcast TV	100,000 –	500,000
	video	5,000 –	30,000
	pay TV	20,000 –	150,000
Western Europe (incl. UK)	theatrical & non-theatrical	50,000 –	200,000
	broadcast TV	50,000 –	150,000
	video	30,000 –	150,000
Eastern Europe	theatrical & non-theatrical	20,000 –	40,000
	broadcast TV	10,000 –	30,000
Central America & Mexico	theatrical & non-theatrical	10,000 –	40,000
	broadcast TV	10,000 –	50,000
South America	theatrical & non-theatrical	30,000 –	150,000
	broadcast TV	10,000 –	40,000

Children's feature contd. $

Africa	theatrical & non-theatrical	5,000 – 20,000
	broadcast TV	5,000 – 10,000
	video	5,000 – 10,000
Middle East	theatrical & non-theatrical	5,000 – 20,000
	broadcast TV	5,000 – 15,000
	video	1,000 – 5,000
Asia (incl. Japan)	theatrical & non-theatrical	40,000 – 170,000
	broadcast TV	10,000 – 50,000
	video	15,000 – 30,000

Telemovie (90 mins)

Australia & New Zealand	broadcast TV	100,000 – 400,000
	video	10,000 – 40,000
US/Canada	broadcast TV	50,000 – 125,000
	video	10,000 – 50,000
	pay TV	30,000 – 200,000
Western Europe (incl. UK)	broadcast TV	50,000 – 200,000
	video	25,000 – 100,000
Eastern Europe	broadcast TV	5,000 – 15,000
Central America & Mexico	broadcast TV	5,000 – 15,000
South America	broadcast TV	10,000 – 40,000
Africa	broadcast TV	5,000 – 30,000
	video	5,000 – 10,000
Middle East	broadcast TV	5,000 – 25,000
	video	1,000 – 5,000
Asia (incl. Japan)	broadcast TV	20,000 – 100,000
	video	5,000 – 25,000

TV mini-series per hour (45–50 mins)

Australia & New Zealand	broadcast TV	75,000 – 400,000
	video	1,000 – 5,000
US/Canada	broadcast TV	50,000 – 400,000
	pay TV	50,000 – 200,000
Western Europe (incl. UK)	broadcast TV	75,000 – 200,000
Eastern Europe	broadcast TV	5,000 – 25,000
Central America & Mexico	broadcast TV	5,000 – 15,000

TV mini-series per hour (45–50 mins) $

South America	broadcast TV	10,000 –	50,000
Africa	broadcast TV	5,000 –	10,000
Middle East	broadcast TV	5,000 –	10,000
Asia (incl. Japan)	broadcast TV	10,000 –	50,000

Documentaries made for television per hour (45–50 mins)

Australia & New Zealand	broadcast TV	5,000 –	50,000
	video	1,000 –	5,000
US/Canada	broadcast TV	10,000 –	80,000
	video	5,000 –	10,000
Western Europe (incl. UK)	broadcast TV	25,000 –	75,000
Eastern Europe	broadcast TV	5,000 –	20,000
Central America & Mexico	broadcast TV	2,500 –	5,000
South America	broadcast TV	2,500 –	5,000
Africa	broadcast TV	2,500 –	5,000
Middle East	broadcast TV	2,500 –	5,000
Asia (incl. Japan)	broadcast TV	10,000 –	40,000

Short films, including drama, per hour

Australia & New Zealand	broadcast TV	5,000 –	40,000
US/Canada	broadcast TV	5,000 –	30,000
Western Europe (incl. UK)	broadcast TV	15,000 –	50,000
Eastern Europe	broadcast TV	2,500 –	5,000
Central America & Mexico	broadcast TV	1,000 –	3,000
South America	broadcast TV	5,000 –	10,000
Africa	broadcast TV	1,000 –	2,000
Middle East	broadcast TV	1,000 –	3,000
Asia (incl. Japan)	broadcast TV	5,000 –	20,000

Television series per hour (45–50 mins)

Australia & New Zealand	broadcast TV	70,000 –	200,000
US/Canada	broadcast TV	100,000 –	300,000
Western Europe (incl. UK)	broadcast TV	10,000 –	40,000
Eastern Europe	broadcast TV	5,000 –	20,000

A GUIDE TO DISTRIBUTION FEES

Percentage of Sale/Deal
%

Theatrical

USA/Canada	25 –	30
World	35 –	40

Non-theatrical

World	40 –	50

Television

Pay cable (USA)	15 –	30
Network (USA)	10 –	20
Syndication USA	30 –	40
World	30 –	40
Video	30 –	40

THINK LIKE A DISTRIBUTOR

Try to answer the following questions:

* Without describing plot or characters – what is the film about?

* What will the audience feel when leaving the theatre?

* Describe a typical member of the audience.

* Name the three most likely markets for the film.

* List the main protagonists. *Are they box office stars?*

* List the main antagonists. Are they *box office stars?*

* Name three other films that are most like your film.

* Where is the turning point in the film? *Has it got a happy or positive ending?*

* What censorship rating is it likely to get?

* What are the merchandising possibilities?

* In a sentence, what goes under the title on publicity material? Is it the best possible title?

* What is the film genre? Comedy, horror, children's, etc.?

* What is the optimum release date?

85

PRE-PLANNING FOR SUCCESS

As early as possible in the film's life you should be getting it into a position of strength. The film will fail or succeed on its financial returns. Films, by nature, are sold individually and require promotion to suit their particular needs. Audiences have to be courted and actively pursued to get them into the cinema or to watch the program on television. Even before this, distributors, exhibitors and television network executives have to be warmed to the financial potential of the film.

As producer it is your job to give the film its best chance. Early promotion and publicity all assist in convincing the distributors and sales agents of its potential value. Keep them informed. Invite them on set. Send them photographs and press cuttings. Have meetings with them.

THE ROLE OF THE UNIT PUBLICIST

Prior to and during the shoot, a unit publicist can assist the producer in early promotion of the film to investors, distributors, sales agents and the general public. The unit publicist will also develop the materials which will be required to market the film when it is released. The unit publicist will organise:

* location visits: media, public relations, distributors, investors;

* trade press releases: *Encore, Cinema Papers, Film News, The Business of Film, Screen International, Variety, Hollywood Reporter;*

* press releases generally: daily papers, local papers, *TV Week, New Idea, Women's Weekly;*

* press kits containing synopsis, cast and crew lists, biographies;

* supervision of still photography, printing and captioning of stills, selection of stills;

* exclusives: set up and supervise special interviews for feature articles or TV news items;

* final report: compile a final press kit ready for the distributors and/or sales agents; an electronic press kit may also be made.

THE BOX OFFICE GAME SHOW

This is a lighthearted quiz with a salutary message.

Put your idea/synopsis/treatment/script to the test. Award points after answering each question. Add up the total. Answers at the end.

1.   What is the target audience?
     12–35 3
     18–35 2
     Over 30 1
2.   One of the leading roles is played by:
     A recognisable international box office star 3
     A recognisable international TV star is in the film 2
     There is no recognisable star 1
3.   Your production budget is:
     less than $2.5 m 3
     between $2.5 m and $5 m 2
     over $5 m 1
4.   The distributor is financially committed 3
     The distributor is in place with a small financial commitment 2
     There is no distributor at this stage 1
5.   All rights and territories are available 3
     Some rights and territories are available 2
     Most of the rights and territories are pre-sold 1
6.   Most rights and territories are pre-sold and the film is in profit before
     production 3
     Some rights are pre-sold to 50 per cent of budget 2
     Very few rights and territories are pre-sold 1
7.   The story has universality of theme and would have relevance to most
     audiences 3
     The story should work well in most English-speaking territories 2
     The story will have strong appeal to a smaller audience 1
8.   The producer is willing to change the title and re-edit or re-shot
     sequences after the results of audience surveys 3
     Some adjustments will be possible 2
     No changes can be made 1
9.   There are strong and logical reasons to indicate that the film will succeed
     in the US mainstream cinema 3
     It has a reasonable chance 2
     Its best release will be on the art circuit 1
10. The film is likely to receive a rating equivalent to M in Australia 3
     The film is likely to be a G rating where most of the audience pay half
     price 2
     The film is likely to receive an R certificate 1
11. It will be a box office hit in Australia 3
     It will do average business in Australia 2
     It will take careful handling in Australia 1

12. It is clear that the film will receive distribution advances in four other
countries other than the US 3
Two other countries 2
It is not known at this stage 1
13. The audience will care a lot about the leading characters and want them
to win 3
The characters are appealing 2
The characters are not very appealing 1
14. The locations are pleasant 2
The locations are not an important element 1
15. The director is well known and audiences follow his/her films 3
The director is experienced in this film genre 2
The director is unknown 1
16. How successful at the box office was the precursor to the film? (i.e. you are
now planning a sequel)
Very 3
Moderately 2
Not 1
17. Was the novel or other source of the screenplay a best-seller? 3
Did it achieve moderate sales? 2
Is it unpublished? 1
18. The title has been tested with a potential audience of the film and found
to be very appealing/intriguing 3
There is some evidence that it will draw an audience 2
You like it 1
19. A hit song from the film will be playing on TV or radio just before
the film's release 3
The sound track will be available 2
Music will not be released 1
20. Does the film lend itself to merchandising or other promotional
possibilities?
Yes 3
Not much 2
No 1
21. Is the film's genre currently successful at the box office and do you expect
that this genre will be just as successful in two years time?
Yes 3
Don't know 2
No 1
22. The film is set in the past or future 3
It will date slowly 2
It has contemporary relevance 1
23. Can the film be re-released, e.g. children's pictures every Christmas?
Yes 3
Maybe 2
No 1

24. Does the film lend itself to a release in the peak business period, e.g.
Christmas, Easter?
Yes 3
Maybe 2
No 1

SCORES

66–72 If it's that good someone would have already made it. Go back and answer the questions more realistically.

51–65 May I invest in your film?

35–50 The film has a reasonable chance. Have another look at the package. See if you can improve the film's potential to earn income.

24–34 Don't bankrupt your investors and yourself with this film.

LEGAL ISSUES

Copyright And Other Legal Matters

Ian Collie

Director
Arts Law Centre of Australia
Sydney

Acquisition, control and exploitation ... this sounds very imperial but from a producer's viewpoint these are fundamental aspects of film making. The key element here is not an army of foot soldiers, but some intangible form of property known as copyright that subsists like a benign condition in all original creative works, whether that be a novel, a musical score or the film itself.

Copyright can be a difficult and abstract notion to grapple with, a subject from which only metaphysicians and lawyers seem to obtain any real satisfaction Its importance, though, cannot be understated. It is the golden thread, legally speaking, of the film business and a failure to understand the nature of copyright and the scope of the rights inherent in it could lead to a film project coming unstuck.

As we greet the emerging information superhighway, there will be many opportunities and pitfalls for the producer to be aware of. Technological innovations such as digital compression and optic fibre are paving the way for new products like multimedia and introducing broadband services such as pay television and video on demand.

Digitalisation provides greater ease with which to manipulate and access copyright material without the owner's consent. The development in high compression techniques will soon see CD-video on the market (only a standards dispute is delaying its entry) and, more threateningly, recordable and erasable CDs that could see a significant increase in home taping and piracy. Computer digital imaging is also raising interesting ethical and moral rights issues. Two Swiss computer scientists are currently producing a film that will feature the digital recreation of James Dean, Elvis Presley and Marilyn Monroe.

It is essential, therefore, that producers have a basic grasp of copyright and associated film rights. This chapter provides a primer looking at copyright, contractual issues and other legal matters, focusing primarily on the development phase of a film project.

The Nature And Scope Of Copyright

Copyright is a member of the class of property known as intellectual property. In contrast to other types of property, like real estate, the property rights are in the right to reproduce or copy a work (and hence its name 'copyright') rather than in the physical work itself. The two are quite separate property rights. So if I buy a video I can essentially do what I want with it: re-sell it, dispose of it, add it to my vast collection of videos. But unless I buy or acquire a licence to the copyright to the video I cannot copy the subject matter on video or deal with any of the other exclusive rights belonging to the copyright owner.

Despite their differences all forms of property have the same basic principles when it comes to dealings. A property owner can sell (or assign) the property outright; can lease (or license) the property subject to certain conditions relating to time, cost, etc.; and can leave the property in a will for the benefit of others.

So what is copyright? It is the exclusive right to do, and authorise or prevent others from doing, certain acts in respect of the subject matter that is protected under the *Copyright Act*. The subject matter protected are 'works', which refer to the traditional creative works of literature, drama, music and art, and the imaginatively titled 'subject matter other than works'. The latter, sometimes referred to as neighbouring rights, consist of sound recordings (e.g. CDs), films and videos, television and sound broadcasts) and published editions (i.e. typesetting). They are independent and separate to the underlying 'works' that may be embodied in the subject matter. Thus, an infringement of the copyright in a film may also be an infringement of the musical work, in the form of a soundtrack, that is synchronised to the film. Copyright protection was accorded to producers and publishers of these neighbouring rights primarily to encourage and reward investment in the creative works. (It wasn't until 1969 that film actually became a separate category of copyright material.)

The acts that are the exclusive domain of copyright owners in relation to literary and dramatic works, music and art are:

✳   to reproduce the work in a material form – for example, to record music onto a record (known in the music industry as the mechanical rights); to make a film of a book (known simply as the film rights); storing a copy of a photograph or other artistic work on CD-ROM;

✳   to publish the work – that is, to supply or distribute copies of works to the public whether by sale or otherwise;

✳   to perform the work in public – the obvious example is the live performance of a theatrical work or music. (Note the qualifying expression 'in public'. The right does not apply if it is a performance in domestic circumstances but performance in public has been defined by the courts very broadly – for example, performance of a play to a members-only club and with no admission can still be considered a performance in public);

✳   to broadcast the work – includes television, radio and some satellite broadcasts;

✳   to cause the work to be transmitted to subscribers to a diffusion service – better known as cable rights;

✳   to make an adaptation of a work (apart from artistic works) – this covers making a screenplay from a novel, a foreign translation, an arrangement of an orchestral score, amongst others.

93

In relation to films and video, in contrast to the underlying creative works that are comprised in the film, the following exclusive rights are protected:

* to make a copy of the film – for example, to make a video cassette of a film;

* to cause a film to be seen or heard in public – the most obvious being the theatrical exhibition of the film;

* to broadcast the film;

* to cause the film to be transmitted to subscribers to a diffusion service (cable rights).

(It is anticipated that the *Copyright Act* will soon be amended to provide for a new right of transmission to the public. This right will encompass the existing broadcasting right and replace and extend the cable right. It will apply to both works and other subject matter.)

Of course when it comes to the real world, most deals acquiring rights tend to use language that is more industry specific and shorthand than the rights listed above. Hence expressions like film rights, television rights, CD-ROM rights, videocassette rights are simply different media formats for the reproduction rights in works.

Copyright in film lasts for 50 years from the first publication. For the underlying works to the film – music, script, etc. – the usual rule of thumb is the life of the author plus 50 years. This period of copyright will still apply even if the author is no longer the owner of the copyright. Once the 50 years after the death of the author has expired, the work enters the public domain and anyone can use or copy it without infringing copyright. The copyright to 'Beatrix Potter' has recently expired. Those film producers with a taste for bunny movies ...!

EXPRESSION OF IDEAS

One of the basic tenets of copyright law is that there is no copyright in ideas, opinions or facts as such, but rather in the expression or form of those ideas.

The distinction is important but notoriously difficult to apply in practice, especially in relation to infringement of copyright (discussed below). The general rule is that there is no copyright in the central idea or theme of a story but rather in the combination of situations, events and scenes which constitute the particular working out or expression of the idea or theme.

Therefore, for a work to obtain copyright protection, the idea must be reduced to writing or some other material form such as being fixed on film or tape. Furthermore, the literary, dramatic, musical or artistic work produced must be original. (Interestingly the Act is silent on whether this is a requirement for film.) The degree of originality required, at least from a creative angle, is not great – that copyright subsists in racing programs, trade catalogues and blank Kalamazoo accounting forms is testimony to that requirement – but it must be the product of the creator's own skill and effort and not be copied. Finally, the author of the work must be a citizen or resident of Australia or of a country to which Australia has promised copyright protection through its international treaty obligations.

Copyright protection is automatic and there is no need to formally register the works or film as with other forms of intellectual property like patents or trademarks. Once the three elements exist – material form, originality and qualified person – copyright will immediately subsist. It is advisable, though not mandatory, to give notice of the copyright by the familiar copyright symbol © followed by the name of the copyright owner and year of first publication. Such notice is a requirement for protection in some countries and importantly, advises users that the work is protected and who to contact if permission is sought to use it.

In those situations where your ideas or concepts have not been reduced to material form, protection may still be afforded through the law relating to confidential information. For a court to enforce an action for breach of confidence there must exist three essential elements: (i) the information has the necessary quality of confidence – this excludes trivia or ideas that are public knowledge, (ii) the information was disclosed in confidence, and (iii) there has been an unauthorised use or threatened use of the information. As to the first element, the court will examine such factors as to the extent to which the idea is known or has been disclosed to others; the ease with which those ideas could be independently duplicated by others; measures taken to keep the idea secret; and the value of the idea to the author.

The type of situation in which the law of confidential information may assist is in that initial contact with, say, a TV network to interest them in an idea for a new program. It is advisable to ensure that the recipient of the information understands its confidential nature. The Arts Law Centre has devised an information sheet on this subject which includes a sample confidentiality letter that should be forwarded to the recipient before divulging the confidential information. As a rule, though, it is far safer to express your ideas on paper, in the form of a concept document or treatment, and add both the standard copyright notice and a 'private and confidential' warning.

INFRINGEMENT OF COPYRIGHT

Infringement is the use of a substantial part of a work or film without the permission of the owner, unless the work is in the public domain or a special exception applies.

What is 'substantial' in any particular case is a question of fact to be determined having regard to all the circumstances. The most important factor is the quality of what is taken in relation to the work as a whole. If it is a vital or essential part of the work or film, even though only a small part in quantity, it may nevertheless be considered to be an infringement. Other factors that the courts consider are whether what is taken is so important that the sales of the copyright owner's work might be affected, whether the infringing person is attempting to take an unfair advantage of the author's work and skill; and the originality of the part taken (a film based on historical facts is less likely to infringe than one based on an original work of fiction, although if the copyright goes to the actual selection and arrangement of facts, the inference of deliberate copying and hence infringement arise). A rather tired old maxim that regularly pops up in copyright cases is 'what is worth copying is prima facie worth protecting'.

Difficulties arise when a film is based on general ideas or themes inherent in a novel, play or some other work. Copyright protects the wording, the form of expression rather than the ideas themselves. The idea/expression distinction is often difficult to draw and the courts need to balance the public interest in maintaining the free flow of ideas and facts available to all to use and the private interest in protecting an author from unfair appropriation.

An illustration of this is where Universal City Studios sued the Italian producers of a film *The Great White*, an imitation of *Jaws*. The Italian filmmakers argued that their film about a shark terrorising a local community was merely a genre film and that there was no copyright in ideas. The court disagreed. It held that the combination of events and characters were so markedly similar as to give rise to the inference that a substantial part of the literary work and film of *Jaws* had been reproduced.

ACQUIRING THE RIGHTS

As a producer you will need to obtain, whether by assignment or licence, the rights to all the underlying works to the film. These works are the original screenplay or an adaptation of an existing play or book, as well as the treatment, outlines, synopses or drafts of the script and the music for the film. If artistic works are included you will also need to obtain a licence to use such works.

The difference between assignment and licence is that the former involves the sale or transfer of the copyright and the latter gives the user (the licensee) the right to use the work but not actually own it. The licence agreement will be tailored to fit the needs of the licensee in terms of whether it is exclusive or non-exclusive, the period of use, the territory, what uses are permitted and so on. Assignment, on the other hand, is generally the loss by the author of both ownership and control of their work, although even assignment agreements can still be limited by time, territory and whether it is some or all of the rights that are assigned. Both an assignment and an exclusive licence agreement must be in writing to be enforceable.

The general practice in the film industry is to acquire by assignment the film and ancillary rights in all underlying works, except published music in which usually a non-exclusive licence is granted by both the music publisher and the record company. Arguably an exclusive licence agreement for the full term of copyright is just as effective and can be drafted to give the producer full control over the rights. Assignments tend to be favoured by investors but even these types of arrangements transfer only partial rights – authors usually reserve novelisation and stage rights – and sometimes include reassignment clauses for a material breach of the contract – for example, if principal photography has not occurred within five years of the grant of film rights.

So in acquiring these rights the first question is identifying the owner of copyright in the work. The author of a novel is not necessarily the owner of the film rights to that novel. In the publishing contract the author may have granted an exclusive licence to the publisher to sell the film rights. The first port of call in acquiring rights to an existing literary or dramatic work is the publisher. If the publisher does not have the rights or the work is unpublished contact the writer or his/her agent or his/her estate if the writer is deceased.

There are several possible options for soundtrack music: library or production music, using pre-recorded or published material or commissioning an original soundtrack. The rights owner will vary in each case.

Locating the rights owner for library music, general music specifically written and recorded for use in advertising, television and films, is through AMCOS (Australasian Mechanical Copyright Owners' Society Limited), a copyright collecting society for music publishers.

For existing published material you need to obtain two licences: one from the owner/s of the musical work and the other from the owner of the sound recording. If the recording is a CD or LP record then check the back cover or insert that provides the © and (P) notice, the latter being the universal symbol for copyright ownership in the sound recording. [(P) stands for Phonograph.] Usually a music publisher will own the music copyright pursuant to a music publishing agreement between the composer and the publisher. Either contact the music publisher direct or via AMCOS. If the composer is still the owner, s/he will need to be contacted or, if there is a composer and lyricist, the two separate owners. APRA (Australasian Performing Right Association) should be consulted for assistance here. And if the published material is an arrangement or an adaptation of an original work contact the original composer (or publisher) as well. By this stage your chain of title of copyright is beginning to resemble a genealogical tree!

For use of the copyright in the sound recordings, contact ARIA (Australian Record Industry Association) or the record company direct. (*The Australasian Music Industry Directory* has an up-to-date and comprehensive listing of record companies, music publishers and music associations.) Check that the record company has obtained the performer's consent for the recording to be used on film. If not, a performer's release will need to be obtained from each performer. (The Arts Law Centre has a sample performer's release to assist.)

Acquiring the various rights to a film project is part of the chain of title sought by investors, film finance bodies and insurers to ensure that there will be no obstacle in exploiting the film. Permissions and rights clearances will need to be obtained from all the appropriate parties, otherwise the film could be an infringement of someone's copyright, exposing the producer to legal action and risking delays to the distribution and marketing of the film. It is so important that you carefully scrutinise the book publishing and music industry contracts to ensure that the rights owner actually has the rights to give. If it is a book publisher and they do not have the film rights, obtain a release or quit claim acknowledging this and ensure it is drafted broadly so as to cover not just the film rights but the ancillary rights sought. If it is a music publisher check that they are able to provide a synchronisation licence (term for applying recorded or published music to film) – they may only be a local sub-publisher and permission will need to be sought from the overseas head publisher. Other points to consider:

∗   are there any underlying rights to the literary, dramatic or musical work? – it could be an adaptation or use extracts from another work;

∗   that there has been no default by the publisher which would permit termination or reversion of rights that could prejudice any assignment or licence to be granted;

∗   that the underlying work is unencumbered to any third party – for example, an unpublished screenplay may be subject to a proprietary interest to the investor who provided script development funding;

✳   that if any rights clearance is executed by an agent, manager or power of attorney that they have the appropriate documentation that authorises their capacity to act;

✳   that all performers' releases have been obtained;

✳   if the work is potentially defamatory check if any legal opinion was obtained by the author or publisher;

✳   if the rights are given by an estate of a deceased author, obtain a copy of the will to ensure that the person granting the rights has the power to do so.

The rights concerning artworks will also need to be cleared. If sets and designs are created in the course of employment, the employer will own copyright. If they are commissioned the general rule is that the artist/designer retains copyright unless the parties agree to the contrary in contract. Therefore, a letter of agreement or contract in which the artist assigns or grants an exclusive licence will be needed here. The use of artworks in a film is permitted if it is incidental otherwise you will need authorisation from the artist if s/he is the copyright owner. Finally, for photographic works, such as films stills, the general rule is that the commissioning party rather than the photographer owns the copyright in the works. A letter to the photographer confirming this arrangement should be sent.

The clearance of rights concerning the filming of performers and people are discussed under the heading 'Other rights' below.

To state the blindingly obvious, there can be a lot of work involved in properly obtaining all the rights to the component parts of a film project. It is essential that you keep and properly manage all the documentation to this chain of title. It is the foundation from which investment and distribution will result. Any glitches and the project can come unstuck. Accordingly, it is advisable that you retain an experienced film lawyer to assist you in this stage. If your film is a low budget film, documentary or short film and you do not have the budget or financial capacity to afford the services of a private lawyer then take advantage of the advisory services offered by the Arts Law Centre of Australia and the Australian Copyright Council, both organisations funded by the Australian Film Commission, to fill this need.

FILM CONTRACTS

GENERAL PRINCIPLES

Whether it is acquiring rights or retaining cast and crew, the deals or arrangements you make will be underscored by the principles governing contract law. The aim of contract law is to instil certainty to the business deal by requiring a party to the contract to perform what s/he undertook to do. If s/he reneges or fails to fully perform the task, the other party has certain legal remedies available, such as monetary compensation (known as damages) to address the situation.

A contract is a legally binding agreement. There is no requirement that it be in writing except in the case of an assignment or exclusive licence of copyright. A verbal agreement is enforceable

– something that Kim Basinger discovered to her cost in her failure to perform in *Boxing Helena* – although certainly not encouraged due to the evidentiary difficulties in enforcing such a contract in a court of law. Fortunately it is standard practice in the film industry to use written contracts although sometimes there is slavish reliance on precedent and standard contracts, some of which are still replete with wheretofores and whereofs and other tired forms of legalese.

Contracts are flexible instruments that should be adapted to accurately reflect the terms agreed by the parties. There is no science to their drafting although it would be very unwise to attempt complex transactions like production investment contracts or distribution contracts without the assistance of an experienced film lawyer. The format is generally one identifying the parties at the head of the contract, a preamble (often referred to as the 'recitals') providing a brief statement as to the background to the contract and the intention of the parties, the body of the contract in which with precision and clarity you identify and express in plain English all the terms agreed to by the parties and conclude with the execution clause to which both parties sign. For very simple contracts often a letter of agreement will suffice.

Contracts arise when one party makes an offer and the other accepts. There is a further need for a price or benefit to be attached to the contract, what is known in legal parlance as consideration. It explains the contrivance you sometimes see with release forms in which the token amount of $1.00 may be paid, say, to a performer to ensure that the release is not unenforceable due to lack of consideration.

The distinction between pre-contractual negotiations and a concluded agreement, the latter being legally enforceable, is not always evident. Deal memos tend to fall into either category. They may only be an intention to enter into an agreement or they may be so vague and uncertain as to not be a binding agreement. Although the courts may imply terms into a contract to reflect commercial reality and industry practice, generally, if deal memos or other shorthand forms of written or verbal agreements are plagued with imprecise language and incompleteness the courts will be reluctant to enforce. A recent US case on this point involved the pop star Mariah Carey. Her stepfather took legal action to enforce a verbal licence agreement to permit him to merchandise 'Mariah dolls'. He based his claim on the fact that twice in the family car and once on his boat he had told Carey 'Don't forget the Mariah dolls' and 'I get the Mariah dolls' and she had either responded 'okay' or had smiled and nodded. The US District Court found that on the evidence both parties did not intend to form a concluded agreement, in particular, essential terms such as price, territory, duration and right to approve the dolls had not even been discussed.

It is therefore essential to use clear and precise language to define exactly what rights are being acquired or granted, what type of medium (film, video, etc.) the term, the territory, the mode of payment and so on. You don't want to repeat Disney Studio's mistake where they hired Peggy Lee to sing in *The Lady and the Tramp* but did not acquire sufficient rights. When they released the film on video 40 years later, Lee sued and received more than US$3.2 million in damages for infringement of her video rights.

Once a contract is created it will either expire with the effluxion of time after both parties have performed their obligations under the contract or it will be terminated by mutual agreement, an unforeseen event (e.g. strike or lockout) or by breach of one of the parties. If one party defaults the other has certain remedies available to it depending on how significant and essential the term is that has been breached. For example, in the case of Bettini v Gye, an Italian tenor was in breach of his contract for services by being a number of days late for rehearsals. The English opera company sought to terminate his contract but the court held that the breach was not sufficiently material to warrant such a remedy. Rather the company had to keep the contract on foot and were restricted to a claim for any damages that they could prove they had suffered. If terms relating to payment or time are essential then this should be stipulated in the contract and a termination clause provided in which the defaulting party has a certain period within which to rectify the breach otherwise the contract automatically terminates.

Finally, it is suggested that a disputes clause be included in which both parties have recourse to a disputes resolution forum such as mediation. The Arts Law Centre has a mediation program which is tailor-made for the film industry and is much cheaper and quicker than traditional avenues like litigation.

OPTION AND PURCHASE AGREEMENT

If the budget of your film or your finances permit, a film lawyer should always be retained to assist with the drafting of the various contracts to your project. The commercial reality for many producers, however, is that during the development stage of a film, and especially if it is a low budget film, the luxury of retaining a lawyer is just not feasible.

There are a number of useful organisations which can assist with sample film contracts and advice. For example, the Australian Writers' Guild has option and purchase agreements and screenwriters agreements, the Media and Entertainment Arts Alliance has crew agreements and actors contracts, the Australian Guild of Screen Composers a music commission agreement, the Australian Screen Directors' Association a directors contract and the Arts Law Centre has sample option and purchase agreements, performers release forms, music commission agreements, licence agreements for artistic works and so on. For further guidance, a list of reference texts is included in the bibliography section of this book. As mentioned, the Centre, the Guild and the Australian Copyright Council can also give advice on these contracts. The AFC/AFTRS *Production budgeting and film management manual* also carries copies of many of these contracts.

One important document is the option and purchase agreement where a film is based on an existing literary or dramatic work. Firstly, the producer takes out an option on a novel or book or even an existing screenplay so as to buy time whilst exploring the various avenues to raise finance for the film. The option period will usually be for a period of twelve months with one or two further renewal or extension periods of twelve months each. The option fee, like the purchase fee, will vary with the reputation of the author but a rule of thumb is between $500 and $1000 for each option period, or 5 per cent of the actual purchase price for each period. These fees should be non-returnable if the producer does not exercise the option as the author has had to forgo selling the rights to other prospective buyers.

Other matters to include in your option agreement are:

✱ correctly identifying the rights holder – does the author or the publisher own the film rights?

* warranty and indemnity that the author (or publisher) owns the work and has not licensed the rights to any third party (note an existing screenplay may be subject to a prior interest held by a film finance body);

* identifying the work. If it is an unpublished manuscript, state the working title. If it is an idea then describe in detail the idea in the recitals or attach as a schedule to the option agreement;

* what, if any, development of the work, e.g., first draft screenplay, can be made during this option period and who owns copyright in the developed or adapted work if the option is not exercised?

* if rights to develop or adapt the work were granted during this period, define with clarity the scope of these rights (this is usually done by referring to the rights granted in the annexed purchase agreement);

* clearly state the date by which the option should be exercised and how it is to be exercised.

The option agreement must state that the exercise of the option shall automatically give rise to the annexed purchase agreement and that the author will be obliged to execute the agreements. It must be annexed to the option agreement at the time the parties sign the option, otherwise you may not be able to bind the author to accept the terms of the purchase agreement.

The purchase price for the film and ancillary rights will vary with the reputation and bargaining clout of the author and/or publisher. As a rule of thumb it tends to be around 2–3 per cent of the budget. If the budget is not ascertainable at the time of entering into the option agreement, apply a sliding scale of fees depending on the budget with a maximum and minimum ceiling. The purchase price will usually include a share of the producer's share of net profits from the film (and this expression should be defined with precision) less any option fees paid.

The purchase agreement should cover the following points:

* a clear statement of the rights acquired, e.g., right to adapt to make a screenplay, treatment, etc., right to reproduce generally and exploit as a film in specified or all media, right to make sequels and remakes, merchandising rights; right to licence for multimedia and other electronic/digital publishing media. Normally an author will reserve publication, live stage and radio rights although he/she may not be able to exploit same within a certain period without the producer's consent (referred to as a 'hold back' provision);

* are the rights acquired by way of assignment (partial or full) or by exclusive licence?

* warranty by copyright owner that they own copyright; it is original and does not infringe other copyright; and is not defamatory;

* the territory for which the rights are granted – with satellite transmission of film don't be surprised to see not just 'world' but 'universe' rights in many contracts;

* the term of the assignment or licence – usually for the full period of copyright;

101

* a credit clause for the author – this should state exactly how the author is to be accredited and in what circumstances the attribution will and will not apply;

* there should be a termination clause in which rights can be reassigned to the author for an agreed sum if principal photography of the film has not commenced within, say, five years, or the author has not been paid within the agreed time, after due notice to remedy the breach;

* a disputes clause should be included for resolution of disputes between parties, such as disputes concerning accreditation. The arbitration committee of the Australian Writers' Guild and the Arts Law Centre Mediation Service are two suggested services.

Other Rights

Performer's Rights

Performer's rights were introduced in the *Copyright Act* in 1989 to give performers (including musicians and singers) some limited rights over uses of their performances. It enables the performer to prevent others from using their performance without their permission. The period of protection is 21 years from the end of the year in which the performance was made.

Performer's rights prevent the following unauthorised uses of a performance:

* recording, whether directly or indirectly, the performance;

* broadcasting or re-broadcasting the performance, either directly from the live performance or an unauthorised use of it;

* transmitting by cable the live performance or an unauthorised recording of it;

* commercial dealings in unauthorised recordings of the performance.

Generally, the performer's rights are exhausted with the first recording of the live performance, unlike copyright in which the author or composer can control subsequent uses of their work. Only with respect to the use of a sound recording in the soundtrack of a film is further permission required, unless the performer's initial consent to the recording extended to this use. This should be checked with the record company concerned and an undertaking given by them to that effect.

Both the Media and Entertainment Arts Alliance and the Arts Law Centre have sample performer's releases that may be of assistance.

Moral Rights

In contrast to the economic rights inherent in copyright, moral rights are non-economic or personal rights of an author to be accredited for the authorship of their work and to prevent the alteration, debasement or derogatory treatment of their work which prejudicially affects the author's reputation. These rights, known as the right of attribution and the right of integrity respectively, acknowledge the intimate bond that exists between a creator and his/her creative work and therefore, unlike copyright, cannot be assigned. They may, however, be waived, an aspect of the proposed moral rights legislation that is likely to render such rights ineffective as it is anticipated that it will become standard practice in the film industry for all authors (including directors) to waive their moral rights. This has been the situation in the United Kingdom since the introduction of moral rights in that country in 1988.

At the date of writing this chapter a moral rights regime has yet to be introduced in Australia, although the 'Creative Nation' cultural policy statement (October, 1994) has made a commitment to introduce such legislation. A discussion paper on the moral rights issue has been released and there has been much vigorous debate, particularly in the film industry, on the subject especially concerning who can assert moral rights (the director? the scriptwriter? the producer?) and the scope of the right of integrity. To give an illustration of the latter, Italian film directors were successful in a moral rights action against television networks that interrupted the broadcast of their films with excessive advertisement breaks.

For further reading on moral rights, see the Commonwealth's discussion paper 'Proposed Moral Rights Legislation for Copyright Creators' and the seminar paper 'Auteur or Author? Moral Rights and the Film Industry' available from the Arts Law Centre.

PERSONALITY RIGHTS

Personality rights (or publicity rights, as they are known in the United States) refer to the right of a person to prevent their name, likeness or biography from being used in the commercial exploitation of a product without their consent. In the United States there have been a number of look-alike and sound-alike cases in which celebrities such as Woody Allen and Bette Midler have successfully asserted their publicity rights to prevent unauthorised appropriation of their reputation.

Australia does not have a legislative scheme of personality rights although there are remedies available under the tort of passing off and trade practices legislation that may assist an individual whose personality or reputation has been used to sell products. Paul Hogan successfully prevented the maker of Grosby Leather shoes from using a television advertisement parodying the knife scene in *Crocodile Dundee*. The Court found that a viewer would be misled into believing that Hogan had endorsed the product.

The 'rights' are important with respect to the marketing and packaging of the film, as well as with the promotion of any ancillary merchandising products. As a producer you will need to negotiate in both your rights agreements and key personnel agreements the use of the name, likeness and biography for these purposes.

Multimedia Legal Issues

Stephen Peach

Partner
Gilbert & Tobin
Sydney

There is a scene in the film *Stand By Me* where the central characters are seated around a campfire pondering what must have been one of the major issues for children in the fifties. If Mickey's a mouse, Donald's a duck and Pluto's a dog, what the hell is Goofy?

Many people ask a similar question about multimedia – they have a vague idea as to what it is (or what it is not) but they are not entirely sure. See Ben Cardillo's chapter (pp. 55–64) on multimedia for a definition of it.

Multimedia is (or can be) many things, but essentially all multimedia products (as they are rapidly and unimaginatively becoming known) share the following elements:

✳ they contain a mixture of visual images (often including moving footage), audio and text;

✳ the data is stored in a digital form;

✳ the products are interactive and non-linear in the sense that responses, and the nature of responses, are dependent upon the interaction by the user.

Current everyday examples of multimedia products are most often found in the CD-ROM format used in personal computers. These products range from high level computer games to 'infotainment' products (such as compendiums of film reviews complete with movie footage, still photographs and theme songs) to educational products such as interactive encyclopaedias.

So why are we talking about multimedia in this book about the film business? Principally because multimedia producers will often look to film to form part of a multimedia product. Also, as Ben Cardillo describes in his chapter, film producers will look increasingly to produce products especially for multimedia. And, of course, film is an 'early' form of multimedia combining as it does visual images, audio and text (in the form of a screenplay). As such, many of the issues that confront multimedia producers have already been confronted by traditional film makers.

This discussion will focus upon the position of the film maker in the multimedia world. However, the position of the multimedia producer (if that is who you are) will be fairly easy to see.

OBTAINING CLEARANCES

Many multimedia products incorporate moving footage which is often shot specifically for that multimedia product. However, just as often, the multimedia producer will want to use someone else's film, or at least parts of it, in that product. In that case, the multimedia producer will need to obtain a licence from the owner of copyright in the film or footage.

As the copyright owner faced with a clearance request, there are a number of major issues to consider, including:

✳ **whether you are obliged to grant a licence.** In short, no. There is no statutory entitlement on the part of the multimedia producer to use your film irrespective of your consent, provided that the film is still subject to copyright protection. The period of copyright protection for a film is generally 50 years from release.

✳ **whether you have the right or ability to grant a licence in any event.** While the film producer or production company will often own the copyright in the film, this will usually not be sufficient if the film incorporates other material (music is a good example) the copyright in which is owned by others. While film production companies often take a complete assignment of copyright in, for example, the screenplay, they are just as often restricted in the extent to which they can use, say, the music synchronised with the film. Therefore, you as the film producer need to verify or clear all underlying rights before granting any licence to a multimedia producer. Frequently, the right to digital or multimedia use of such underlying or associated copyright material is reserved to the copyright owner and you will not be able to licence your film, or parts of it, without getting a clearance from that original owner of copyright. Contracts with the actors and performers in the film may also prohibit or restrict such use.

✳ **the amount of licence fee.** This is almost literally the $64,000 question. The difficulty with multimedia use is that it is extremely difficult to gauge the extent of intended or possible use of either the footage or the multimedia product into which it is incorporated. Also, given that it is such a relatively new form of exploitation for film, many people are still feeling their way. At this stage, it is difficult to distil any objective criteria for setting appropriate licence fees. However, what is almost certainly true is that, for multimedia use, less is definitely more (or rather, less is definitely worth more). Given the objective of most multimedia products (to incorporate many different elements) and the current technological limitations of the CD-ROM format (which has a physical limitation on its capacity to store and reproduce footage), most multimedia products will typically only use a relatively small proportion of any film. However, the potential success of any multimedia product is such that the limited footage being used is more valuable, at least to the multimedia producer, than the film as a whole (or, at the very least, is worth as much as the whole film). As a general rule, given that the potential success of a multimedia product is difficult to gauge from the outset, any licence deal should ideally be structured on the basis of a cash advance against a percentage of each unit sold or licensed.

✳   **other issues.** You should also consider whether the licence is to be limited in time or territory or whether you want to restrict use in some other way. For example, you may want to ensure that the footage is shown in full or, perhaps more relevantly, that the images contained in the footage are neither manipulated by the multimedia producer nor capable of manipulation by the user.

UNAUTHORISED USE OF THE FILM

As with almost any other use of a film, unauthorised incorporation into a multimedia product will almost always be an infringement of copyright in that film. The trouble is that many multimedia producers either don't realise that it is an infringement (many think that because it is technologically possible to do something, it must be legal) or deliberately choose to ignore the copyright laws (often because tracking down the copyright owner and obtaining the necessary clearances is either difficult or expensive or both). Don't be blinded by science – unauthorised use, even in a multimedia product, is still a copyright infringement and you are entitled to all of your remedies at law for such unauthorised use.

UNAUTHORISED USE OF THE MULTIMEDIA PRODUCT

Unauthorised copying of the multimedia product presents one of the most significant difficulties for the multimedia producers. As the *Copyright Act* stands in 1994, multimedia products are probably not, in themselves, subject to copyright protection. However, the constituent elements of such products such as software programs, text, audio, film, etc. will almost certainly be protected even if incorporated into a multimedia product. So, while unauthorised use of a multimedia product may not infringe any rights of the multimedia producer (unless he or she created part of that product), it will almost certainly constitute an infringement of copyright in the constituent elements of the product.

The practical difficulty is that the multimedia producer is often neither the owner nor the exclusive licencee of copyright in each constituent element. If that multimedia product contains an excerpt from your film, then only you can do something about it. The multimedia producer will usually have no right under the *Copyright Act* to sue a copyright infringer for the infringement of copyright in your film.

As such, you should ensure that your licence agreement with the multimedia producer does one of the following two things (and preferably both):

✳   provides that the multimedia producer has to pay your costs of taking action to prevent copyright infringement caused by the unauthorised use of his or her multimedia product;

✳   requires the multimedia producer to sue the copyright infringer and authorises the producer to commence any legal action in your name provided that he or she pays any costs or other expenses to which you may be exposed as a result.

MORAL RIGHTS

During 1994, the Federal Government announced its intention to introduce moral rights for, amongst others, film producers. A discussion paper was released and legislation may be implemented in 1995. The current proposals for moral rights can be summarised as:

* a right of attribution;

* a right of integrity.

If these are implemented (and the manner in which they may be implemented is still the subject of much discussion), the former could probably be satisfied by the licence agreement providing that sufficient acknowledgment is to be included in the product and its packaging. However, it is the latter right that is more problematic for film producers and multimedia producers alike. That right is intended to preserve the integrity of a film. However, multimedia often relies upon (and, indeed, often promotes) the ability to break down and manipulate the images contained within film. It is likely, therefore, that many multimedia producers will seek a waiver of this right on the part of the copyright owner (assuming that the law will allow the waiver of that right).

No guidelines can be formulated until the proposals are firmed up. Nonetheless, it appears that moral rights, in at least some form, will be introduced in the short to medium term and will almost inevitably need to be considered in any licence granted to a multimedia producer.

The Legal Ladder

Lyndon Sayer-Jones

Entertainment lawyer
Lyndon Sayer-Jones and Associates
Sydney

Step 1: Engaging Your Lawyer

Just as any person forming a business needs an accountant, the producer should also engage a lawyer early in the development phase to advise on the legal aspects of a film project. Film making is contract obsessed – lawyers are a necessary evil. Accept this reality and develop the realisation that contracts are put in place because sometimes people disagree and/or break their word. You need to be protected.

Find a lawyer with a good reputation who specialises in the film and television industries. You should feel comfortable with that person and the legal firm – check out performance with other producers.

If your funds are tight, by all means do all the preliminary negotiations and legal legwork yourself (even preparing draft agreements) but seek legal guidance before finalising and signing documents. A specialist lawyer will be able to guide you on what is industry practice and identify any deal points or contractual terms which may prove problematic when you are seeking finance.

Although the incurring of legal costs in the development stage may appear to be 'risky' expenditure the cost should, in the long term, be justified. It is usually easier to reach agreement in the preliminary stages rather than when the cameras are about to roll.

To get the most out of your lawyer it will assist if you have a basic understanding of the points at issue. Ask your solicitor questions, read documents and keep your own files and copies of all contracts. If in doubt about any of the advice given, feel free to seek a second opinion. Lawyers are not infallible – far from it. A healthy scepticism should be maintained for any advice that doesn't 'ring true' to your producer instincts.

The whole process of film making, from script development through actual production to final distribution, requires the co-ordination of a large number of people and companies to a common purpose. The financial magnitude of that process makes its contractual documentation complex. Just as a producer needs to understand the creative requirements of a script, so it is also necessary that he/she is aware of the legal issues.

SOME SUGGESTIONS FOR KEEPING LEGAL COSTS DOWN

To keep legal costs down:

* Be well prepared when giving instructions. Avoid paying for professional time if the preliminary work can be done by you (such as compiling a chronology of facts and supporting documentation).

* Give your lawyer all relevant information. Failure to do so may result in a waste of professional time and your money.

* Consider using the fax machine to confirm an instruction rather than another telephone call. This is sometimes cheaper and more precise.

* Don't skimp on the fundamentals, especially chain of title, as it will save you money in the long run.

* Ask for an estimate of the costs for professional work to be done. Note that most lawyers will only give a 'ball park figure' as it is difficult to estimate the time that will be involved in negotiations with third parties.

Allow your lawyer to spend sufficient time on your affairs (i.e., be prepared to pay a sensible price to get the fundamentals right). However, if you have a limited budget for legals, be honest about it. Many lawyers will try to do the work for the money available.

STEP 2: THE PRODUCER – ESTABLISHING THE DEVELOPMENT ENTITY

There must be a legal entity, 'the producer', which will control the script rights and other film elements relevant to the development of the project. As will be discussed later in this chapter (Step 5), raising a project's budget may well need a corporate structure and, for a prospectus, possibly a public company.

In the early stages of script development a producer may prefer to contract in a personal capacity (in his/her own name). This involves few legal formalities. Or, the producer may choose to operate through a company. This is safer from a liability point of view – remember film making is a very risky business.

Where two or more people are jointly developing the project there will need to be a proprietary limited company, a joint venture or a partnership. An appropriate agreement should be put in place to define the relationship of the parties (e.g., a partnership agreement or a shareholders' agreement). In the absence of such an agreement, a project may falter where, for example, the parties have a falling out, become ill, etc.

This agreement should:

* define the functions and duties of each party;

* specify any cash commitments from the parties;

109

✳ address the rights, powers and obligations of the parties;

✳ cover the possibility of one of the parties withdrawing (whether through illness, disability or otherwise);

✳ provide for a dispute mechanism;

✳ specify the manner for sharing of fees and profits;

✳ specify the activities of the partners/shareholders which come within the scope of the venture (be careful of 'catch all' clauses which deem all the activities of the shareholders/ partners the property of the company/partnership);

✳ provide a buy-out mechanism (if one party withdraws or cannot continue through illness or death) which should accommodate economic realities with provision for reasonable time to pay.

Some suggestions:

✳ Proprietary limited companies are usually the most favoured vehicle, mainly to limit liability. This is important where a contract involves substantial financial obligations. With a partnership each partner is jointly and severally liable for the debts and liabilities of the partnership.

✳ It costs about $1000 to set up a company. There are also ongoing annual costs and you usually need the assistance of an accountant for the preparation of annual returns.

✳ Consult your financial advisers on the best tax structure.

✳ It may be wise for the initial working arrangement, be it a partnership, joint venture or company, to be limited to a specific project. If things work out, then new projects can be added.

✳ Try to maintain control, especially if you initiated the project.

Step 3: Project Development

It is necessary to secure all the elements that are essential for the film project at the outset. Apart from, for example, obtaining an option on a novel, it may be critical to secure a director, an actor, a particular piece of music or even a location to make a project viable. These elements will make up the package for which the producer will seek to raise the finance.

All parties engaged during the development phase should have a written agreement, including the writer, script editor, consultant director, storyboard artist. These agreements need not be long, provided that the essential terms are covered including the specification of required services, time frame, fee, rights granted/acquired, credit entitlement (if any). Comprehensive agreements can rarely be drafted on a page or two. Although short form agreements may seem attractive, as a rule they can lead to more disputes than complete agreements.

THE SCRIPT SOURCE

The screenplay for a project may be an original work commissioned by the producer, or developed from an existing literary/dramatic work (e.g., novel or play) or a draft screenplay written by a writer and subsequently presented to the producer.

If the project is to be developed from an existing work (often called 'the underlying work'), the producer will usually take out an exclusive option over the underlying work. The option agreement is between the producer and the author (the owner of the copyright) and, if necessary, also the publisher. If a literary work has been published but the author claims to control the film rights it is prudent to examine the publishing agreement and to obtain a 'Quit Claim' from the publisher. Otherwise the so-called 'chain of title' may not be clear. Authors sometimes do not know the legal position themselves.

An option agreement should always have attached to it the agreement setting out the terms of the purchase of the film rights. This rights agreement comes into effect if the producer exercises the option.

The basic terms that need to be addressed in the option agreement are:

* the period of the initial option and any extension periods;

* the option fee and extension fees payable by the producer (and whether these fees are to be deducted from the agreed purchase price, if the option is exercised);

* the right of the producer to exclusively develop the project during the option period and any restrictions on this (e.g., the author of the first draft script being optioned requiring to be engaged as the writer of the second draft screenplay);

* the effect of non-exercise of the option, in particular in relation to the material developed by the producer during the option period (e.g., the rights in respect of the second draft screenplay, i.e., who owns it?).

The rights agreement (annexed to the option agreement) should specify:

* the rights assigned/licensed by the owner to the producer – that is, whether the owner assigns copyright or assigns/licenses specific film rights (for one film only or also for sequels, re-makes, etc.);

* the purchase price, including how much of this fee is payable on exercise and how much is payable at a later date (such as on commencement of principal photography of the film);

* the credit entitlement of the owner;

* appropriate warranties with respect to ownership, originality, exclusivity, etc.

SOME HELPFUL HINTS ON OPTION/RIGHTS AGREEMENTS

The following hints may be helpful:

111

✳   Check that the rights are free (e.g., by having the writer's publishing agreement cleared).

✳   The period of the option and extensions should provide adequate time for the producer to 'get the project up'. The AFC standard requirement in its script development agreements is for the producer to secure an option (plus extensions) totalling three years. Try for four years, as you may well need the extra time.

✳   Option fees vary on perceived value (writer's reputation/best seller performance, etc.) and range from a low of $500 to $5000 plus per option/extension period. The initial fee is usually credited towards the purchase price (if the option is exercised) but sometimes extension fees are not. The purchase price is often 2–3 per cent of actual production budget, but there is obviously a wide range of variables which affects the negotiated price.

✳   The rights granted to the producer and the rights reserved by the owner are always negotiable. However, financiers (including the FFC) and distributors want the producer to acquire spin-off, sequel rights and merchandising rights wherever possible. If certain rights are reserved by the owner (e.g. stage rights) a 'hold back' should be negotiated so that confusion in the marketplace will not adversely affect the release of the film.

✳   Where a government body is providing development funding it is generally possible (and advisable) to submit contracts in draft form for its comments.

✳   An arbitration clause for disputes on credits is a sensible idea; nomination of the Australian Writers' Guild as arbitrator is common.

WRITER'S AGREEMENT

The producer will also need to finalise the terms of engagement of the writer of the screenplay.

The major points to be addressed in the writer's agreement are:

✳   the fee (including any deferred fee payable on commencement of principal photography);

✳   the delivery date for the relevant draft of the screenplay;

✳   the nature of the engagement (usually on a draft by draft basis);

✳   the rights acquired by the producer (usually a full assignment of copyright where the work is commissioned by the producer);

✳   credit entitlement;

✳   appropriate warranties with respect to originality, exclusivity, etc.;

✳   waiver of potential moral rights.

Note: The above lists are not intended to be exhaustive.

GENERAL CONTRACT PROVISIONS

There are some contract provisions that a producer will usually insist upon being included in a development agreement in order to ensure that the chain of title is acceptable to the ultimate financiers of the film, the completion guarantor and, with development funding, the government or private development body. For example, the rights and benefits of contracts should be capable of assignment to third parties, (e.g., the production company, completion guarantor). Ideally, such assignments should not be conditional on the third party assuming the obligations of the producer as this is often unacceptable to the third party.

SPECIAL CONSIDERATION WHEN OFFERING A SHARE OF NET PROFITS

Profit splits to writers, directors, etc. (so-called 'points') are expressed as a percentage of either 100 per cent of net profits or as a percentage of the producer's share of net profits. The agreement should provide a definition of 'net profits' or 'the producer's share of net profits'. If a producer agrees to give a share of 100 per cent of net profits he/she needs to be careful not to overestimate the producer's likely share of net profits, because it is from the producer's share that the third party participants are usually paid. You should not assume that the producer's share will be the usual 50 per cent; in some instances the share of a project's net profits will be considerably less.

STEP 4: SECURING PROVISIONAL CERTIFICATION AS AN AUSTRALIAN FILM

If a film project is to be eligible for the 10BA tax concessions and/or FFC investment, it is necessary for the film to qualify as an 'Australian film' as defined in Division 10BA of the *Income Tax Assessment Act*. This initially involves the lodging of an application to the Federal Department of Communications and the Arts ('DCA') for a Provisional Certificate. The application form is quite detailed and should not be lodged at too preliminary a stage as many facts will be unknown. Questions that need to be answered include:

❋ the sources of finance (including any overseas financing);

❋ the sums to be expended on non-Australian elements;

❋ distribution arrangements;

❋ the manner of sharing income from the film (including any entitlements of overseas participants);

❋ the nationality of all cast and crew.

A budget and script must also be supplied to the Department.

Application forms for Provisional Certification and information can be obtained from DCA, the AFC or any of the state film bodies.

Once the Provisional Certificate is obtained it is important to make DCA aware of any major changes in the production (such as title, budget, etc.) and, in particular, all changes to non-Australian elements (e.g., cast, locations, foreign investors). Ensure that DCA has recorded these changes without objection.

Note that following completion of the film, once the audit has been carried out, it is necessary to apply to DCA for final certification.

A NOTE ON CO-PRODUCTIONS

DCA provides a short-form application for projects that have been accorded official co-production status by the AFC and the equivalent overseas authority. It is first necessary to apply to the AFC for Official Co-Production status. The AFC (Film Development) provides written guidelines and application forms.

STEP 5: RAISING FINANCE FOR THE PROJECT

An approach to the AFC, a state film funding body or the FFC are the main ways for an Australian producer seeking to raise the finance for a film project. Each such body has published guidelines available. You should note that the FFC does not fund 100 per cent of a film's budget and it is necessary for the producer to secure a percentage of the budget by private investment, and/or a distributor's investment, pre-sale or distribution guarantee (that percentage varies but averages 40-45 per cent for most projects).

A producer must be extremely cautious when seeking to raise finance from associates and/ or the public within Australia. The corporations law requires such approaches to be made by special documentation – a prospectus. The main purpose of such documentation is to protect prospective investors by ensuring that there is adequate disclosure of all relevant matters. There are some special exemptions for single investments in excess of $500,000 and for offers made to family members, executive staff and to very wealthy individuals and so-called institutional investors (such as banks, superannuation trustees) in control of funds which exceed $10 million.

Australians traditionally resist investing in high risk enterprises such as film productions, unless there are tax incentives and guaranteed returns which reduce most of the risk. In the current financial climate, and given the level of the tax incentives, it is difficult to raise money from 'the punters'. Further, with the high costs associated with the preparation of a prospectus (including public and trust company management fees, legal fees, printing costs and publicity expenses, underwriting and brokerage fees), relatively few Australian producers seek to raise finance from the public by way of public offer.

Instead, most producers attempt to put together an attractive pre-sale/guarantee package (possibly with some private investment) for presentation to the FFC. The AFC also funds a small number of low budget feature films and a mix of documentaries, short films, animated films and experimental films each year. The state funding bodies also provide varying levels of production investment funds.

A Guaranteed Return: Pre-Sale, Distribution Advance/Guarantee

A secured return can take the form of a pre-sale from a licensor/distributor (such as an Australian or overseas television broadcaster). With a **pre-sale** certain rights (e.g., UK free television rights) are pre-sold to the licensor. The purchase price is usually paid on delivery of the film. With a **distribution advance** a distributor acquires certain distribution rights (e.g., Australasian rights for all media) and is willing to put up an advance against future income from the exploitation of these rights. A third possible way a producer may secure a return is by way of **distribution guarantee**. The appointed distributor guarantees to investors that the film returns will reach a certain dollar amount at a certain date(s); in the event that film returns are lower than this amount the distributor makes up the difference.

The guaranteed return (whether by way of pre-sale or distribution advance/guarantee) should ideally be secured, especially from overseas distributors or smaller local distributors by Letter of Credit from a bank. This may well be a requirement of the FFC as well.

Note that often pre-sales and distribution advances are expected to cash flow the production and accordingly make up part of the finance to meet the budgeted cost. If this is unacceptable you may need to raise a loan secured against the distribution contract – this is known as 'discounting' – this can be both difficult and expensive.

Step 6: The Production Contract

The AFC and FFC production investment agreements usually also provide the contractual parameters for any additional investors – either the additional investors are parties to the main agreement or enter into ancillary investment agreements.

Obviously, the AFC and FFC production investment agreements adopt a standard format and terms and conditions. Variations to standard documents are possible but often difficult to negotiate. Your lawyer should protect your interests and minimise obligations that are impractical or unreasonable for you or your production, but not alienate the 'backer' in the process. Ensure sufficient flexibility within the production contract for the reallocation of budgetary amounts and variation to time schedules. The terms for the exploitation of sequel and spin-off rights may also vary on a project by project basis.

The investors will require that all 'major' production contracts are approved by their lawyers, including chain of title documentation, completion guarantee agreement, pre-sale agreements and any other marketing agreements.

It is important that the producer is familiar with the obligations specified in the production and investment agreement including the required bank accounts (and their operation), reporting obligations, what matters require the prior approval of the investor(s) (e.g., lead cast and key crew), the manner of keeping of financial records, insurance requirements and required approval of budget reallocations.

Step 7: Legal Considerations During Production

During the pre-production period (if not already finalised beforehand to secure the production finance) your lawyer should prepare and finalise documentation to secure:

* producer and director;

* principal cast;

* key locations;

* completion guarantee;

* leases of premises (film studios, production office);

* script clearance re defamation, etc.

Your lawyer should also draft the composer's agreement, any footage licence agreements and any music synchronisation agreements.

It would also be prudent to have your lawyer look over the proposed pro forma agreements to be used by the production office including:

* cast agreement, particularly to review any required Special Conditions and to confirm the buy-out of rights (non-Award provisions should be discussed with the MEAA first);

* crew agreement;

* location agreement;

* insurance details, particularly to ensure compliance with the production and investment agreement (be careful of standard exclusions: special cover is needed for stunts and filming involving aeroplanes and watercraft).

Errors And Omissions Insurance

This is a vital insurance which is intended to protect the producer, the investors and any distributor from claims for breach of copyright, defamation and other contractual breaches relating to incorporation of literary, musical and other materials. It is important to ensure an Errors and Omissions Insurance Policy will be issued for the project before its first release in accordance with the requirements specified in the production and investment agreement with the investors. It is wise to submit a shooting script to the insurer in pre-production and obtain a written undertaking that 'subject to the film following the script' the policy will be issued upon payment of a specified premium. Errors and Omissions policies are invariably a requirement of investors and overseas distributors and should be for a period of at least three years from first release of the film. For features it is expected to offer indemnity in the order of US$3 million in the aggregate and US$1 million for any one claim. An international title clearance will be required – the US trademark/copyright searchers Thomson and Thomson are often used, and if a legal opinion is required, the US attorneys Brylawski, Cleary and Komen offer a well-respected service. The cost of this search alone can be US$600.

SOME SUGGESTIONS REGARDING E&O INSURANCE

When taking out E&O insurance, keep the following in mind:

* The legal clearance procedures required are extensive and cover all the literary and musical works, location agreements, footage agreements, title checks and can also involve consideration of court transcripts, interviews with witnesses, newspaper reports and behind the scenes cross checking and verification. If the clearance procedures are not carried out by the producer the insurer may refuse to pay on a claim. It is advisable to get your lawyer to review the clearance procedures and give you a written assurance that this review has been carried out.

* With 'risky' projects it may be wise to consider taking out E&O insurance from commencement of pre-production. An injunction against the production during the shoot can be disastrous.

* E&O policies specifically exclude claims that result from the failure of the production company to perform any contracts or other obligations. Your own negligence is not covered. Also excluded are claims by employees, partners, joint venturers relating to the supply of copyright material.

COMPLETION GUARANTEE

A completion guarantee is a contractual arrangement whereby completion of the project is guaranteed should there be a cost overrun. In many respects it is like an insurance policy. Usually the investors require a completion guarantee (except for very low budget films, short films, and in some instances, documentaries).

Note that certain overages are not covered by the completion guarantor, including cost overruns on cast and crew living expenses, legal fees, and overages due to so-called 'enhancement' of the film.

The completion guarantor has a number of rights, including the right to take over the production and to appoint a receiver, effectively removing production control from the producer. Like investors, the completion guarantor requires approval of key agreements (including financing agreements, chain of title, principal crew and cast, distribution agreements). A producer must also provide regular financial and production reporting in accordance with the completion documents.

A completion guarantor should be a financially strong company, which should be backed up by reinsurance through a major insurance conglomerate. Actual film production experience of the guarantor's representative is, of course, very important, as is a good reputation for prompt payouts.

If a production is produced on time and within budget it is common for a rebate to be made

117

to the producer and this can sometimes be as high as 50 per cent of the fee itself. Often it depends on the producer's track record with previous productions, similar to a 'no claim bonus' in motor vehicle insurance. Also be careful about delivery items and their synchronisation with a distributor's requirements.

Note that when the cameras start to roll, everyone's mind should be focused on the project itself. All major contracts should be fully signed, dated and completed during pre-production except perhaps the composer's and the music licence agreements for non-critical music. Be very careful about unrealistic stop dates for key personnel (cast or crew). Think and plan early about what will be needed.

REPORTING

The producer must give regular progress reports to the completion guarantor, the underwriter (if applicable), the FFC and other investors, the distributor in accordance with the relevant contract arrangements. The frequency and content of required reports may vary. Each report must be dispatched on time. A failure to do so may render the producer in breach of a key financing or insurance agreement.

CREDITS

The area of credits is where many disputes are generated. Some suggestions:

* Negotiate credit provisions very carefully. Scrutinise the standard wording found in most contractual documentation. Look at the exclusions (such as advertising limitations, spin-off product exclusions).

* The exact wording of the credit and whether it is to be in the front or end credit sequence should always be specified. For front credits, position and size should usually be specified.

* A usual provision is that the producer will not be responsible for any 'inadvertent omission' of a credit. This is reasonable in circumstances where an innocent mistake has been made. However, it is also reasonable to require the producer to take reasonable steps to rectify omissions.

* The Writers' Guild offers dispute resolution procedures for disputes with writers. An objective arbitrator is a sensible precaution to break deadlocked negotiations.

* An appropriate disclaimer, copyright warning and copyright notice is necessary at the end of the titles.

The copyright notice should read: © (name of owner) (year).

COMPOSER'S AGREEMENT

A film may include an original musical score and also incorporate previously released musical items. The composer's contract is often a complex agreement. Many film composers have arrangements with music publishers and, if so, the publisher should be made a party to the agreement or provide a quit claim/release.

The contract needs to be absolutely specific on the rights acquired by the producer in respect of the original music (either by an assignment of copyright or a licence) and what rights, if any, are reserved to the composer.

The music soundtrack may be utilised as a separate marketing tool (e.g., a soundtrack album). It is essential to agree on the royalties payable to the composer in such an instance.

The contract should also specify the fee payable to the composer and the manner of paying for recording costs (whether budgeted to be paid out of the composer's total 'fee' or payable by the production company). The delivery items (including tape format, cue sheets, etc.) and the delivery date must also be specified.

SOME MUSICAL SUGGESTIONS

* Make sure the pre-existing publishing agreements as well as recording contracts allow the composer/performer to grant the relevant rights in the music as well as provide the appropriate services. Do not just rely on warranties.

* Ensure that all pre-recorded music is properly cleared through reputable agents and/ or AMCOS. The recording itself will need a synchronisation licence from the record company.

* Ensure all the appropriate rights have been obtained from musicians, producers, performers. Usually distribution agreements hold producers responsible for any residual fees payable.

* If using pre-recorded material be aware of the possibility of it also being the jingle for next year's dog food commercial.

* Be extremely careful in allocating royalties for soundtrack album use. Check whether the production and investment agreement provides that soundtrack album royalties be first applied against recoupment of production costs.

* Finally, don't leave music legalities to the last minute, especially if your film or program depends on a particular piece of music. Like all things, the price depends on demand. If you paint yourself in a corner the price will reflect your desperation.

STEP 8: DELIVERY, MARKETING AND DISTRIBUTION

The production agreement and the distribution agreements will specify a list of delivery items which need to be delivered once the film is completed. It is essential that these are delivered on the due date.

Ideally, the producer will maintain a substantial degree of control over a project's marketing. However, because of the need for the producer to acquire pre-sales and distribution guarantees, it is often difficult for him/her to retain control over key territories.

Because the production budget for Australian films often only provides for minimal marketing expenditure, the producer seeking to market the film may need to secure additional funds for promotional and marketing expenses. A marketing loan (for example, from the AFC) attracts interest and is usually repayable out of first returns (after deduction of distributor's commissions and marketing expenses). As a marketing loan ranks in priority ahead of investors, it is necessary to obtain the prior approval of the investors to such a loan.

All agents/distributors commissions and expenses are also deducted prior to the investors receiving any share of gross proceeds from the film. A sales agent works on a commission calculated on the film's gross revenue (usually 15-35 per cent). If possible, particularly where the term of the agency is long, the agency agreement should provide that the agency can be terminated if the sales agent does not perform to a level agreed to as satisfactory. A performance clause could specify gross revenue required to be earned from the sales agent's efforts over a fixed period. Some sales agents (like executive producers) will try and secure pre-sales for a producer.

Often sales agents require an exclusive agency arrangement. Sometimes the producer may also be permitted to negotiate sales.

IMPORTANT ELEMENTS IN A MARKETING/DISTRIBUTION AGREEMENT

Important elements in a marketing/distribution agreement include:

* scope of the appointment (what rights/media and which territories);

* term, including a performance clause;

* proper reporting conditions for sales/distribution progress and revenue accounting, with the actual form and frequency of these reports specified;

* adequate producer consultation and consent. Approval rights of deals for major territories and major rights (theatrical, television), as well as decisions such as packaging a project with other films or cross-collateralisation of revenues. Don't let your strong film subsidise somebody else's failure;

* a clearly defined basis for the deduction of marketing expenses. Sometimes approval rights apply before expenses can exceed a specified amount. To understand the impact of such deductions, use a test example: take a fictitious total film rental received from the film's distributors (based on, say, 35 per cent of actual box office) and allocate particular amounts to each deductible marketing item (e.g., promotional costs, prints, freight, travel, etc.) and then also deduct the agent's commission. Have your lawyer confirm a final net figure;

* note that relevant provisions in a distribution agreement should also include a P & A (prints and advertising) commitment from the distributor.

A sobering fact to remember is that many distributors are currently returning to the owners of a film/television project only 12-15 per cent of gross income (from box office takings, television, video, etc.) even with successful films. There is an increasing tendency to cross-collateralise all revenues for the purpose of distribution fee/costs deductions. From a producer's point of view, the important thing is to get a fair deal, given market realities. Expert international advice may be necessary in some cases.

SUMMARY

The legal ladder has to be climbed often on several rungs at the same time. Getting things right from a legal point of view has direct commercial and, indeed, personal benefits. It is in the producer's interests to make sure every issue is addressed so that the critical and commercial success of a project can be enjoyed and translated into investors' assistance for your next project.

FINANCIAL MATTERS

Finance

Damien Parer

After decades of inactivity in Australian feature film production, in 1970 the federal government established the Australian Film Development Corporation, which in 1975 became the Australian Film Commission and in 1988 the Australian Film Finance Corporation was incorporated. The early 1970s also saw the establishment of the first of five state film bodies. These bodies play a vital role by assisting film and TV projects at various stages of development, production and marketing. Their presence on a project and their ability to give professional assessment also provide a certain security factor for the private investment sector.

Script and Project Development Funding

The Australian Film Commission, state film corporations, business corporations, government departments and television networks all have a history of providing script and project development money for projects that meet their individual criteria. There is no guarantee, however, that your application will be successful. The only way to find out if your project is suitable for development is to put up a proposal. Simply apply to the donor of your choice for the relevant application form, or make a presentation to them.

Government Sources Of Development Funding

A description of the funding available from each of the federal and state funding bodies can be found commencing on page 128.

Other Sources Of Development Funding

Other sources of funding include:

* Television networks may provide development funding for television projects. Sometimes funding may be shared with a government body.

* Larger film companies, e.g., Village Roadshow or GUO, may provide funding.

* Deferrals: some of the development costs, e.g. part of the writer's or producer's fee, may be deferred until production. This reduces the money required for the development stage.

* Production houses may advance money on a promise to use their facilities when the film goes into production.

124

* Private investors don't usually advance money for development, but it's worth a try.

* Don't forget relatives and friends.

* Bank loan: as producer you may be able to borrow from a bank. But you'd have to put up some collateral.

Development contracts should always contain a clause which allows the property to return to you if production (or development) does not proceed. One year is usually sufficient time. If after that nothing has happened, you should be able to take back the rights to the project so that its development may continue in a different manner. In the USA, this is called a turnaround clause.

DEVELOPMENT COSTS

Development costs should be included as a cost of the project's production. Therefore, keep an accurate account of all your development costs so that you can claim them back when production finance is found. Development costs can include:

* an estimate of the value of your time

* office staff

* typing and duplication costs

* research materials, books, tapes etc.

* office rental

* telephone, FAX, postage costs

* legal cost of the option on a book or script

* all transport costs e.g., own car, air travel, taxis, etc.

* budget preparation and attendant costs

METHODS OF PRODUCTION FINANCING

Once the project has been developed or 'packaged' with elements including script, lead actor and director, the next step is to raise the money for its production. You may decide to use an agent to find production funds. A commission will be charged, perhaps 10–15 per cent. You could work with an executive producer who would also charge a fee, and who might also assist with finding a pre-sale. Otherwise you might wish to consider trying one or more of the following:

* **Sponsor or client.** Commercials and corporate videos or films are funded directly by the user or client. The whole budget usually comes from one client source. However, it may be necessary to fund from two sources. If so, clients may have to agree to share credits or, if they won't, you may make two sets of titles for them.

125

* **The Australian Film Finance Corporation.** The FFC requires pre-sales and/or equity investment but operates like any other financial institution. Pre-sales can come from exhibitors, distributors, TV networks, video distributors and others.

* **Bank loan.** This can be a secured loan against pre-sales or distribution guarantee. Remember, banks charge interest but they don't take any of the profits.

* **Equity investors.** Equity investors may be drawn to a commercial proposition. They will look at the financial aspects of your proposal, especially the pre-sales, but they are fully aware of the high risk nature of film investment. They may be attracted by the glamour of being part of the movie, even though they may not say so. Storyline and stars play a big part in the decision process. Profit share is usually 50/50 with equity investors.

* **Investor bias.** It may be possible to structure the finance around a situation which gives the private investors their money back first. Institutions or government bodies may be willing to take second place under special circumstances. This will give the private investors a position with less risk.

* **Co-production agreement**. A co-production agreement may mean that you only have to find half the budget. It can be within Australia or international.

* **Government bodies.** Direct investment and distribution guarantees are sometimes available from the AFC or Film Victoria, etc.

* **Television sale.** For series production, the Australian television sale would generally need to cover the whole budget, but mini-series can seek pre-sales from elsewhere, e.g., overseas TV sale.

* **Public company.** Form a company which is listed on the stock exchange and raise capital by share issue.

* **Line of credit.** A bank or lending institution will, in certain circumstances, establish a line of credit for film production. This operates like a bank overdraft in that a maximum level of borrowing is established and funds are drawn as needed.

* **Pre-sale of some kind.** A minimum distribution guarantee or any other commitment backed by irrevocable letter of credit will reduce investor risk and lead to film financing.

* **Output deal**. An agreement is reached where a distributor takes all the output of a production house. The production slate is financed through deals already established between the distributor and various outlets, e.g., theatre, TV, video.

* **Independent association.** Films from a group of producers are financed by preset deals with distributors. Cross-collaterisation of returns would reduce the risk over all the films.

* **Interstate rivalry.** Money from any source can sometimes be forthcoming because of the film's major location, e.g., Perth-based films can more easily be funded from Western Australia if they are shot there.

* **Distributors and exhibitors.** Distributors and exhibitors may sometimes be willing to finance films. Generally, though, they will offer a minimum distribution guarantee.

* **TV sponsoring.** A major TV advertising client may be able to persuade a TV network to pre-buy your program.

* **Theatrical agent.** In the USA, agents will sometimes assist with securing finance by packaging their clients, e.g., actors, director or writer.

* **Negative pick-up.** A US studio may guarantee to purchase all rights to the film on delivery of the negative. Certain conditions will apply, usually involving sharing creative control and budget constraints. Sometimes studios have actors or directors on contract and they may be looking for suitable films to attach them to.

* **Entertainment lawyer.** An entertainment lawyer can sometimes help introduce producers to investors. They may also be involved in financing properties for a fee.

* **Grant.** Occasionally benevolent institutions or government bodies may grant money for film production. They may see value in a film about social welfare or defence, or anything really. The whole or part of your budget may be found here.

* **Donation.** A donation is a possibility if your subject matter is seen to be so powerful that the commercial world avoids it. An important issue being suppressed by the media generally may draw funds from a concerned public.

* **Part of a package.** Join other films in a package. A producer may be able to fund thirteen documentaries in a package more easily than one.

* **Rich uncle.** Don't fail to review your family and friends as a source of finance. Generally this is easier money to obtain than from elsewhere.

* **Product prominence.** You may have a script set in a glamorous resort hotel. You may be able to negotiate free accommodation, or accommodation at substantially reduced rates if you feature the hotel prominently in the film. Goods and services, seen in a favourable light, may be enough to convince manufacturers to put up cash or substantial assistance.

* **Record company.** A film which promotes the sale of music may be able to get finance from the record company involved.

* **Deferrals.** Some individuals or facilities may be willing to defer fees or a portion of them until after the investors have been repaid. You may have to offer a higher fee or larger percentage of profit. Producers, directors, writers or labs, post-production facilities, studios, may be agreeable to deferrals.

* **Contra deals.** Contra deals may save you money in the budget, e.g., airlines, hotels, hire cars, locations, etc.

* **Producer's money (Gulp!).** If all else fails, put up the money yourself.

Government Sources Of Finance

The Australian Children's Television Foundation

See p. 277 for contact details.

The Australian Children's Television Foundation is a national, non-profit organisation created to encourage the development, production and dissemination of television programs, films and other audiovisual media for children. The Foundation acts as an executive producer to initiate projects which push forward the boundaries of children's television and to encourage their distribution by any form of technology. It undertakes, initiates and encourages research and provides an authoritative source of information on all aspects of television, film and other audiovisual media relevant to children. It stimulates interest in, promotes and improves the quality and suitability of children's television, film and other audiovisual media. It also provides support to projects developed outside the Foundation by independent producers.

Since its establishment in 1982, the Foundation has invested in both the script development and production of telemovies, mini-series and one-off dramas and encouraged the top writers, producers and directors of the Australian film and television industry to become involved in production for children. It has produced 115 hours of programming which has sold into more than 90 countries around the world.

The Foundation's programs have received more than 45 awards both nationally and internationally, including the AFI Award for Children's Drama each of the three years following its inception in 1991; an international Emmy in 1988 for the film *Captain Johnno*, and two further Emmy Award nominations for the film *Boy Soldiers* (in 1991) and the series *Round the Twist* (in 1993); and the Prix Jeunesse Award for an episode of *Round the Twist* in 1994.

The Foundation also develops books and teacher/parent materials to accompany all of its programs. To date more than 650,000 publications associated with Foundation programs and 65,000 videotapes have been sold in Australia.

Applications for script development or production investment are assessed quarterly and must be submitted on forms made available by the Foundation. Deadlines for submission are also available upon request. In its assessment procedures, the Foundation gives priority to high-quality children's television projects which are submitted by experienced teams, including an experienced producer. Projects should be entertaining, child-focused and essentially Australian in character. Commercial viability is also a criterion.

Australian Film Commission

See pp. 277-278 for contact details.

The Australian Film Commission (AFC) is the primary development agency for the film industry in Australia. With revenue earned mostly from film investments and interest on deposits, and an annual federal government appropriation, the AFC provides financial assistance and support for the development of new talent, as well as the production of film and television programs. Under its charter the AFC can only invest in Australian creative personnel and projects. The

AFC is a federal statutory authority and maintains three offices located in Sydney, Melbourne and a European office in London.

It undertakes six main activities: Indigenous, Film Development and Production Assistance, Marketing, Policy, Industry and Cultural Development (ICD) and Official Co-Production.

FILM DEVELOPMENT

The objectives of the Film Development Branch are to:

* support the development and production of projects which reflect a diversity of genre, format, budget and audience, and

* encourage and foster the development of work and individuals likely to make a significant contribution to the future of film and television in Australia.

Investment is in both filmmakers and films and the AFC welcomes applications from both individuals and creative teams.

Through its **Development Investment Program**, the AFC provides financial assistance to cover the range of costs associated with script and project development, research, securing of production financing and market placement of Australian film and television programs, and caters for projects emanating from all sectors of the Australian industry and culture.

Assistance is available for the development of feature films, mini-series, telemovies, documentaries, short films, animation programs, experimental programs, and works utilising new technologies. Due to the substantial costs involved, prospectus preparation costs are not eligible for AFC support.

Through its **Production Investment Program**, the AFC provides production investments to a diverse range of exemplary projects, including low-budget feature films, documentaries, programs utilising new technologies, animation and short films. Particular emphasis is given to work that is exploratory and innovative and is geared to lower budgets. Although filmmakers may identify a significant audience for their project, it will be unlikely to find finance in the commercial marketplace. By virtue of content, approach to form, and/or level of experience of key members of the creative team, projects supported through this program represent high-risk, yet informed, investments. As such, the objectives of this program complement the other federal film agency providing production investment, the Australian Film Finance Corporation.

Through its **New Image Research Program**, grants are provided for small-scale works (up to $20,000) which are innovative experiments in form and technique, with an emphasis toward, but not limited to, projects utilising new technologies.

Under the federal government's **Distinctly Australian Initiative** (1993–1997), the Branch provides support for producers and the development of screen writing, through a range of strategies designed to be complementary to the **Development** and **Production Investment Programs**.

CO-PRODUCTION PROGRAM

The Australian Film Commission, through its **Co-production Program**, is the authority **129** empowered to consider applications for programs to be approved as Official Co-productions with other international parties. The AFC role is administrative only. As at January 1995, the Australian government has entered into co-production treaties with the United Kingdom, Canada and Italy; less than treaty arrangements have been made with New Zealand and France. The AFC anticipates co-production treaties will soon be concluded between Australia and the Republic of Ireland, Israel, the Russian Federation, the Republic of Germany, and Japan.

Financing is not available through this program. Productions granted official Co-production approval by the AFC may then apply to the Department of Communication and the Arts for certification under Division 10BA of the *Income Tax Assessment Act* in order to access Australian finance for their productions.

INDIGENOUS BRANCH

In order to foster and develop Aboriginal and Torres Strait Islander filmmakers, the objectives of the Indigenous Branch are:

*   to facilitate effective participation in all levels of the Australian and international film industries whilst promoting the quality and diversity of indigenous films;

*   to maintain and improve their competitive standard and widen audience appeal.

MARKETING

The AFC is the major film agency in Australia engaged in the international promotion of Australian film and television programs and creative talent. It achieves this objective by:

*   publishing information on Australian programs for distribution at the major film and television markets;

*   entering films in selected international festivals;

*   curating special events in developing markets;

*   undertaking a range of targeted promotional activities which increase the profile of Australian talent and programs.

AFC Marketing support also includes:

*   devising financing and marketing strategies with producers;

*   commissioning and disseminating market intelligence;

*   co-ordinating attendance at international markets;

*   contributing a market perspective to AFC funding deliberations;

*   providing marketing loans, and travel grants to directors and actors.

From this area, expert advice is also provided to government, industry and the public. Policy activities include regulatory and structural issues of importance to the industry.

Industry And Cultural Development

The ICD Branch supports the development of an active, diverse and informed film culture in Australia. Funding is provided to national and regional resource organisations which serve as a focus for the independent film and video community by their involvement in production, distribution and exhibition. The ICD Branch supports publications, awards, festivals and conferences which aim to encourage critical debate and analysis in the film and wider Australian community.

The Research and Information Unit of this branch collects and publishes data and research on the Australian film, video and television industries.

The Women's Program is responsible for initiatives which increase the participation of women in all areas of film, video and television production.

Australian Film Finance Corporation Limited

See p. 278 for contact details.

Background

The Australian Film Finance Corporation is the federal government's main agency for financially supporting the Australian film and television production industry. It was established on 12 July 1988 as a wholly owned government company.

The Corporation invests in feature films, telemovies, mini-series and documentaries that are 'qualifying Australian films' provided there is support from either private sector investors or marketplace participants (e.g., broadcasters, distributors, sales agents).

In addition to investments the Corporation provides production and print and advertising loans aimed at facilitating the theatrical release of feature films.

The Corporation provides production assistance. Development (e.g., script) and marketing assistance (other than print and advertising loans) is provided by the Australian Film Commission and in some cases by the state agencies in New South Wales, Victoria, Queensland, Western Australia and South Australia. These bodies also provide limited forms of production assistance either in collaboration with the Corporation or in areas outside the Corporation's responsibility, such as short films, training films and films by new or inexperienced filmmakers.

The Corporation receives an annual appropriation from the federal government. Through this and revenues earned from investments in previous years and with the collaboration of private investors and marketplace participants in individual projects, the FFC is able to support a diverse range of Australian film and television production.

Decreasing allocations from the government over the past few years have pointed to the need for the FFC to maximise co-investment opportunities and to earn increasing revenues on its investments to make up the shortfall. For 1995/96 an indicative amount of $50 million has been allocated to the FFC. The outcome of a government review of the FFC, held at the end of the 1994 calendar year, would determine the level of FFC appropriations for the next few years.

131

The Corporation's responsibilities are set out in a contract with the Commonwealth of Australia, and its powers and functions are determined by its Memorandum of Association. This contract is due for renewal at the end of the 1996 financial year and the recommendations of the government's review of the FFC were due early in 1995 – i.e., too late for any changes to the Corporation's operations or guidelines to be incorporated into this publication.

FUNCTIONS AND OBJECTIVES

The Corporation's principal functions are to:

* invest in qualifying Australian films, which are feature films, mini-series, telemovies and documentaries certified as Australian under Division 10BA of the *Income Tax Assessment Act,* i.e., made wholly or substantially in Australia with significant Australian content, or as an official international co-production;

* make loans, provide guarantees and underwriting for qualifying Australian films;

* lead or participate in loan syndicates for the production of qualifying Australian films.

In exercising these functions, the objectives of the Corporation are to:

* underpin a production slate at a high level in each financial year;

* support projects with demonstrated market interest and budget levels commensurate with the potential market and realisation of returns;

* secure an appropriate return on each of its investments;

* achieve a balanced production slate between cinema and television projects, including documentaries;

* assist towards financing a body of qualifying Australian films which in the opinion of the Board reflects the diversity of cultural, creative and commercial endeavour in the Australian film and television production industry.

QUALIFYING AUSTRALIAN PRODUCTIONS

The Corporation is only permitted to provide financial assistance to feature films, mini-series, telemovies and documentaries which are 'qualifying Australian films' as defined by Division 10BA of the *Income Tax Assessment Act,* as follows:

* films made wholly or substantially in Australia with significant Australian content, and

* films made pursuant to treaties or other forms of government or quasi-government arrangements (official international co-productions).

Each qualifying Australian film or television program must first receive a provisional certificate as required by Division 10BA from the Department of Communications and the Arts (DCA).

For official international co-productions, DCA issues a provisional certificate taking into consideration advice by the Australian Film Commission (AFC) that the film satisfies the criteria of an official co-production. These criteria are determined by the AFC in consultation with the unions and guilds active in the film and television industry.

INVESTMENT GUIDELINES

The Australian Film Finance Corporation has a Board of ten directors including the Chief Executive. Board members are appointed by the Minister responsible for the Arts.

All investment decisions are made by the Board, which has regular monthly meetings. Additional meetings and committees may be convened to attend to urgent investment applications, administrative matters and applications to vary previous investment decisions.

The Corporation is not permitted to fully fund any project with the exception of the Film Fund. In the Corporation's investment guidelines, producers are given guidance regarding the expected level of private sector participation for various budget thresholds and production categories.

These published guidelines are revised annually after consultation with industry representatives and are available from the FFC along with an application form.

METHODS OF FUNDING

The FFC can fund projects in a number of ways. However, the overwhelming majority of FFC funding is by way of equity investments.

On a case-by-case basis the FFC will also provide other forms of financial assistance such as production loans, underwriting, print and advertising loans and guarantees. As there are a number of limitations on the FFC's powers to provide these forms of financial assistance, producers are advised to obtain advice from the FFC on alternative methods of funding.

PRIVATE SECTOR PARTICIPATION

The FFC was expected to attempt to secure an overall private sector participation level of 40 per cent in its funded production slate through 1994/95. The level for 1995/96 cannot be confirmed until the government review is complete. This is an aggregate target. The FFC has the discretion to reduce the level to as low as 15 per cent in individual projects provided it meets the aggregate 40 per cent target.

Private sector participation includes 10BA investments, distribution advances and pre-sales used to finance the production, and equity investments from non-public sector bodies.

The overwhelming source of private sector participation has come from the marketplace: distributors, broadcasters and sales agents. Producers are required to secure appropriate marketplace attachments when structuring the project deal. These may be pre-sales, distribution guarantees or advances from other market participants which ensure that the project has recoupment prospects and a guaranteed audience.

RECOUPMENT

The Corporation expects to share in returns from the worldwide distribution of the projects in which it invests and will not accept a recoupment formula confined only to a high risk territory, such as North America; nor will it agree to recoup exclusively from a distributor's or sales agent's overage.

Ideally, the FFC should have an entitlement to a reasonable level of guaranteed returns as well as an entitlement to revenues from unsold territories. This is particularly desirable in relation to higher budget feature films and adult television drama.

The FFC accepts that expected returns for documentaries, particularly those with specific cultural relevance to Australian audiences, are likely to be low.

PRODUCTION SLATE

The FFC's brief is to support a diverse range of culturally relevant material. The FFC also has targets for its investments to ensure a spread of product across the various production categories. The targets are:

* 45–55 per cent for feature films;

* 40–50 per cent for television drama;

* 5–15 per cent for documentaries.

The FFC monitors its investments in order to achieve these targets, but recognises that market factors will influence their achievement.

The FFC expects to commit no more than 10 per cent of its investment funds to co-productions. This level may be exceeded where there is a large proportion of Australian majority co-productions.

FFC OFFICES AND STAFF

The Corporation has offices in Sydney and Melbourne. Filmmakers are invited to consult with the FFC's Investment Managers while structuring their projects.

Generally the Sydney office is responsible for New South Wales and Queensland projects and the Melbourne office is responsible for projects in all other states. Regular visits to states outside New South Wales and Victoria are made by the Chief Executive, Investment Managers and other key staff.

The Corporation's Investment Managers:

* assist the producer to frame an application for funding;

* assist the producer's negotiations with distributors and private sector participants to ensure an investment and recoupment structure acceptable to the Corporation;

* present a proposed investment structure to the Board with an analysis of the recoupment prospects for the Corporation;

* monitor the project, with the assistance of the Budget Analyst, during the production process;

134 * liaise with the producer about the marketing of the film and distribution proposals.

The Corporation's Budget Analysts review the production budget of the project to ensure it can deliver the requisite on-screen values and is realistic, given the project's expected returns from exploitation in the marketplace.

The Business Affairs staff is responsible for the contracting of all projects, including variations to investments, according to the Board's decisions and policies. They also review and upgrade the FFC's standard form production agreements and negotiate licence, distribution, sales agency and completion guarantee agreements.

The Distribution Manager advises the Corporation on distribution aspects of the film investment proposals, particularly the projects' marketing prospects and their potential returns. The Manager may recommend sales strategies where appropriate and, together with the Distribution staff and relevant Investment Manager, liaises with producers and distributors to monitor the performance of projects once they are delivered and in the marketplace.

Further information is available from the Public Relations Manager and the Policy Officer who liaise with the industry, media and government regarding the FFC's policies and activities.

THE APPLICATION PROCESS

Producers are invited to discuss their projects with Investment Managers as the first step in their financing strategy. Producers can then obtain direct advice on how best to structure the project to secure FFC support.

Application forms need to be lodged before a project is formally accepted as an application for funding. The producer should discuss their project with the FFC before lodging an application form.

The Investment Manager will guide the project through the assessment process and advise the producer when the project is ready to be considered by the Board. The Board makes all investment decisions, generally following Investment Managers' recommendations.

A project will generally proceed to the Board six weeks following application. This may take longer if the elements in the project are complex or if there are difficulties in securing the commitments from the co-financiers and marketplace attachments.

INFORMATION

The FFC publishes a regular newsletter. The Newsletter publishes the dates of Board meetings and provides other information in relation to the FFC. Copies are available from the FFC.

FFC staff also participate in industry seminars, conferences and workshops on request.

FILM QUEENSLAND

See p. 294 for contact details.

Film Queensland, a branch of the Office of the Arts and Cultural Development, is committed to the support of film and television production in Queensland. Assistance is offered through a wide range of programs, incentives and equity investment.

Programs of Assistance are divided into five major categories:

* Project Development

* Creative Development

* Cultural Development

* Professional Development

* Production Finance and Incentives

Project Development and **Creative Development** funds are provided for the development and production of feature films, telemovies, mini-series, series and serials, documentaries, animation and short films intended for production in Queensland.

While funding through the **Project Development Program** is also available to credited applicants from interstate, the **Creative, Cultural and Professional Development Programs** can be accessed only by Queensland residents.

Production Finance is available for feature film and television drama projects based in Queensland. The producer, director or writer must be Queensland residents.

INCENTIVES

The following **Production Incentives** are available:

* The **Revolving Film Finance Fund** (RFFF) provides a loan facility of up to 20 per cent of the budget to a maximum of $1,000,000 to support film and television production in Queensland.

* **Wages Subsidy for Queensland Cast and Crew** provides cash rebates to all substantial productions employing Queensland resident cast and crew. Rebates are designed to encourage productions to employ Queensland cast and crew and to help establish and retain a pool of qualified film personnel in the state.

* **Payroll Tax Incentives** - full rebates of Queensland payroll tax are available to film productions and television series expending a minimum of $3,500,000 in Queensland.

FILM VICTORIA

See p. 294 for contact details.

Film Victoria's major objectives are to assist and promote quality film and television projects that are both innovative and marketable. The Corporation provides investment for all stages of the production process including development, production and marketing. It also operates a range of marketing and financial support services to assist film and television production in Victoria. Film Victoria is also committed to encouraging the development of multimedia, including CD ROM applications and interactive projects.

Film Victoria supports a broad range of activities through the following programs:

* **Script Development.** Investment is provided for the development of quality scripts for a range of film, multimedia and television projects.

* **Production Assistance.** Film Victoria offers production investment for television, feature film, multimedia and documentary projects.

* **Marketing Assistance.** Marketing assistance is provided to companies and individuals to assist in the promotion and marketing of projects.

* **Producer Support.** The Producer Package Scheme provides financial assistance for producers to develop and/or market projects in Australia and internationally.

* **Cultural Activities.** Film Victoria actively supports film organisations and events by encouraging programs and initiatives that promote Victoria's film culture.

* **Independent Filmmakers' Fund.** The fund aims to develop new creative talent by providing a development opportunity for emerging filmmakers.

* **First Time Directors.** Film Victoria offers production assistance to promising first time feature film or documentary directors.

* **Documentary Mentor Scheme.** This scheme creates an opportunity for emerging documentary filmmakers to develop projects with a consultant attached.

* **New Writers Scheme. This fund** provides assistance for new writers to develop a script for a feature length project.

* **The Government Film Unit.** The GFU liaises between government departments and Victoria's independent filmmakers for the production of high quality, appropriate and accessible government films.

* **The Melbourne Film Office.** The recently established MFO is a film industry marketing and locations advisory service for local, interstate and international producers.

* **Committed Funding Facility.** The CFF cash flows distribution guarantees and pre-sales offered by a distributor, television network or sales agent.

* **Prints and Advertising.** Film Victoria offers loans to assist with the cost of prints and advertising for the theatrical release of local feature films.

New South Wales Film & Television Office

See p. 296 for contact details.

The New South Wales Film & Television Office (FTO) is funded by the NSW government to support the film and television industries.

The FTO has existed since 1988. NSW is the traditional centre of the production industry in Australia, attracting about 60 per cent of all production in Australia, including foreign production. It invests directly in production and the development of TV and film projects and assists the film and television industry in a variety of other ways.

137

The Office invests about three quarters of a million dollars each year in script and project development and $1,000,000 in production investment. It encourages local producers to co-develop projects with overseas partners.

The Office also actively supports production and assists overseas and local producers through its location liaison service.

The FTO acts as executive producer for the research, scripting and production of films and videos for the NSW state government and its agencies.

Each year the FTO funds a number of cultural organisations and film events and the promotion of the industry as a whole. It has been responsible for a number of research projects and sponsors seminars for information exchange among industry personnel.

Based in Sydney and with wide experience and contacts in the industry, the FTO is well situated to extend services and advice to local filmmakers and visiting producers.

Screen West

See p. 302 for contact details.

Screen West, the Western Australian Film and Television Office, is the primary government agency responsible for assisting the development of an artistically vibrant, commercially viable and forward-looking film industry in Western Australia.

Its main focus is to provide development loans, marketing loans and strategic investments as a means of bringing marketable film and television projects to fruition and helping film-makers to attract full production finance. Through these funding mechanisms it supports a diverse range of projects, including feature films, telemovies, television drama series, mini-series, documentaries and animated films.

With access to its own Production Investment Fund and the Lotteries Commission Film Incentive Schemes, Screen West is able to draw on a total funding pool amounting to some $3,000,000 annually for Production Financing and Incentives. These funds are intended to provide real incentives to producers who are looking to complete the financing of their projects and are seeking competitive funding arrangements. The funds can be used to complement sources of finance from the commercial sector, private investors, broadcasters or government funding bodies. Screen West can tailor its funds to suit the needs of an individual production, and funding may be available from a combination of schemes.

Proposals from interstate and overseas producers are welcome, but in order to qualify for assistance projects must involve substantial West Australian elements, be filmed principally in WA, and yield measurable benefits to the state.

In addition to its entrepreneurial role, Screen West runs a Creative Development program with the aim of fostering new ideas and talent, and encouraging fresh and innovative approaches to film making. Funding schemes available under this program include the Film Extension Fund, New Screen Writers' Bursaries, Documentary Research Packages and Tele-visionaries.

The agency also offers financial assistance to West Australian filmmakers to extend their skills and professional development by participating in conferences, workshops, seminars or other training activities, and provides grants in support of a variety of screen culture activities and film industry events.

Screen West has taken over responsibility for administering the Lotteries Commission Film Incentive Schemes. These Schemes support the employment of West Australian film practitioners, the development of low-budget feature films, and the provision of awards for excellence.

SOUTH AUSTRALIAN FILM CORPORATION

See p. 302 for contact details.

The Film Development Office of the South Australian Film Corporation provides financial assistance for filmmakers to develop projects to market readiness, provides limited production investment funds, and has a range of programs to assist the development of a viable film and video industry in South Australia.

To be eligible for assistance applicants need to demonstrate and deliver benefits by way of employment opportunities for South Australian cast and crew, use of locations and facilities as well as cultural benefits to the state.

PROJECT DEVELOPMENT

The following assistance is available:

* **Script Development Loans.** Script Development Loans are available for the researching and development of feature films, telemovies, mini-series, long form drama and documentaries which have a theatrical or television broadcast market. Loans will be recouped on the first day of principal photography with interest.

* **Marketing and Project Development Loans**. Marketing and Project Development Loans will be available to projects which have marketing potential and can cover travel costs, producing marketing materials, preparation of budgets and schedules and cast nego-tiations. Loans will be recouped on the first day of principal photography with interest.

* **Production Financing and P&A Loans**. Production financing, either as equity in-vestments or loans, is available to a maximum of $200,000 in any on production or 10 per cent of the total production budget. The SAFC may, from time to time, increase this level of investment. Production investments will normally be recouped pro rata and pari passu with other investors.

    P&A Loans will be provided to assist the filmmaker in attracting a distributor to the project. The loan will be recouped with interest from the first dollar returned, before investors.

* **Cash Flowing of Distribution Guarantees.** The SAFC will provide loans to the producer of up to $200,000 to cash flow distribution guarantees into the budget. The loans are subject to interest and an administration fee. The producer and the distributor will need to assign the payment of the distribution guarantee directly to the SAFC.

* **Creative Development Fund**. The Creative Development Fund aims to support the **139**

creation of new and innovative ideas and the development of new filmmakers. Eligible projects include experimental and avant-garde, animated, drama and documentary short films. Multimedia projects are also considered. Projects can be either on film, video or computer formats. Both script development and production applications will be considered.

Applying To The Film Development Office

The Film Development Office will accept applications throughout the year. There is no specific deadline with the exception of the Creative Development Fund and Cultural Organisation funding.

Depending on the amount being requested, the applicant will be informed of a decision within four to six weeks.

The SAFC will accept applications on a selective basis from producers who are not residents of South Australia for script development, market development and production financing (including P&A Loans and cash flow loans). For the SAFC to consider supporting a non-resident project, significantly more than 50 per cent of the film will need to be shot and post-produced in South Australia (unless it is a co-production). The investment level will be commensurate with the level of benefit to the State, and will be influenced by the use of South Australian cast and crew, and the use of locations and facilities.

Ideally the SAFC is looking for projects which have a likelihood of going into production within 12–18 months.

The SAFC will not consider applications for the Creative Development Fund from non-South Australian residents.

Other SAFC Services

Other SAFC services are:

*   **SAFC Studios.** The SAFC maintains Studios which provide facilities including sound stages and sound mixing/editing facilities which, combined with those of other South Australian companies, meet the full range of production and post-production needs.

*   **Government Film Fund**. The SAFC provides film and video services to the state government, including executive production of short documentaries and dramas for educational and promotional purposes, seeking tenders from independent production companies and providing advice to state government departments and agencies.

*   **Marketing**. The Marketing Office provides support for South Australian producers and promotes the industry and the wide range of locations available in South Australia.

Using a Financial Agent

Hal McElroy

As the American market (or more specifically Hollywood), gets more xenophobic and egomaniacal, as the budgets get bigger and the list of 'A' list players get shorter, everyone outside that inner circle gets left out. And left out in a big way.

In fact, I'd go as far as to say that these days unless you live and work in Hollywood then by definition, you are 'out'. Clearly, therefore, most people reading this are definitely out and will always be so. But so is everyone else in the world. So don't slash your wrists.

A world outside Hollywood? Hard to imagine if you live in Hollywood, but there is a world of non-American filmmakers and we're an important part of it in Australia. Why? Because we're English-speaking, our budgets are still relatively low and we seem to combine the best of substantive English drama, the romanticism or poetry of 'European' cinema, the individuality of Scandinavian filmmakers and the energy and 'don't give a damn' of the American independents. That makes for a pretty interesting mix.

The same is true of television. Arguably we're the finest and cheapest non-American producers of quality television drama be it for children or adults.

So enough of the self-congratulations. Why am I saying this? Because Australia has become a very attractive co-production partner, because of the good creative and economical work we do here and because the penny has dropped and we're welcoming co-productions.

In the old days, there were basically three television buyers in North America and, say, six or seven, or maybe eight, studios. That's it!

Same in microcosm here. Way back, there were three commercial networks (forget the ABC) and one or two film distributors/exhibitors. Nowadays in Australia (with the recent boost for SBS), there are five viable TV buyers with one, possibly two, pay TV buyers coming on stream. The exhibition/distribution options have expanded here to as many as four.

That exact scenario has repeated itself time and time again, right across the world, but it is particularly true of America. For example, in their heydays, the big three US networks commanded, among them, 95 per cent of the available audience. Today it's 65 per cent odd – a loss of 30 per cent of their audience.

This multiplication of options for both consumers and US producers also means fragmentation of the market. Smaller pieces means a consequent diminution of the revenues and therefore the licence fees paid in television.

What does all this mean to us? Nowadays, most TV sets in America carry 20 plus channels. Some carry 50; 150 will be available in a few years. Smaller, less monolithic buyers are less powerful, therefore less demanding and more open to collaboration with outsiders.

What must we, as outsiders, do? We must start forming strategic alliances to help cobble together the patchwork quilts of a production budget and distribution arrangements necessary to make what we want to make and the various new buyers want to buy.

Again in the old days, distributors would insist on automatically obtaining all rights, all media, worldwide and refuse to accept anything less. Today with fragmentation leading to lower individual revenue streams, but rising cost structures for production, the most common result is split rights and most buyers (with varying degrees of good grace) are beginning to accept this new reality.

Let's examine a single deal, with three different partners. First partner, a broadcaster, may get certain broadcast rights (and pay up front), and then perhaps s/he may get a certain share of profit from sales in other territories, while second partner, a distributor, may acquire limited rights in certain territories that s/he advances money against. A third partner (perhaps a cable system), could retain video rights in their territory (in addition to cable) to help them cover their downside risk and reduce the licence fee outlay.

Three different buyers, with three different agendas all agreeing to get into bed together on the one production. Why? Because none are putting up 100 per cent of the financing. So if they want product, it's only deals like this that give them product at the right price.

In this increasingly complex deal-making environment, particularly overseas, there has been an increase in the importance and number of independent agents who can be marriage broker, circus ringmaster, packager of talent or money, or all of the above. In other words, a lifesaver.

The Creative Artists' Agency (CAA), and indeed all the big agencies in Los Angeles, have a packaging fee which is a standard. It's call a '5+5 deal'.

In TV, they retain 5 per cent of the licence fee, as a cash repayment for their work, plus 5 per cent of producer's net profits as a continuing interest. Now on a successful TV series, that can add up to a huge river of money.

Less powerful agents, particularly if they're not providing 100 per cent of the funding or key creative elements, will accept a position a lot less than that. So it gets down to very individual negotiations specific to a project to figure out any ownership or entitlement.

An independent agent makes his or her money in exchange for packaging certain pre-sales or equity investment, cashflowed against future sales by seeking:

* an executive producer credit; or

* a share of producer's profit; or

* a fee out of the budget; or

* retain certain distribution rights for his/her own exploitation; or

* a combination of all four.

Before you start signing up with an independent financing agent, because you think this person is your lifesaver, I suggest you do a couple of things:

* seek from them their professional history, a CV or biog or whatever, and ask them to effect introductions for you to talk with previous clients of theirs – and do it! Check them out carefully and personally.

The old saying that success has many parents, whilst failure is an orphan, is never truer than amongst packaging agents in the film and TV industry. Some agents will make the most outrageous claims about the pivotal nature of their role in any previous success within a hundred miles of their office.

Remember that this guy or gal is going to promise to deliver money to you at some point in the future. You, in turn, without seeing the money first, are going to rely on those assurances to get other people to put up money or spend your own. You may seek investment from the FFC or spend thousands, tens of thousands even hundreds of thousands of dollars, of your or other people's money in further development or legal fees, to contract for that money. So if s/he lets you down, and there's no money when you're waiting for it, you've got a huge credibility problem and maybe a big hole in your pocket. Worse, you may not discover this for months and months.

A little anecdote…When I was trying to finance *The Sum of Us*, Kevin Dowling arranged for me to meet with two Chicago-based lawyers, who became co-EP's on the film. They introduced to me a real estate billionaire, Jerry Wexler, Darryl Hannah's stepfather. Lovely man. He agreed to put up two or three million for the film. Perfect! Unfortunately he died of cancer before we were able to complete the deal.

So we had to go out again in America, looking for money. You all know that feeling…ghastly!

We were introduced to one guy, yes, no problems, the money was available amazingly as a loan, no collateral, except for revenue from the film and the interest rate was very reasonable. He takes a fee of 7.5 per cent of the money raised, everything's fine. Just sign a piece of paper, giving him exclusive rights to raise the money for a 90-day period. So I got my lawyer in New York to check out this guy whose office address was the World Trade Centre. There was an address all right, in one of the twin towers of this famous building, a mailbox, but no office. His corporation effectively didn't exist. So forget him.

Next, a female independent producer in NewYork. She could get the money she said. She checked out. She was OK. Then she introduced me to another guy, her partner, who introduced me to a third guy. No problems, same deal, 7.5 per cent commission, money as a loan from a well-known Californian Bank, against future revenues of the film. Sounds terrific.

So I rang my Los Angeles lawyer, to check the deal out. Immediately he said, I know the bank, I know the key officers, there's no way they'll do that deal – no way. I said, do me a favour, ring them and ask them just an 'in principle' question, no names no pack drill, will they do the deal the New York broker promised he had agreed to do. One hour later, my lawyer rang back – definitely no.

We confront the broker and pull out. He screams no, not true, threatens to sue. The female producer and her partner believe the broker not me, and spend months chasing me to do the deal which I now know can't be done! This leads me to the second piece of advice:

✻   Don't sign a piece of paper, a contract, giving anybody rights to finance or pre-sell a picture unless you do the following:

–   As I've said, you've checked them out.

143

- There's a definite time limit on the contract, the shorter the better. A year is OK, 90 days is better.

- If possible, set in writing definite performance targets in terms of a calendar and dollars. For example, let's agree that within 30 days of the end of the next Cannes Film Festival, if you haven't raised X dollars against Y territory, it's off.

- Clear agreement on the territories and rights they are selling or pre-selling, preferably limited in some way to their own professed area of expertise. For example, Continental Europe.

- Requirement for regular and full disclosure of progress, ideally monthly, in writing. That way you know who's seen your project and who has passed.

- Most importantly, a clear and automatic revision of all rights back to you at the conclusion of the period, or failure to achieve agreed targets.

- No money is paid out – never give them money. All their fees and reasonable receiptable expenses are only recoupable from ideally the budget, or less ideally, deducted from the presale or investment they deliver – not before.

Of course any agent is entitled to a free run, an exclusive. There is nothing worse or more destructive than two different parties selling the same project at the same time. So exclusivity is OK, providing it's within prescribed and pre-agreed territories or rights, there's a clock running, you get the rights back when the time expires, and you have a clear picture of what they have or have not done.

Don't forget almost by definition it's your project. It's your money you're spending. Don't hand someone a project on a platter for nothing and not know what's happening to it or how or when you'll get it back if they fail.

THE WRITTEN PROPOSAL

DAMIEN PARER

You have developed the project to the point where you are now ready to go out into the market to raise production finance. The following are some ideas which may help to sell your film. Not all the elements are essential but, as producer, you will best serve the production by preparing and planning them as early in the process as you can.

THE WRITTEN PRESENTATION

It is very useful, indeed mandatory, to set out the project in written form which you can leave with people with whom you have discussions or post to them to excite their interest prior to a meeting. Some producers go to the extent of making glossy brochures with photos or drawings. Whether you do this or not will depend on whether you have the funds and whether you think it will help the sell.

The written presentation can follow the format of the concept document (see 'Preparing the concept document', by Gilly Lowndes) and can include the following information:

∗ **Disclaimer.** You should make it clear that the information that you provide at various stages is not intended to be an offer to the public, i.e., prospectus or similar.

∗ **Working title of production.**

∗ **Contents page.** A contents page makes reading the proposal so much easier if there are a great number of pages.

∗ **Contact address, phone and fax numbers.** How the reader can find you to talk some more.

∗ **What is it?** Describe length. Is it film or videotape? How many episodes? Is there a possible precursor or sequel or on-going series?

∗ **Property.** Offer proof of right to represent the property.

∗ **'Selling' synopsis.** A one-pager, including some story elements and a lot of enthusiasm.

∗ **Synopsis, outline, treatment or script.** This should be available as a separate document.

∗ **Character descriptions.** Not more than half a page each, written interestingly.

∗ **Cast.** Biography and perhaps photographs, especially if they are known to the reader. Suggestions of possible cast may be useful; expressions of interest from cast would be very effective.

∗ **History of the production company involved.** Emphasise the successes and personnel involved.

145

* **Creative personnel.** Provide details of producer, director, writer and any other key creative personnel – biographies or CVs.

* **Background.** Reason for making the production. Why is it needed or different? One or two pages will usually do it.

* **Successful films of similar genre** may make a good comparison. Identify target audience or suggest time slot for broadcast.

* **Readers' reports.** Any material favourable to the project can be useful. Readers' permission may be required.

* **Book.** If the project is adapted from a book, novel, short story or poem, give details of book sales or critical acclaim. Copies of the book, short story or poem may be useful to give away.

* **Locations.** The project may be very dependent on these. Photos may work here.

* **Home town loyalty.** Investors, including government funding agencies and sponsors, may be drawn to a project coming from or being shot in their home town. Ethnicity or special subject matter may appeal to a particular group of investors.

* **Marketing proposal.** Some ideas about the marketing campaign, advertising, release time. Who is the target audience? What censorship rating will it receive?

* **The financial deal.** Any pre-sales or discussions with potential buyers. Any money committed so far. Any government involvement. Order of recoupment of percentage of profits.

* **Income projection.** A timetable showing expected returns from all possible sources.

* **Distribution deal.** Any commitment or interest from distributors or exhibitors.

* **Development funds to date.** List the organisations or people who have been involved so far and describe the stage the production is at now.

* **Tax advantages.**

* **Production schedule** showing start dates, various major items and especially delivery dates for completed film or videotape.

* **Budget summary.** Point out any deferrals or items which affect the deal.

* **Cash flow requirements.**

* **Accounting procedures.**

* **Auditor.**

* **Lawyer.**

* **Insurer.**

* **Banker.**

* **Completion guarantor.**

✳   **Accompanying material.** You may consider making a short video or audio tape to promote and sell the idea.

✳   **Art work.** A professionally presented proposal will work in your favour. You could consider using drawings or photographs. A professional layout makes reading it easier. An index is always welcome.

WHAT IS MEANT BY...?

To help you understand what people are expecting when they ask you for a specific piece of information about the project and its plot, the following definitions may assist:

concept   aka idea, premise. A one-page teaser containing anything which intrigues, titillates and causes someone to ask for a ...

synopsis   One to three pages explaining the plot and characters which is so exciting that you are asked for an ...

outline   About three to ten pages. It's an expansion of the synopsis. At this stage the story needs to have a shape, structure and be sufficiently viable to lead to a ...

storyline   You will need ten to fifteen pages here. Much more detail of how the plot works. All characters should emerge in the right proportion and the resolution should be clearly defined. The emotional content of the story should also be reflected in this document which leads to a ...

treatment   aka story treatment, extended treatment. For a feature film, TV or documentary series this can be 20 to 60 pages. The treatment is the hardest part of the whole process. Treatments must be tightly crafted around a strong structure. Characters must be clearly drawn and developed. It can contain some dialogue if you want. The theory is that the first draft screenplay should emerge from the treatment without too much angst. But there is a downside to this. It is very difficult to convey in the treatment the emotional elements of the story. If you have to provide a treatment you should ensure that it is written in a style which is lively and which will engage the reader's keen interest throughout.

scene breakdown   aka scene by scene breakdown. A treatment which has a separate brief paragraph for each scene.

first draft   About a minute a page of screen time. Full scenes, full dialogue and necessary descriptions.

NOTE

Some filmmakers use the word 'outline' to mean concept.

The Spoken Presentation

As the person putting the financial package together for the project you will need to be able to present the project eloquently and succinctly to investors, distributors or agents personally or on the phone. Here are some suggestions to perfect your 'pitch'.

Sell the film to yourself first. Make sure that you believe in its potential and viability. You can't sell anything until it's obvious to the listener that you believe in it. Try out the idea informally on friends and acquaintances.

Make sure that you can talk comfortably about the elements in your written proposal. Stumbling around when asked specifics will not help your sell.

Devise a very brief, clever handle or hook to explain the appeal of the film to audiences. This gives investors an idea to hold onto. Films are sold on concept, not screenplay. Is the concept unique? Does it compare to other successful films of a similar genre?

Equity investors, when they are individuals, like to be seduced by the logic of the presentation but they may also be interested in the perceived glamour of the enterprise. They tend to know that film investment is high risk but they may be willing to put up money because it's more fun than investing in most other high risk areas.

Talk about all the potential income from the film. If there is a possible sequel it becomes more attractive.

You are as good as your last picture. Make capital out of any success or notoriety you may have acquired. Don't be shy about mentioning your proposed cast (particularly if it has 'star' value) and crew if they have had successes. The investors may be impressed by a meeting with a well-known actor or director at the meeting. Their presence endorses the film and makes it a more solid proposition.

A short videotape or still photographs may help sell the project. Well-known actors saying on tape that they like the project can be helpful. A dramatised sequence from the script or a demonstration of skills may be useful.

Suggest a time frame: give investors a deadline so that they make up their minds relatively quickly.

Make it possible for investors to say 'no'. It's no use assuming that they are interested – give them the opportunity to commit or drop out. You must keep seeking funding until contracts are signed.

If your potential investor says 'no', at least try to get the names and contacts of other people that he or she feels may be interested.

The *Trade Practices Act*

You should be aware of the Act and its amendments. It covers all of a producer's activities, but particularly:

*   Investors:

-     don't tell investors the film qualifies for 'Australian film' until you have a Provisional Certificate;

-     pre-sales must be contracted before a producer can state that they exist;

-     other elements in the package must be secured before a producer can guarantee them to the investors.

*   Distributors: misrepresenting aspects of the film to distributors or exhibitors is against the law.

INSURANCE

NEIL McEWIN

The insurance requirements for shorter films and video tapes do not differ greatly from those offered to major feature films. The basic difference is obviously the size of the budget which can, in some cases, lead the producer to discard or ignore some covers purely because the budget cannot cope with the cost.

It is therefore imperative that the production company understands the insurance covers that are being offered, in order that an understanding is reached on the areas in which the production company itself is going to bear the risk.

It must be strongly pointed out that, when dealing with these insurances, the production company should ensure that the underwriter or broker is conversant with the covers in order that correct covers are obtained and, just as importantly, that correct advice is given.

FILM PRODUCERS' INDEMNITY

This class of cover, also known as cast insurance, provides cover for the increased costs incurred by the death, injury or illness of nominated personnel. Ascertaining whom to insure can, in some instances, prove to be extremely difficult; as a basic guideline the production company should only insure those personnel who are integral to the completion/continuation of the production. Obviously in most cases the director is the most integral and, invariably, the director is always insured under this policy, together with lead artists. Other key personnel can be a narrator or a cameraman. If the shoot is occurring overseas then often several other members of the crew would be insured on the basis that they would not be easily replaced.

The period of cover under this class is basically split into two sections:

* pre-production;

* shoot.

The pre-production period – with the personnel insured under it – is another area which can vary enormously. Again, the director is usually insured for the longest period, that is, from the first day of pre-production. However, the director may be insured several months before commencement of pre-production on the basis that it would be difficult to replace him or her without causing delays to the production.

It should always be remembered that the insurance underwriters will require a medical examination to be completed before affording the nominated person with illness cover.

The policy is variably subject to a deductible (or excess), the size of which is usually related to the budget. For example on a budget of $100,000 the deductible would usually range from

150

$1000 to $2500 for each and every claim. On a large feature the deductible would be up to $10,000 for each and every claim.

The policy contains very few exclusions, the most important being:

* flights where the insured person is actually piloting the aircraft;

* hazardous stunts where the underwriter is not notified beforehand. However if the underwriter is advised about the stunt before it occurs, and if approval is given, this exclusion can be avoided.

The premium is based on 'Net Insurable Costs', which are estimated as follows:

> total budget *less*   story and script rights
> music rights
> brokerage
> post-production
>> − offices and administration
>> − editors' rooms
>> − laboratory
>> − sound
> owned wardrobe, sets, props, equipment
> premium for the film producer's indemnity

i.e., all costs incurred from the initiation of the project through to completion of the shoot, excluding underlying rights and royalties.

NEGATIVE FILM RISK

Cover is provided for increased costs incurred by loss of, or damage to the negative, and includes the risks of faulty stock, camera and processing. When arranging the cover, consideration should be given to the following points:

* Cover should be arranged to commence one week before the shoot in order to include damage to raw stock being collected beforehand.

* It should be remembered that the period of cover should be taken to the estimated date of the answer-print, plus at least one month, in order to obviate the need for extensions.

* Should it not be possible to test the camera before commencing the shoot, then the broker or underwriter should be notified in order that cover can be correctly extended.

Once again the policy will often have a deductible, but this is usually only on faulty stock, camera and processing claims. Where the frequency of rushes is irregular this deductible will invariably increase.

The sum insured is based on the total budget, less story and script, music and brokerage costs, i.e., 'gross insurable costs', though the premium will probably be based on the declared 'net insurable' and will be rated according to the period of insurance, frequency of processing and location of the filming.

MULTI RISKS

This particular cover, which used to be entitled 'all risks', is basically split into two sections:

* props, sets and wardrobe, which can also be extended to include, if nominated, items of jewellery and office contents;

* cameras, lighting and electrical equipment.

It should be remembered that the sum insured on each of these sections must represent the full value, and thus the figures given in the budget will invariably be incorrect as they will usually include items that are being hired.

The basic exclusions under this class of cover are:

* wear, tear and gradual deterioration;

* shortage of inventory;

* rain, sleet, snow and hail damage to property stored in the open;

* damage caused intentionally or at the direction of the insured;

* in respect of camera, lighting and electrical equipment, mechanical breakdown or derangement is also excluded.

There are other exclusions to the cover and care should be taken to ensure that the correct cover is obtained when initially arranging the policies.

It must be established before commencement of the shoot as to whether items owned by specific crew members are covered by the production or by the owner who is hiring them to the company.

The insurance company must be informed if equipment is to be taken in boats or helicopters, or used for stunts, and it should be remembered that intentional write-offs may not be included in this cover.

For all multi-risk insurance, average will apply if the full value of items is not insured. The period of cover must include pre- and post-production until the return or sale of all items.

The policy always has a deductible, which is usually around $250 for each loss on smaller sums insured. For larger sums insured, a deductible of possibly $500 may be offered.

EXTRA EXPENSE

This cover, which is usually only used on features or larger documentaries, provides cover to the production company for the increased costs incurred by loss of or damage to props, sets and/or facilities.

The basic thing to consider under this cover is that it is not necessarily covering only those items which are insured under the multi-risks cover such as props, sets and wardrobe. If the production is being shot in a studio then the studio is considered to be a facility. If the studio were to be destroyed by fire then the production company would obviously incur increased costs in moving to another studio or location. This would result in a claim under the extra expense policy.

The sum insured will be an estimate of daily costs to a maximum number of days required to relocate or replace unusual sets, scenery or equipment, and up to approximately 25 per cent of the net insurable as a maximum. Any claim would be subject to a deductible of around $1000 for each and every loss.

Public Liability

The policy covers the production company for claims made against it by third parties for acts of negligence resulting in property damage or injury or death to persons, other than employees of the production company.

The cover extends to include loss of use, which is usually of great interest to production companies in that it provides cover for such items as cameras, where the hiring company maintains a weekly rental charge whilst a damaged camera is being repaired. This, of course, could result in large additional costs being incurred.

It is extremely difficult to ascertain a sum insured for this cover as invariably, on larger claims, it is the courts who award the settlement figure. It should be remembered, however, that one of the largest settlements awarded by the courts in Australia was just under $3 million, and this was an instance where the insured only had cover for $500,000. The standard cover is $5,000,000 although some councils are now requesting $10,000,000.

A deductible of usually $1000 will usually apply to property damage claims.

Workers' Compensation

This class of cover is compulsory to protect employees of the production company. The cover provides a weekly benefit to the employee (in New South Wales this benefit is the Award rate of pay) and also includes cover for common law claims where negligence is proven against the employer.

Although this policy is compulsory for all employees, there are a number of personnel within the film industry who have formed their own companies and who therefore provide their services to the production company as contractors. In this case, care should be taken to ensure that such contractors have arranged their own workers' compensation insurance.

If the production is being shot outside the state of residence of the production company, a workers' compensation cover should also be effected in that state to protect personnel who may be hired interstate and who elect to claim under their own state's *Workers' Compensation Act*.

In New South Wales the premium is based on a rate applied to the total payroll of all employees.

MONEY INSURANCE

This cover must be written to include money or negotiable instruments in the care, custody or control of the insured and/or authorised personnel, to provide protection at all times. The sum insured should be the maximum at risk at any one time. It will exclude theft by employees.

PERSONAL ACCIDENT AND DISABILITY INSURANCE

This may be required for those crew or cast who at any time during the production may be in hazardous situations including filming in light aircraft, helicopters or balloons. Stunt persons may also require additional cover.

MOTOR VEHICLE COMPREHENSIVE INSURANCE

Vehicles which are hired will most probably be insured by the owners, but in some circumstances cover will need to be taken out by the production company. In these cases the vehicle details including registration and value must be given to the insurer, and it should be confirmed that third party property damage is included in the comprehensive cover. Action and static vehicles will be included under 'multi risks'.

WEATHER INSURANCE

Weather insurance is a very expensive cover that may only be economically viable for specific days for whatever weather conditions are required, when no alternative is possible.

MARINE AND AVIATION INSURANCE

Marine and aviation cover will only be taken out if the script requires special activities involving boats or aeroplanes. They would most probably only be for specific days. Care should be taken to include the production company's name under the owner's policy, should cover be taken out under their policy.

OVERSEAS TRAVEL

Travel insurance packages are available and a producer would be well advised to take out individual covers for all crew and cast travelling overseas.

Errors and Omissions Insurance

Also known as Motion Picture Producer's Liability, this cover provides an indemnity for suits brought against the producer and/or production company in respect of libel, slander, defamation, plagiarism, breach of copyright, invasion of privacy or theft of rights. The cover includes defence costs within the indemnity limit and is usually worldwide. The policy will state a limit on any one claim as well as on the aggregate of all claims. A cover of three years is recommended and a deductible will apply.

The standard cover in Australia, to satisfy US requirements, is $1,500,000 on any one claim, or $4,500,000 in aggregate.

The sum insured is split into two sections:

(a)   a limit on any one claim – usually this figure will vary from $1,000,000 to $1,500,000, although higher figures may be selected if required;

(b)   a limit on all claims in aggregate during the policy period – this figure is usually $3,000,000 to $4,500,000.

The two basic requirements for the cover to proceed are that clearance procedures have been read and approved by the production company's solicitor and that title clearance is obtained. The title clearance, in most cases, comes from the law firm Brylawski, Cleary and Komen in Washington.

Completion Guarantee

The completion guarantee guarantees to the *investors* in a film that the film will be completed and delivered and that, subject to certain exclusions, funds will be made available in the event of an overage.

Approaches for a completion guarantee are usually initiated by the producer in very early pre-production stages. The completion guarantor will require, at that stage, the following documentation as a prerequisite:

*   budget;

*   shooting schedule;

*   script;

*   proposed key personnel such as director, producer, production manager, first AD, accountant and DOP.

The completion guarantor then decides, on the information presented to it, whether the project has a reasonable chance of being completed on time and on budget. If the decision is positive then a 'letter of intent' is given to the producer stating that, subject to certain conditions, the completion guarantor is prepared to proceed with the issuing of a guarantee.

Once the letter of intent is provided, the completion guarantor will, at the request of the

155

producer, proceed to final contracts. At this stage the guarantor will require to know certain other details such as whether:

∗ all financing is in place (the guarantee does not come into effect until this is so);

∗ all rights acquisitions have taken place;

∗ key personnel have been employed;

∗ necessary steps to effect complete insurances have been taken.

The standard rate for a completion guarantee is 5 per cent of the budget, excluding indirect costs. A no claim rebate may be applicable.

The completion guarantor works closely with the production company and has the right to access all production information. Therefore the guarantor will require reports on a regular basis on the progress of the film relating to the shooting schedule and budget. These will include daily progress reports and weekly cost statements.

Care should be taken to select a guarantor who is fully versed in the production area.

Clearance Procedures

The following is a guide – not a complete checklist – for the applicant's attorney who should make certain that the undernoted points have been complied with before final cut or first exhibition of the production to be insured.

∗ The script should be read before production to eliminate matter which is defamatory, invades privacy or is otherwise potentially actionable.

∗ Unless the work is an unpublished original not based on any other work, a copyright report must be obtained. Both domestic and foreign copyrights and renewal rights should be checked. If a completed film is being acquired, a similar review should be made on copyright and renewals on any copyrighted underlying property.

∗ If the script is an unpublished original, the origins of the work should be ascertained – basic idea, sequence of events and characters. It should be ascertained if submissions of any similar properties have been received by the applicant and, if so, the circumstances as to why the submitting party may not claim theft or infringement should be described in detail.

∗ Before final title selection, a title report should be obtained.

∗ Whether production is fictional (and location is identifiable) or factual, a check should be made that no names, faces or likenesses of any recognisable living persons are used unless written releases have been obtained. Release is unnecessary if a person is part of a crowd scene or shown in a fleeting background. Telephone books or other sources should be checked when necessary. Releases can only be dispensed with if the applicant provides the insurer with specific reasons, in writing, as to why such releases are unnecessary and if such reasons are accepted by the insurer. The term 'living persons' includes thinly disguised versions of living persons or living persons who are readily identifiable because of the identity of other characters or because of the factual, historical or geographic setting.

* Releases from living persons should contain language which gives the applicant the right to edit, delete material, juxtapose any part of the film with any other part of the film, change the sequence of events of any questions posed and/or answers, fictionalise persons or events including the release and to make any other changes in the film that the applicant deems appropriate. If a minor, consent has to be legally binding.

* If music is used, the applicant must obtain all necessary synchronisation and performance licences.

Written agreements must exist between the applicant and all creators, authors, writers, performers and other persons providing material (including quotations from copyrighted works) or on-screen services.

* If distinctive locations, buildings, businesses, personal property or products are filmed, written releases should be secured. This is not necessary if non-distinctive background use is made of real property.

* If the production involves actual events it should be ascertained that the author's sources are independent and primary (contemporaneous newspaper reports, court transcripts, interviews with witnesses etc.) and not secondary (another author's).

PRE-PRODUCTION

Casting

SUSIE MAIZELS

The Casting Consultant

The main role of a casting consultant/director is to flesh out the script. Whether it be documentary or fiction, if it required actors, the producer's and director's jobs will be easier if they take their scripts to a casting consultant.

Casting consultants spend most of their time watching performances of actors and, therefore, are constantly aware of performances and availability. After the casting consultant has had preliminary discussions with the producer/director, he or she will suggest various actors. When they have been approved by the producer/director as possible cast, the casting consultant will set up a casting session through the actors' agents.

When casting, keep an open mind and try to see any plays, TV shows or tapes of actors being considered. It is always a pleasant surprise to stretch a good actor instead of going the predictable route.

The Casting Session

When it is agreed that certain actors are a possibility for the parts discussed, a session is set up for the director and sometimes the producer to meet these actors. The script is usually sent to the actors beforehand so that any questions the actors might have regarding the part, and any questions the director might have about their comprehension of the part, can be discussed at this meeting. The director then decides who to get back in for a screen test, and a scene is picked out for the actor to learn. If a screen test is held, i.e. the actor performs and is directed in front of a film or video camera, the Media Entertainment and Arts Alliance (the union representing actors) has stated that a screen test fee must be paid. It is part of the Feature Film Award and could be mooted in terms of dramatised documentaries, etc.

Media Entertainment and Arts Alliance

The Media Entertainment and Arts Alliance (MEAA) is the official union for actors, announcers, musicians, journalists and people who work behind the scenes in the film industry. In relation to film and video production, areas covered by the Alliance include film and television, stunts, ABC and SBS, commercial radio, AFTRS, voice-overs, corporate video, commercials, documentaries, session singers, studio singers, backing vocalists, dancers, opera, theatre restaurants and imports.

Wherever possible, members of the Alliance should be cast. If, however, a genuine butcher, plumber, etc., is to be in his/her professional capacity during a film, television series, commercial or play, it will not be necessary for that person to join the Alliance. The philosophy behind this is that an actor is not losing work because of the employment of a trained person performing their normal professional duties.

Should an actor *not* be a member of the Alliance they should not be discounted. Preference should be given to members, but if the actor is a recent drama school graduate, or has recently arrived in the country and lands a part, he or she is entitled to join the Alliance. When using extras, preference should be given to members. If extras are used on location in the 'country' and are cast from locals in the area, an agreement can be made with the Alliance to make those extras temporary members for that particular job only.

In the case of imported artists (please note that using imported actors will change your film categories), it becomes necessary to advise the Department of Immigration of your intention and a visa is granted *only* after consultation with the Alliance. It is, therefore, very important to advise the Alliance of your plans and furnish them with adequate reasons for the particular overseas actor being given the role over a local actor. There can be several reasons for the import, including:

* it is part of the co-production deal to use an overseas lead actor and it has been requested that a marque name player be used from the particular overseas country involved in the co-production;

* the distributors have requested a name they can sell worldwide;

* it is essential to have a certain ethnic content and there are not enough actors of that particular ethnicity in Australia. In such instances a genuine search must be made in Australia first, with lists furnished to the Alliance of all the actors tested with genuine reasons for their non-selection.

If the Alliance is fully cognisant of your plans, it will be extremely helpful, so make sure you advise it every step of the way.

All negotiations are based on a scale of minimum fees that the Alliance has determined by arbitration and are subject to change, so it is always a wise idea to get the latest fee schedules from the Alliance before setting your budget. If it may be some time before you intend to take your project into production, it would be best to allow a margin for CPI indexation.

NEGOTIATIONS

Some producers prefer to undertake negotiations themselves as they may be more aware of the elasticity of their budget. Others prefer to have their casting consultants do it as the latter are constantly dealing with agents and are usually more aware of the actors' current market value.

When negotiating for film or television it is useful to know exactly what you wish to include in the deal. If shooting on away locations, producers prefer to buy 6 x 10-hour day weeks i.e., 60 hours per week. If shooting in a city where actors are resident, then it is usual to **161** buy 5 x 10-hour day weeks, i.e., 50 hours. In relation to the rights' loadings, your deal for film normally would include Australian television rights for not more than four screenings, Australian ancillary rights, world television rights excluding US network, world theatrical rights, and world ancillary rights excluding Australia. This will add up to 110 per cent of the Basic Negotiated Fee (BNF). Different rights are negotiated for television only: these comprise Australian repeats for not more than four screenings, Australian ancillary rights and worldwide screening *excluding* US network; this will add up to 102.5 per cent of the BNF. For corporate videos and training films, actors work on an hourly rate with a minimum of 4 hours for release over a twelve-month period only. If you wish to buy use rights in non-broadcast areas in perpetuity, then a loading of 150 per cent will apply. Add to this overtime to allow for 10-hour days, and holiday pay. Superannuation must be paid but cannot by law be negotiated as part of the deal. Rehearsal time is calculated on the BNF, i.e., the fee without loadings and overtime. Do not forget to state any post-syncing time, extra workshops or rehearsal periods as actors have to take as much work as possible. Just because you have confirmed them for your project does not necessarily make them totally available to you unless you state exactly when you require them. Always be honest with the agents. They are usually just as eager as you to have a successful project for their clients. Always leave a contingency in your budget. Make sure you discuss and agree on credits at this early stage. With leading actors and actresses it may be necessary to negotiate billing size and order.

CHILDREN

Under the age of fifteen, children are entitled to 50 per cent of adult fees. At this age they must have the permission of the Department of Community Services (in NSW), who should be informed of the shooting dates and times and the payment made to the child. If shooting times are outside school hours they will not be concerned, but as schedules are usually within those hours, you need to provide a tutor who has been approved by the Education Department, and the child must be accompanied by a parent or an approved chaperone such as the director's assistant. The Department must also receive a copy of the script for their perusal. The Alliance would prefer any child performers to become members. Any person over the age of fifteen is automatically considered an adult.

Not all states have a department dedicated to children's employment. However the following organisations should be contacted when filming with children in other states:

* Queensland: Department of Family Services and Aboriginal & Islander Affairs
* Australian Capital Territory: Chief Minister's Department
* Victoria: Department of Business and Employment
* Western Australia: Department of Community Development
* South Australia: Children's Interests Bureau
* Northern Territory: Department of Education

ANIMALS

There are no rules except to make sure that you have handlers and wranglers and that the actors chosen are comfortable with the animals they have to work with.

EXAMPLE –

ARTIST'S INFORMATION SHEET

Name

Address

Telephone

Agent's Name

Address

Telephone

Age: Height: Weight:

Complexion: Hair Colour:

Availability:

MEAA Memebership No:

Drivers Licence No: Expiry Date:

Superannuation No:

Biography

Formal Training:

Work Experience:

Other:
(e.g., accents, languages, special skills – e.g., bike riding, stunt work, etc.)

Budget For Features, Telemovies And Mini-Series

Damien Parer

Budgeting, like high-wire walking, is an acquired skill. Instinct and experience are as valuable as price lists. From experience and wizardry you know that some areas of the budget always cost more than logic dictates. You know that other areas can be reduced as you shoot.

The most important practical consideration in preparing a budget is that you have not underestimated the total cost. A breakdown of the individual elements in the budget will tell you where you go over, but the bottom line figure is what everyone watches.

It should also be said that a budget which grossly overestimates total costs is just as erroneous in its own way.

Administering the budget is also a skill perfected by few. The deciding factor is, does the expenditure help to put value up on the screen, in the release print? As you move through the production, accurate forward prediction is a valuable tool in money management. Life can become very unpleasant for you and the production manager if you start biting into the contingency, or worse, exceeding your budget. Completion guarantors, investors and government bodies will take a closer interest in, a harder look at, the production – so exceeding your budget is best avoided if possible. But if you do get into difficulties, the sooner you assess the problems and ask for help and assistance, the better. Don't hide a problem – start solving it.

A budget is as good as its foundations. If you are budgeting from a synopsis, no schedule, no location survey and no cast costs, then you will be doing a lot of educated guesswork. All you can provide in these circumstances is a 'ball-park' total figure. On the other hand, if you are doing your last budget before the shoot and you have final schedule, cast negotiated, and various set quotes for equipment, post-production, art department and so on, then the budget document will be more accurate.

Preliminary budgets are concocted early and with little fixed price information. What you are doing, in fact, is using average figures from similar situations. Bear in mind the following important points for preparing preliminary budgets:

* Should the film go ahead, the budget will need to have a forward projection of costs built into it. Film production costs are rising at approximately 10 per cent per year.

* Quotes usually have a time limit on them.

* Unwritten quotes can rise. Sometimes crew members and facilities quote verbally on the lower side, so that they will be considered seriously for the job.

164 * Insist on specific answers to your questions to executive producers, directors, etc. Everybody wants money for themselves and no one wants to commit to prices or be responsible for a budget.

*	Everything is negotiable but it is better to estimate as though crew, cast and facilities are hard to get. The director currently under consideration may take a smaller fee than the average, but what if he/she drops out or is not available at the time of shoot? Where are you going to find the extra money needed? Budget average costs.

*	Consult an experienced film production accountant to help you prepare the budget, or to check your figures.

If, on presentation of your carefully considered budget, you are told, 'It's too much, reduce it', then you say, 'Reduce the demands made in the script, and I will reduce the budget'. The whole point of bothering to do a preliminary budget is to allow you to assess the viability of going into production.

Production Budget:
a Guide to Presentation

The standard production budget form used in Australia has been compiled by, and is available from, the Australian Film Commission. The AFC/AFTRS *Production manual* provides a comprehensive guide to the preparation of a budget.

The following notes should be read in conjunction with the standard budget form (see pp. 49–54), and are designed to highlight some items where you'll need to take care.

A Story, Script & Development

As a rule of thumb, the total fees for producing, writing and directing should be approximately 10 per cent of budget, equally divided. The Australian Writers' Guild publishes recommended fees for most categories of work, including script editing.

If you have been involved with the film since its conception you will be aware of all the development costs. Otherwise care should be taken to allow sufficient funds to reimburse those involved.

Development funding buy outs can have various premiums applied, including an interest charge which can be considerable when calculated over 3-5 years.

Script printing can involve 20 copies of each of the drafts; 100 or more copies of the final draft will be required.

B Producers, Director

Expenses for producer, writer and director may be included in either the above-the-line or below-the-line sections of the budget. Putting them in the above-the-line section provides a very clear idea of the total costs of producer or director, whereas putting them in below-the-line item may help you with calculating the contingency, which is based only on below-line-costs.

165

E1 PRINCIPAL CAST

Usually the budget is done before the artists are contracted and so you need to estimate total cost cautiously. However, if principal artists' fees and conditions are already contracted, then all is well. Overseas artists' contracts can have special conditions which require careful budgeting. For example, car with or without driver, caravan, cash in hand per diem, extra air fares, nanny…

Establish which currency the contract with any overseas artist (or director, etc.) is written in, as currency fluctuations can wreak havoc on the budget. Note that you can put in an amount to cover currency fluctuation under the 'Indirect Costs' in Section **Y** (Finance & Legal).

C PRODUCTION UNIT SALARIES

Minimum fees and overtime loadings are set down by the Media Entertainment and Arts Alliance. Most crew members negotiate a fee higher than the award. You are breaking the law if you pay below the minimums.

Consult an experienced production accountant or try to acquire copies of other people's budgets. Make sure that they are current and based on a screenplay not unlike the one that you are budgeting from. The Screen Producers' Association of Australia (SPAA) distributes a guide to current salaries for its members.

I use the rate column to list the negotiated base fee, i.e., 38, 50 or 60 hours. Calculate a total for overtime for the whole crew over and above that, and write it in item **C17**.

Budgets tend to underestimate the need for crew in the pre-production period. Time and money spent then on preparation can save a great deal more during the shoot. The post-production period also needs crew to properly complete work.

Don't forget to allow for crew travel time during and after the shoot. The Art Department always needs time to clean up locations and return props. Sound recordists sometimes need extra time to record wild effects.

The post-production period can range from 10 to 20 weeks. Realistic budgeting is required. A post-production supervisor is a good investment. They can be contracted to do a budget estimate for you

Casting consultants will sometimes quote a flat fee for services.

Some crew members, e.g. camera assistants and wardrobe assistants, consistently require a few more hours overtime than the whole crew. Will you ever be working crew without a 10-hour-break? If so, allowance should be made. Will you be working a sixth or seventh day?

D HOLIDAY PAY & TAXES

Holiday pay is 8.33 per cent (not payable to companies).

Payroll tax varies in each state. Check these. A superannuation levy of 4 per cent of crew salaries and 4 per cent of cast (excluding doubles and stand-ins) is payable. These percentages may increase over time.

E Cast – Principals & Other

Various industrial awards apply to actors. Make sure that you are not paying less than minimums. Rates can sometimes increase during the shoot.

Allow for post-sync work in your calculations. Travel can add extra cost to budgets.

Allow time for wardrobe, make-up and special hair preparation in your calculations.

Stunt loadings need to be negotiated. A stunt co-ordinator can be contracted to do a budget for you.

F Music

Composers will sometimes quote for the whole job, i.e., conception to delivery on tape.

H Sets & Properties

A production designer will also prepare a cost estimate for you if required.

Workshop or stage rental depends on your requirements. You may choose to lease an area which is not soundproofed but is inexpensive. On the other hand, you may use sound stages with construction areas available which may cost $10,000 per week. Make sure you understand what is needed. If your interiors are being used as wet weather cover, then you may need to hire these areas for a long period.

Locations are getting more expensive every year. Local councils usually charge for the use of parks, beaches and streets. Traffic and crowd control costs need to be considered.

In relation to special effects, get advice from a special effects co-ordinator or production designer who has experience in this area.

I Lab Costs – Shooting & Editing

Picture stock prices can be acquired from AGFA-Gevaert Hanimex (Fuji) and Kodak. Laboratories will also supply quotes on request.

Establish the exact requirements for stock footage, video clips and other material which you plan to incorporate into the film. Finding and negotiating for royalties on stock footage can be expensive.

The researcher may have to fly to London to obtain what you want.

Trailer: allow $25,000

Sales tax: allow 20 per cent on film and video

Video stock and post production: get several quotes.

K EQUIPMENT & STORES

Make sure that you understand what the director has in mind. Helicopters and tricky shots eat budgets for breakfast.

Camera departments usually underestimate their needs when you ask them. Be sure they clearly understand the director's requirements.

Obtain price lists from film equipment suppliers. Equipment hired in a whole quote can be, of course, less expensive than hired as individual items. Get a quote and, as always, everything is negotiable.

Individual grips and lighting crew members will generally have equipment and/or a truck available for hire. Their price is usually competitive with the equipment suppliers.

M TRAVEL & TRANSPORT

Several travel agencies specialise in the entertainment business. They can keep the cost down and they understand the needs of production. They offer services like air travel, air freight, accommodation, vehicle hire, air charter, assistance with customs, carnets, and so on.

N HOTEL, LIVING, CATERING

Conditions of accommodation are set out in the various Awards.

O INSURANCES

As a guide, allow 2.5 per cent of total budget. But talk to an insurance broker or specialist film insurance company about the production and get quotes.

COMPLETION GUARANTEE

Refer to the chapter on 'Insurance', by Neil McEwin (pp. 150–157). The fee is calculated generally at 6 per cent (this is negotiable) on both above- and below-the-line costs, excluding indirect costs and the contingency.

CONTINGENCY

The contingency is designed to give you funds to cover unforeseen circumstances. If you spend it, it should be used wisely. It should be seen as an adjunct to the budget, not part of it. It is calculated on all below-the-line costs, not including the completion guarantee, and is generally calculated at the rate of 10 per cent.

SPAA LEVY

168 Production levies for feature films, documentaries, telemovies and mini-series, are calculated at 0.25 per cent of total budget.

PRODUCTION

THE PRODUCER'S ROLE IN PRODUCTION

DAMIEN PARER

THE PRODUCTION TEAM

Essentially, the producer's role is to create an environment in which the full potential of the project can be realised. Not only is the producer responsible for ensuring that the film comes in on time and on budget, but s/he is also responsible for ensuring that the production team has the necessary support and guidance to enable it to function in a collaborative and creative manner.

Three major documents underpin all film, television and video enterprises:

* **Script**. It is essential that the script is finalised before the start of pre-production. It must be the correct length and agreed to by all those who have a say in its content. Script demands which appear to be potential problems should be resolved, not ignored.

* **Budget**. A realistic budget must be drawn up or adjusted from a previous budget before pre-production. If the budget needs to be reduced then the demands of the script must be reduced similarly. It is a complete waste of time proceeding any further until this is resolved.

* **Schedule.** The first requirement is an overall schedule showing major dates, particularly the delivery date to the distributor and the date when videotapes will be available. This is the time, also, to compile your post-production schedule, so that facilities (e.g. mixing studio) and personnel (e.g. sound editor) can be booked. An initial shooting schedule may have been prepared to enable the budget to be drawn up. This will now need to be refined and may take at least half the pre-production period to complete. If the shooting time available is too short to accommodate script and budget – act now. Face the problem and solve it before proceeding.

There are three stages in the production process:

* **Pre-production.** Pre-production can be summed up in one word - planning. The aim is to prepare the ground so that the film can be shot under the most favourable circumstances. Pre-production is where the experienced producer makes or breaks the film by anticipating all the requirements and allowing for all or most of the contingencies. All planning is based on the script, the budget and the schedule.

* **Production.** In production it is the producer's responsibility to ensure that the film keeps to schedule and within budget. The producer also ensures that the highest level of creative and professional excellence is achieved and maintained.

Once shooting commences you (or the production manager) are in charge of the supply lines, supervising the smooth functioning of the production machinery.

There is a range of paperwork to assist you maintain an accurate track of expenditure. The paper trail includes call sheets, daily progress reports and weekly cost reports. Copies of all purchase orders must be retained as well as invoices, receipts and petty cash vouchers. These all provide vital information to the producer allowing full awareness of the cumulative costs. If the information is accurate, which it should be, it will highlight where costs are running above budget and should allow sufficient time to identify where savings can be made without affecting the production.

Information from these sources may indicate that the production is behind schedule and why. Decisions may need to be taken on the spot as to whether to put the crew on overtime rather than lose another day. Having this range of information at your finger-tips or, better still, in your head, will allow quick and accurate decisions to be made.

A successful producer will encourage the cast and crew to utilise fully their skills and talent to create an excellent film. All effort must be aimed at what the audience will see on the screen.

* **Post-production.** Don't be fooled into believing that the pressure and pace of the production will slow down during post-production. Whilst it is true that crew numbers will reduce substantially, and that all the 'action' is confined to the editing rooms, there is a vast amount of work for the producer to do.

Tight financial control must be maintained, deadlines must be met, reports to investors made, marketing matters attended to including ensuring that all the delivery items are being prepared, and attending screenings of the work-in-progress, to name but a few of the producer's tasks.

THE DIRECTOR

Basically the director translates the written word of a script or treatment into images and sound. Directors may be involved in the writing stage and certainly like to have the opportunity to make their creative input into the script. However, while this is not an essential part of the director's role, whether the director does make a contribution at script stage will depend very much on the project and who the director is.

Certainly the director should be party to all the major planning decisions concerning the production, both during pre-production and during the shoot itself. Consequently a producer must ensure that the director's time is scheduled effectively. The director must be allowed time to think.

After production and editing the director will present a cut of the film to the producer. At this point it is the producer's role to ensure that the best possible film has been made and that the investor's or sponsor's best interest has been served. One of the producer's main

171

responsibilities is to ensure that everyone has a clear understanding and agreement about the look and style of the film before it is made, and that 'this' film is the one that is seen after editing. The final decision in the film making process rests with the producer.

The Production Manager

If the workload is heavy and you have a large enough budget, it is wise to hire a production manager. This person may also be called an associate producer or a production supervisor. Whatever the title, your deputy will be in charge of the day-to-day running of the production. The production manager must be capable of acting in the producer's stead when necessary in both an administrative, financial and creative capacity.

Lines of Communication

In the production of any film everyone is responsible to someone. Recognising where these lines of responsibility fall is the first step in ensuring that good and clear communications prevail throughout all stages of the production.

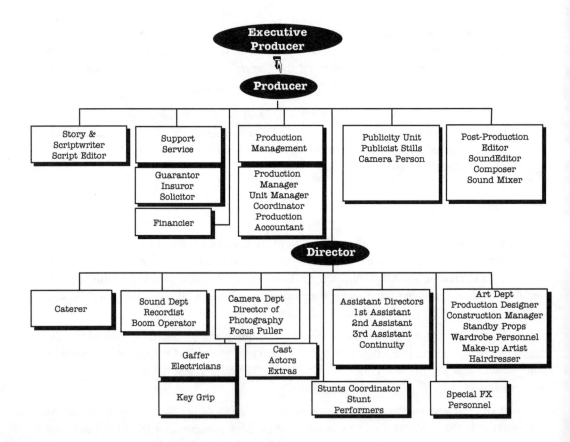

SETTING UP THE PRODUCTION MACHINERY

You'll need somewhere for the production team to work. Space should be found which can accommodate you, the director, the production office personnel, and, ideally, the production designer and art department staff, and the wardrobe department. Remember that the closer you get to first day of principal photography the more people there'll be, and you will start to need space for camera equipment, storage of props, clothes, files and so on. Adequate parking for your staff, probably including trucks too, is a priority need. It's pointless having to have walk miles from the nearest parking station, or having to duck out of the office every hour or so to feed the parking meters. Also, you may need to find space for rehearsals later on.

The next step is to ensure that all the heads of the creative departments have been engaged. It is important to set in motion early the scheduling of the shoot and refining the production budget. You can then pay attention to the other details in collaboration with the production manager. This includes engaging all the technicians needed, casting, hiring the stages and allied equipment, arranging travel and accommodation for the unit, and taking out all the necessary insurance. It is most important that all crew and cast engagements are confirmed in writing before the shoot begins.

If you are filming for any period of time on location, credit facilities with local traders should be arranged and banking arrangements made with a local branch.

SAFETY

Everyone involved in the making of a film has a duty of care towards other members of the team. This is set out under the Workcover legislation in NSW and is being unified throughout Australia. This obligation carries heavy penalties if not observed.

Safety guidance notes have been issued by the Australian Film Commission (AFC), following extensive consultation with individuals and groups, and can be regarded as an accurate reflection of generally accepted industry practice.

However, an important point needs to be made. The guidance notes are recommendations reflecting current safe practices but there may be better ways of working in some circumstances. The notes do not have the status of enacted laws or regulations but, where the notes refer to laws and regulations, those laws and regulations must be observed without exception.

It is the producers' primary responsibility to ensure that no cast or crew member is asked to perform their duties in an unsafe manner; the cast and crew also have their own duty of care towards each other. It is the producers' business to know that what the schedule asks of the cast and crew — and the time allocated to do it — does not compromise their duty of care.

In 1983, The Film Industry Recommended Safety Code set out procedures to assist in achieving a safe working environment. The code was agreed to on a voluntary basis in 1983 between what was then Actors Equity and the ATAEA (now MEAA), and the FTPAA (now SPAA). In 1988, the Code was incorporated into the Motion Picture Production Award between SPAA and the ATAEA (MEAA).

173

The Code has served the industry well and, twelve years later, safety standards are being maintained at generally high levels with the number of serious accidents or fatalities thankfully kept low.

The habit of thinking safety first, together with the world-class skills of our cast, crews and stunt and safety personnel, has ensured safe working methods have developed and become standard industry practice.

Negotiating Salary And Conditions With Cast And Crew

Every employee has their employment rights outlined in legislation. Producers should be aware of the employment acts that pertain in each state.

Minimum pay rates for every employee are laid down in a variety of industry awards. Contact SPAA or the Department of Industrial Relations in your state for these rates.

To assist your negotiations, plan what you need to say to each person before the meeting, and know the salary range you can offer to keep within the budget allocated. The following points may help you plan your discussions:

*   Tell them about the project and why it might different from others they may have worked on.

*   Outline other advantages, e.g. interesting locations, part of the shoot will be overseas, the lead performer is from overseas.

*   Allow heads of department to nominate their crew. The production designer should be involved in all the decisions made in his or her department. Cast members are swayed by information that other members of the cast are of a high artistic standard. Crew members like to work with professional, cordial people.

*   Explain the contract terms: length of contract, basic hours per week – 38, 50 or 60 hours.

*   Explain how they will get paid: day of the week, deposit in bank, etc.

*   Pay retainers in advance. Sometimes senior crew are paid retainers before working. Cast can also be contracted on a pay or play contract.

*   Describe their creature comforts. Will they be housed in first class accommodation with their own room? What will the catered meals be like? Are you paying per diems above the award?

*   Will there be an entertainment allowance for a particular cast member?

*   Consider whether the cast/crew member would be eligible for further work you might have in the pipeline. Is it worth telling them about it, to encourage them to take this job?

* Money might appear in the conversation here.

* Explain superannuation and holiday pay.

* Discuss the screen credits: opening title credits for some; billing and preference order.

* You may be able to offer spouse travel and accommodation. You may be able to offer a crew member a return travel trip home during the course of work. A weekend home may be better than money.

* Can you offer first class or business class travel on aircraft instead of economy?

* Discuss profit sharing: you may wish to share some of the profits with cast or crew.

* Cast may negotiate special payments for nudity or extreme hair cuts or tinting.

* Money might reappear in the conversation here.

* Will the cast/crew member be given their own car or driver?

* Will cast members have their own caravan/dressing room? Make-up artist? Dresser?

* Will the production pay a tool allowance?

* Can the production assist with equipment hire or provide an equipment allowance?

* A VHS copy of the finished production may be requested.

* You may wish to offer the director or production manager part of the rebate from the completion guarantee.

* Post-sync fees for cast should be negotiated up front.

* Bonuses sometimes apply.

* With cast contracts, it is not necessary to purchase all rights in advance. But remember, if a feature film later gets a US network sale or a telemovie gets a feature release, then the cast are due an extra payment.

* Deferrals should be settled in advance.

* If the cast/crew member has still not reached an equitable and reasonable fee by now, then I suggest that you suspend the meeting and try again later. Don't agree to a fee which you consider too high.

* You may consider it appropriate to mention a few house rules here:
  - The safety code forbids the use of liquor and drugs during working hours. Instant dismissal is the only possible solution.
  - Telephone and liquor bills and motels are the responsibility of the user.
  - Motor vehicles are to be driven within the scope of road regulations.
  - Publicity is to be referred to the producer.
  - Overtime is to be applied for in advance.

175

EXAMPLE –

CREW INFORMATION SHEET

Name:

Address: .

Telephone:

Company Name:

Worker Comp:

Superannuation No:

Insurance –   Company Name:

                    Expiry Date:

                    State:

Service Agreement Dated:

Union Membership:

No. & Expiry Date:

Tax Exemption Certificate (or Company Registration):

Medical Insurance Form:

Date of Birth:

Next of Kin: Telephone:

Special Food Requirements:

Smoker/Non Smoker:

PAY DETAILS

Cheque/Cash: (Give breakdown for wages each week)

Name of Account:

Bank:

Branch:

Account Number: (Cheque/Savings)

State of Health:

Do you suffer from any recurrent medical problems (e.g. asthma, epilepsy, diabetes, back injuries, etc.)...
If yes, please detail ...

If yes, please ensure that medications, etc., are discussed with the producer, production manager, first assistant or unit nurse before principal photography.

Are you allergic to any drugs? (e.g. penicillin, morphine, etc.)
If yes, please detail ...

Other allergies (eg, bee stings, food, etc.) ...

Blood Group ...

Vision: Please detail problems with your eyesight, need for prescription lenses, long sightedness, short sightedness, problems with night vision ...

176

PRE-PRODUCTION CHECKLIST

There is no particular order in which actions are taken in the pre-production period. Whatever suits your particular enterprise is best. This *aide-mémoire* may help remind you of items which you may have temporarily overlooked:

* **Film production company structure.** If you are going to use, or set up, a company separate from your own, has it been legally constituted, and has it sufficient powers to cover all the needs of the film during production?

* **Assignment of rights.** Does the production entity have all the rights legally to proceed into production? Are the creative elements all contracted to it? Copyright requirements, director, cast and crew, etc.?

* **Production company logo, letterhead.** Graphic design requirements should be arranged early.

* **Development costs.** Have you finalised all the payments due? Accounts in any area should be paid promptly. Have these costs been included in the budget?

* **Production office.** To achieve maximum effectiveness the office should be comfortable to work in with good lines of communication. People are going to inhabit it for at least ten hours a day. Make sure that staff are able to work efficiently at their desks. Maintain a good spirit of co-operation. Have a few laughs.

* **Film financing.** Are all the requirements of the funding completed? Are there any other documents to be attended to? What are the periodic reports required during production? Is one due now?

* **Screenplay.** Is the final draft finished? Has everyone with input into the script completed their contribution? Do you expect that many changes will be made during the rehearsal period? How flexible are your investors about changes? What does the writer think?

* **Timing of the screenplay.** Is this the final timing? Do the director, production manager and first assistant agree?

* **Writer.** Remember to keep the writer informed of proceedings. Depending on circumstances they may be actively involved in pre-production, rehearsals, rushes and various stages of post-production. The script is your most valuable asset – look after its author.

* **Director.** Believe me, it can be lonely being a director. Keep in touch. You are the director's main confidante. Leave time for discussions and remember a little encouragement goes a long way. Meetings should be planned to make best use of the director's limited time. Take the director to dinner from time to time.

* **Production manager/supervisor/associate producer.** Remember he or she is your second-in-charge. In an emergency they should be able to take over production. Keep them informed, even about ideas you had in the shower. They also perform better with encouragement from you.

177

✳ **Contracts and forms.** These should be cleared by your lawyer and bulk printed by a commercial printer. The production office should not spend half the day printing forms. Printing on different colours for different forms may assist in easier identification.

✳ **Order books.** Essential to tracking expenditure. Information should include:

– supplier

– price

– sales tax exemption clause

– specific area of the budget for debiting

– description of goods or service

✳ **Police liaison.** This should be done early. Find out who really has the power to assist your production. Talk to them to gain Police Department co-operation.

✳ **Local liaison.** This is particularly important if filming in a country town. A local contact with tact, influence, nous and commonsense can be extremely helpful to the production. They can speed up activities and allow faster access to facilities. Politicians, councillors and community leaders should be consulted. You may wish to speak at Rotary or hold a public meeting to inform the community about filming. The local newspaper may run a story about the filming.

✳ **MEAA.** The union should be kept aware of progress on the production. Consult the relevant awards again to make sure that you are conforming to the terms and conditions. Look again at individual contracts. Actors, extras, stunt personnel, stand-ins and doubles must all be members of MEAA.

✳ **Casting.** Apart from the principals and other speaking parts, there will still be plenty of work to do. Extras, doubles and stunt personnel require your time. You may need to engage an 'extras casting' person to assist you and the director.

✳ **Locations.** Have key crew seen and approved them all? Are they all locked down and signed up? Do you have alternatives in an emergency?

✳ **Two locations for the price of one.** Seek out the advantages of re-using a location. Sometimes an area can be redressed, or another location can be found adjacent. The savings in money and time can be considerable.

✳ **Getting to location.** Do you require any special arrangements to get equipment to location? Low loaders, ship or train? Do access roads need grading?

✳ **Accounting.** Have you kept the accountant informed of changes? His/her experience can be most useful to the smooth running of the production.

✳ **Banking.** Are you using all the facilities of the bank to your best advantage? Do you keep your bank manager informed of progress? Have you given the bank enough signatories to ensure that production is not held up suddenly?

✳ **Accommodation.** People's preference should be sought. Factors like noise and the ability to darken rooms can be essential for rest after night shooting. Make sure that services, like cleaning, are kept up, and that personnel are comfortable.

✳ **Schedule.** Is there an overall schedule for the whole of production including the post-production period? Are you working to the delivery date requirements?

✳ **Budget.** Are you regularly monitoring expenditure? Are you still on budget or are you simply hoping that you are?

✳ **Provisional Certificate.** Have any of the elements listed in the proposal for a final certificate changed since you applied? You are obliged to inform the federal Department of Communication and the Arts of changes.

✳ **Lawyer.** Have you spoken to the film's legal adviser? There may be other matters to cover.

✳ **Interest on loan.** If production funding is by a loan or line of credit, then the more precise your cash requirements are the less you have to pay in interest. A delayed post-production period can be very expensive if pre-sale funds are only released on delivery of the completed film.

✳ **Hired equipment.** Make sure that equipment is hired only for the minimum period required. Crew are inclined to hold onto equipment 'in case' it is needed again. The production office should keep a register:

– description of equipment

– owner

– attached to which department

– date of hire

– return date

– cost of hire

– replacement value

– insurance

✳ **Meetings.** One of the most effective tools of management is the pre-planned, well-run meeting. Those called to a meeting should be informed about the agenda. Meetings should be as short and specific as possible. Minutes of meetings can be useful records, particularly where people have to take action by specific dates. The minutes can serve as 'reminders'.

✳ **Art department cost control.** It is sometimes advisable to employ an art department co-ordinator for planning and cost control; essential on higher budget productions.

✳ **Copyright.** Is the production company now in possession of all the assignment of copyright it needs?

✳ **Storyboard.** A useful tool for director and heads of departments. An effective storyboard can save time and money. Do you need one?

✳ **Safety report.** Periodic reference to the safety report is essential. Make sure that elements have not changed since the initial report. Remember you are ultimately responsible for cast and crew safety.

✳ **Transport.** A transport manager/captain or mechanic is sometimes needed, particularly when there are a large number of vehicles involved in the production. The production office should maintain a current register of vehicles showing:

- owner
- usual driver
- driver's licence and expiry date
- insurance on vehicle
- usual place of parking overnight

✳ **Assets register.** Items purchased during the production need to be listed:

- description of asset
- department they are in
- purchase value
- insurance

✳ **Insurance.** After policies are in place, insurers will require reports and information. Workers' compensation claims must be reported. Hazardous flying insurance may have special conditions regarding prior reporting.

✳ **Shooting schedule.** How realistic is it? Have you allowed an extra day or two as contingency? Are you and the production manager familiar and comfortable with it? Would a minor rewrite help with locations?

✳ **Contra deals.** Arrangements should be clearly stated in writing to avoid misunderstandings later. Try to avoid specific promises regarding product placement and prominence. Companies can be credited in the end titles.

✳ **Cash flow.** Accurate, up-dated reports are essential to the smooth running of the production. Steps should be taken to ensure that you do not run out of funds. Public holidays can interrupt your cash flow.

✳ **Archival footage.** Stock footage can save you time and money. It should be selected well in advance. Libraries need advance notice of your requirements. Allow time for negotiation. Footage will only be released after contracts are signed and money paid.

✱ **Music clearances.** Music heard playing on location, such as in lifts, cannot automatically be included in your film without permission and probably a fee. Arrangements must be made in advance with the copyright holder or their agent

✱ **Composer.** Composer's contracts take time to negotiate and draft. You may wish to involve the composer during the shoot. You will therefore need to settle contractual matters early.

✱ **Cast rehearsals.** Director and cast need clean, quiet, comfortable rehearsal areas. Tea and coffee should be available. Some props and costumes may be needed during the rehearsal period.

✱ **Production office staff.** Sometimes a 'them and us' mentality develops between crew on location and people in the production office. This should be nipped in the bud if it happens. Put on drinks after work. Find out what or who is causing the problem … talk to them.

✱ **Take care of your people.** Your greatest asset is the people you work with. They respond to your interest in them. Shout a few drinks after work now and then. Take time to talk to everyone.

✱ **Alcohol and drugs.** You must instantly dismiss any cast or crew member found to be drunk or drugged during work time. If you don't, you are in breach of the Film Industry Safety Code, several of your insurances, and the various industrial awards.

✱ **Audit.** Be aware that audits will take place at various stages during production. Accounting systems which allow easy access to auditors will save time and money.

✱ **Petrol, oil, diesel.** It is advisable to detect any unusual or excessive use of fuel. Crew should sign for fuel or supply receipts.

✱ **Security.** The production office or art department may require guard or alarm systems to protect them. Locations will sometimes need security, even after filming is completed and the equipment is cleared, because the location agreement may not expire for a further day or days.

✱ **Boats/trains/aeroplanes.** Some props just don't stop when you tell them to, nor do they turn around very easily. Things can go wrong even with a lot of planning. Be prepared. Make extra allowance for things to go more slowly than anticipated.

✱ **Animals** require:
- handlers, wranglers
- trainers
- housing and feeding (and removing the results)
- drugging by qualified personnel
- separating to prevent loving and hating
- delivery and despatch

181

–   insurance: doubles, and sometimes triples (animals tire easily. And they get bored too!)

*   **Stars/principal artists.** Sometimes their contracts require you to supply special facilities. A rest area or 'green room' is advisable. Cast need to relax while not on set and they need an area to rehearse. Chairs on set for the cast are a necessity.

*   **Children.** Are you in possession of the relevant state *Child Welfare Act*? Are all your principal crew aware of its conditions? (Working hours and conditions are particularly relevant.) Do you have tutors, teachers, nursemaids, chaperones, dialogue coaches?

*   **Publicity.** Publicity plays a crucial part in the success of a film. Publicity and still photographs are essential promotion and marketing materials. Give them the priority attention they deserve. Still camera personnel must be given special access on set and assistance where required.

*   **Press.** Do you have a policy for dealing with the requirements of press, and for publicity generally? Who should speak to members of the press? Is a press kit available? The trade press should be informed of production details early in pre-production.

*   **Completion guarantee.** Your guarantor requires various forms, assurances, reports. Make sure you are supplying those as soon as possible rather than the guarantor having to ask for them all the time.

*   **Credits.** Cast and crew credits should be negotiated up front. Credits can also be given to services and in lieu of payment. Logos may also be required. Arrangements should be in writing to avoid anguish later.

*   **Post-production schedule.** It should be set before the start of shoot.

*   **Laboratory.** Have you kept them informed? Have they appointed a liaison officer? What system for rushes will be the most effective? How will negative reports be sent?

*   **Rushes on location.** If you will be screening rushes on film then you will require a double-head projector. Sound will be greatly improved by a baffle or sound-proofing system. Video rushes have the advantage of being able to be re-screened easily. Cassettes can be kept throughout the shoot for reference.

*   **Firearms.** Various state Acts regulate the use of firearms and must be observed. Armourers experienced in film production with appropriate licences are available for contracting on a daily basis.

*   **Portable toilets.** Will they be needed? You need to plan ahead to book them. Also, which unit vehicles can tow or carry them?

*   **Visitors on location.** Visits to location should be co-ordinated by the production office. Visitors should be noted on the call sheet. Let the director know. As a general rule visitors should be escorted. The first assistant director should be contacted immediately they arrive on set. He or she will need to know:

– who they are

– if there are any specific people or things they wish to see

– who is escorting them

– how long they will be staying

– parking and catering arrangements.

* **Dismissals.** It's never easy. Try to do it humanely and with dignity. The person to be dismissed should be given the opportunity to answer any accusations. Union regulations regarding dismissals should be observed. The unions should be informed. Actors' agents should be informed. A written report would be wise. It should include statements by other crew involved.

* **Location first aid.** Depending on circumstances, you may need various emergency services on stand-by, for example, an ambulance or doctor. Larger productions have a full-time unit nurse. If you need only a first-aid kit, then make sure that:

– it is fully equipped

– it is always stored in a place known to cast and crew

– someone on the crew has had some first-aid training

– the first assistant is aware of any cast or crew with specific medical problems

* **Sound.** Do any FX or music require pre-recording or playback facilities? Have you allowed for effects recording time after the shoot? Are you going to post sync after each day's shoot?

* **Second unit**. The second unit requires careful planning and liaison with the main unit director. Second unit should not be confused with second camera, which is an extra camera temporarily attached to the main unit's camera department. Difficult or unusual shots can be completed before principal photography. If they are an essential element in a sequence, then it is better to know in advance of any difficulties or unexpected differences with the special shot.

* **First day of principal photography.** Various contractual payments are due on that day. Make sure that the payments are made.

* **Investors' reports.** Apart from the various financial reports that are required, it is advisable to keep investors and interested parties advised of progress. A newsletter can be useful in informing people about cast and crew, locations, schedules, visits to the set, and even the little amusements that lighten the day.

* **Film vaults.** Have you made contractual arrangements? Do the post-production crew know all the requirements of labelling material?

* **Delivery requirements for distributors.** Do you know all of them? Do the post-production staff know what delivery items are needed? Will you be able to deliver them all on time?

183

* **Catering.** Do you occasionally sample the food? Do you ask the cast's and crew's opinions? Is it possible to vary the menu? Does anyone ever thank the caterer? Do you?

* **On location amusements.** If a location is remote, then the production office will need to think about recreational needs. Videos and games (both indoor and outdoor) will assist in keeping morale high.

* **Laundry.** If hotels and motels don't provide the service on a regular basis then the production office will have to make suitable arrangements.

* **Merchandising.** Remember merchandising needs one to two years advance run-up to coincide with the film's release date. The time at which release prints are available may be too late.

* **Deferrals/deferments.** Is there a schedule clearly stating order of preference, and the terms and conditions? Cast and crew who have agreed to deferrals should be kept informed of the financial status of the production office after the release of the film or TV program.

* **Marketing strategy.** Early discussion and planning is always the most effective course of action. Some of the cast and crew may be required for the marketing. Discuss this with the distributor and then with the people involved. Show reels of 6-10 minutes can sometimes be used by the sales agent or by the distributor prior to release print. Publicity and stills should be tailored to fit this strategy. Scene clips will also be required. Plan which scenes, and when they'll be needed.

FOREIGN LOCATION CHECKLIST

The following checklist may be helpful:

* Is script approval required in a foreign country?

* What bonds are required – or guarantees, carnets?

* Personnel and equipment list – are bags numbered including personal baggage?

* Re-entry of equipment into Australia – what clearances are needed?

* Are location permits required?

* What local laws may affect the filming?

* Film and rushes arrangements need to be made.

* Foreign country union clearances need to be checked.

* Ensure that everyone has current passports, visas and health certificates. Make airline and travel arrangements. Pick up the tickets.

* Organise excess baggage.

* Do you need travellers cheques or cash, banking arrangements?

* Check livestock, firearm and explosives permits.

* Arrange international driver's licences.

* Do you need an interpreter?

PRE-PRODUCTION CHECKLIST – NON-DRAMA

The following points may be helpful:

* Finalise script.

* Finalise budget.

* Contract crew.

* Crew meeting.

* Location contracts.

* Shooting schedule.

* Indemnities.

* Any casting.

* Book equipment.

* Props and wardrobe.

* Graphics, special signs.

* Publicity, stills.

* First aid.

* Wet weather cover.

* Contacts list.

* Transport.

* Accommodation.

* Rushes arrangements and sound transfers.

* Music clearance on location.

* Cash facility for production expenses.

* Telephone, credit cards.

* Notify police.

* Wages payments.

* Travelling allowance, per diems.

* Insurance.

* Excess baggage.

* Unscheduled flights.

* Overtime arrangements.

PRODUCTION CONTRACTS CHECKLIST

Make sure you have remembered all the contracts you will need:

* Application for a Provisional Certificate.

* Contract between the producer and the production company.

* Contract with the writer.

* Contract with your script developer.

* Option agreement.

* Contract with the Film Finance Corporation.

* Contract with investors.

* Contract with sponsor/client.

* Contract with the original source, e.g., novelist, poet, short story writer.

* Bank accounts.

* Production loan.

* Contract with the director.

* Contract with MEAA.

* Individual contracts with the cast, doubles, stand-ins, extras and stunt personnel.

* Contract with the insurance company.

* Contract with the state Workers' Compensation Insurance.

* Contract with the composer.

* Crew contract.

* Location agreements.

* Contract with completion guarantor.

* Contract with suppliers, e.g. laboratory, post-production facility, car rental, accommodation, etc.

* Contract with the distributor.

* Contract with the exhibitor.

* The marketing loan contract.

186 * Contract with the merchandiser.

*   Contract with the sales agent.

*   Contract with television networks.

*   Contract with the video distributor.

LAW AND THE FILMMAKER

Various acts and conventions have particular reference to filmmaking, such as:

> *Trade Practices Act*
>
> *Income Assessment Act*
>
> *Workers' Compensation Act* (state law)
>
> *Export Market Development Grants Act*
>
> *The Australian Film Commission Act*
>
> *Conciliation and Arbitration Act*
>
> *Sales Tax Assessment Act*
>
> *Pay Roll Tax Act* (state law)
>
> *Child Welfare Act* (state law)
>
> *Stamp Duties Act* (state law)
>
> *Local Government Act*
>
> *Noise Control Act*
>
> *Occupational Health and Safety Act (NSW)*
>
> *Patents Act*
>
> *Environmental Planning and Assessment Act*
>
> *Heritage Act*
>
> *Designs Act*
>
> *Berne Convention*
>
> *Universal Copyright Convention*
>
> *Employment Protection Act (NSW)*
>
> *Company Act* (state law)
>
> *Fire regulations*
>
> *Theatres & Public Halls Act*
>
> *Construction Safety Act (NSW)*
>
> *Theatres Act (VIC)*
>
> *Public Health Act (TAS)*
>
> *Public Entertainment Licensing Act (QLD)*

> Places of Public Entertainment Act (SA)
>
> Health Act (WA)

You should also be aware of the laws relating to firearms:

> Firearms and Offensive Weapons Act (QLD)
>
> Local Government Act (NSW)
>
> Firearms Act (NSW)
>
> Firearms Act (VIC)
>
> Police Offences Act (TAS)
>
> Firearms Act (TAS)
>
> Firearms Act (SA)
>
> Firearms Act (WA)

and by-laws, ordinances, mandates, canons, customs, the golden rule, edicts, caveats, bushido, rules, mitzvah, bulls, Aboriginal law, charters, regulations and the Ten Commandments. Good luck.

COMMUNICATION AND FREIGHT

✳ **The telephone.** You and the production office will spend a great deal of time on the telephone. Make sure you have enough lines to enable your work to be done efficiently and effectively. The phones must have STD and ISD.

✳ **Facsimile.** A good quality, reliable fax machine is essential.

✳ **Air express courier service.** Various companies offer same-day or overnight services between major towns and all capital cities. A parcel lodged by early evening will be delivered the next day or parcels can be express-delivered during the day.

✳ **Taxi.** An account, e.g., Cabcharge, with your preferred taxi company is very useful.

✳ **Courier.** Short distance, long distance.

✳ **Domestic airlines.** Offer express courier, overnight air freight and standby services for freight.

✳ **General carrier.** For equipment, props, furniture.

✳ **Ship.** Ships travel slowly so allow plenty of time!

✳ **Train.**

✳ **Postal services (within Australia)**
   – air mail
   – priority paid
   – certified mail (must be signed for on delivery)

- express post (fast delivery – a certified mail service)
- security post (includes proof of delivery and insurance)
- fax post (Australia and overseas) – a fax system which can be combined with express delivery
- imagegram (a fax system for drawings)
- E-Post (letters can be delivered within a few hours. Electronic Post Centres will accept handwritten letters, type them on your letter head and fax them. They can be phoned in also. Letters can be express delivered or mailed for next day delivery).

* **Postal service (outside Australia)**
- sea mail – allow twelve weeks for delivery
- SAL (surface air-lifted mail) – allow one week for delivery
- international express post – between two and four days delivery
- overseas express delivery
- Intelpost – facsimile service
- registered post – advice of delivery and proof of receipt; $75 maximum; insurance available on request.

* **Air cargo** – special rates for film.

* **Accompanied baggage** – excess baggage.

* **Unaccompanied baggage** – make sure it is properly labelled.

COST CUTTING AND SAVING MONEY DURING PRODUCTION

Some ideas:

* Step right back and apply broad and lateral thinking. Hiring the costumes from London may be less expensive than making them. Hiring crew from another state may be better economically than crew members from your state.

* Everything is negotiable, from the completion guarantee fee to postage rates. If you can reduce budget items by an average of 2 per cent over a $2 million budget, then you have found an extra $40,000 to spend as needed, or you can save it for marketing or return it to investors.

* Shoot only what is required to achieve the agreed fine-cut length, tempered by artistic consideration as well. Six minutes of screen time more than you need is probably two to three days' extra shoot. A day's shoot with cast and crew is the most expensive item in any budget.

* Shoot special insert material early and save simple shooting for a second unit or greatly reduced crew.

189

* Avoid Sunday travel. Don't start your shoot on a Monday on an 'away' location unless that is the best day to start. Other start days may be economically better.

* Make the pre-production period work for you. Plan and prepare everything. Urge the art department to prepare as much as possible before the start of shoot. Ensure that the director has conveyed clearly what she/he intends to do.

* Reduce script changes to a minimum after the start of pre-production. Major script changes can mean changes to schedule, casting and locations. This can absorb valuable time and money.

* Shooting period should coincide with the best weather conditions. Also try to avoid Christmas, Easter and public holidays. Shoot scenes with children in school holidays if feasible.

* Review expenditure often. Check areas such as art department and equipment hire. Use the order book system. Question anything unusual. Be fair but firm with the crew.

* Monitor short-term hire equipment. Crew are inclined to keep it 'in case' it may be needed. Send it back as soon as possible and re-hire it if required.

* Prepay costs if possible, to obtain better rates and receive a discount for staying in credit.

* Seek out contras and free goods. You may offer credits in return for discounted or free goods and services.

* Use locations well. Can they be used in more than one way?

* Resaleable assets should be sold off as soon as possible. Even used raw stock is saleable. But keep a register of assets. Things get lost somehow.

* Overtime should be applied for in advance – not claimed one or two weeks after being worked.

* Hold lots of short, to-the-point meetings. Follow them with short memos confirming the action to be taken.

* Storyboard the script, especially action sequences, so that everyone can gain a clear understanding of what is planned. This will assist in making better use of the shooting time.

* Spend time talking to cast and crew. Ask them how to save money in their departments.

* Spend money to save money. Sometimes adding an extra assistant, or providing a piece of equipment, may save more time and money in the long run.

PLANNING THE CREDITS

Use the following as a guide:

* **Opening credits** should be kept to a minimum. Viewers are not as interested as you are in seeing a list of names, mostly unknown. Opening credits can be a bargaining device to obtain a better deal on lead cast or cast and crew costs. Perhaps even a location fee can be reduced by offering an end credit. Contra deals usually involve a credit also in the end titles.

* **Actors' credits.** Lead or well-known actors, through their agents, will attempt to negotiate the best and most prominent position for their credit. Once you have agreed to the style, size and order of the credits make sure that it is clearly specified in contracts.

* **Specific requirements.** Your client, co-producer or major pre-sale source may have specific requirements or logos. Reach agreement early about these requirements as they can slow down your post-production and cost you money. Be aware that a distributor may wish to add their logo and credit to the front or end of your film or videotape.

* **Artwork.** Special art work may be required or may have to be brought from overseas.

* **Titles.** It is important to choose a typeface which is clear and legible. Certain colours and typeface styles will bleed and break up after duplication. You must choose whether to shoot your titles on film or videotape.

* **Film.** Titles shot on 35 mm are the optimum quality. Their registration is sharp and when superimposed on a background scene will not appear to move. For use on 16 mm production they are reduced in the laboratory. Titles can also be shot on 16 mm.

* **Video.** Titles are superimposed or added to videotape productions by using a character generator. A wide range of typeface styles is available. This method allows the producer to preview the effect and placing of titles.

INVESTOR CONTACT

It is always advisable to keep your investors and sponsors informed of progress and new developments. A newsletter written in a conversational style will serve to keep them informed and interested. The investors have probably funded your film because of your liaison with them on a previous film or because their last producer kept them informed. Inviting them to visit the set and meet key personnel is always a valuable public relations exercise.

Scheduling

Mark Turnbull

A **film schedule** is the daily shooting order of the scripted scenes. It is also a declaration of intent by the production of how much shooting time is to be allocated to each scene. A schedule reflects the budget a producer has raised, the time a director needs to shoot and the logistical problems of the script.

The running time of a script affects all elements of the schedule. If a script is too long for its intended market, then a decision must be made to either shoot it over-length and edit out the additional material in post-production, or cdit it out in pre-production and shoot it to time. The obvious difference is that if the project is running over-length and shot accordingly, then there is less time to shoot each scene. An over-length script often shows up in a shoot as frequently worked overtime, scenes dropped from call sheets, and unrealistic expectations on the cast and crew to work faster. The length of a script is the producer's decision. It is the basis of the schedule.

When the producer is satisfied with the script it can be scheduled. The script should have scene numbers for each new set or location and be explicit about the cast in each scene, where it takes place, what takes place and at what time of day, ie, day, dusk, night, etc.

In an ideal world a film should be shot in script order to allow for dramatic continuity. The scheduling is begun on this premise, then tries to get the most shooting time out of the weeks or days that the budget can afford.

Safety And The Schedule

Everyone involved in the making of a film has a duty of care towards other members of the team. This is set out under the Workcover legislation in NSW and is being unified throughout Australia. This obligation carries heavy penalties if not observed. Safety guidance notes have been issued by the Australian Film Commission (AFC).

It is the producers' primary responsibility to ensure that no cast or crew member is asked to perform their duties in an unsafe manner. The cast and crew also have their own duty of care to each other. It is the producer's business to know that what the schedule asks of the cast and crew (and the time allocated to do it) does not compromise their own or anyone else's duty of care.

The Order Of The Schedule

The following are the major variables affecting the order of the shoot:

192

* **Locales.** If a film is set in Alice Springs and Sydney, then Sydney may be shot in a block, and Alice in a block. Frequently, a first schedule will suggest what scenes can be 'cheated' from one locale to another, minimising the crew's time away from their base city and therefore minimising accommodation and per diem expenses.

* **Locations.** Within a locality, locations are grouped to minimise crew travel and maximise shooting time. The exception is a studio. This is discussed later under 'Wet weather cover'.

* **Sets.** A location may have several sets. For instance, a house may have a kitchen and bedroom scripted. Time and money can be saved by shooting bedroom scenes in a block and kitchen scenes in a block. A producer may decide to forgo these savings for dramatic continuity, and budget for lighting both rooms at the same time and allow the extra time it takes cast and crew to shuttle between sets. This is rarely the case and normally sets are grouped.

* **Exteriors and interiors.** As with localities, locations and sets, exteriors (Exts) and interiors (Ints) are normally grouped. It is usual to use interiors to 'cover' for the exteriors. If it rains you go inside. If, however, the exteriors have to be shot at a special time of day, say dusk, then the interiors would be manipulated to allow for this.

* **Day and night.** Note that the cast and crew cannot be asked to report for work without having had a ten-hour break. This means that a schedule's ability to change from night shooting to day shooting is governed by the ten-hour turnaround. By calling on the ten-hour turnaround, it is possible to go from night shooting at the beginning of the week to day shooting at the end, but it has a physical price on the cast and crew similar to jet lag, and nobody's best work will result (not least the director's). There is a strong argument in favour of blocking night shoots or, if possible, blocking half-day half-nights, although this is frequently impractical. When filming interiors, night scenes can be shot during the day by blacking out windows. This gives rise to the term 'day for night'. Likewise it is sometimes possible to light interiors to look like day although filmed at night, 'night for day'. It makes sense to block day and night interiors to minimise lighting changes and so allowing the maximum time for filming.

* **Special climatic conditions.** It is very rare for a schedule to be arranged around particular weather conditions, like wind or rain. These can be created for the camera. The usual conditions to be scheduled around are the tide and the moon. Never film near water without knowing what the tide is doing. Tides flatten at certain times of their cycle, and it is much easier to film a minimum tide variation than the maximum.

* **Cast.** Actors' contracts are drawn up to take account of the number of days they work. With an expensive actor it makes sense to minimise the number of days worked. The schedule will try to reflect this for all the cast, in order of the most expensive down. Obviously there is a limit to what can be done, but in dealing with the principal cast it is an important consideration. If an actor works three or four days a week, it may be best to contract him or her on a weekly basis, which would allow for schedule changes and possible additional days for wet weather cover.

193

✳ **Cast availability.** Although this may not affect a preliminary or budget schedule it frequently affects a shooting schedule. If a producer and director want an actor badly enough they will often cast that person with restricted availability and then schedule accordingly. There is a very short limit to this, as it does not take long to reach an impasse between conflicting availability of cast in the same scene. Recasting is sometimes the only way out and is an expensive solution. A contract with limited availability should only be entered into when the producer is fully aware of the ramifications to the schedule. A problem of schedules that go over is that some cast may not be available after the original completion date, forcing a reschedule to clear them at the expense of all else.

✳ **Location availability.** Many locations are day sensitive, that is, they must be shot on a particular day or at a particular time. Restaurants are usually Mondays, banks Saturdays, pubs in the morning, business offices at night, etc. It is a rare location that doesn't have some requirements for a specific day or time of day, and the schedule must take account of this. Locations make bad wet weather cover as they are not available at short notice – the sort of notice you get when it rains.

✳ **Wet weather cover.** Most scripts do not require rain for their exteriors. It is hard to film in real rain and it is usually not sufficiently consistent for a sequence to be completed with a uniform rain 'look'. It is also dangerous to film in rain on roads or when using a lot of electric lighting. The best wet weather cover is interiors on the same location as the exteriors, preferably with the same cast. As this is rarely the case, another solution must be found. As previously mentioned, locations make bad cover as they are not available at short notice. Likewise, scenes that involve cast with availability problems, or who are not contracted to work, are also bad cover. Scenes with principal cast on a picture deal and sets in the studio are the best scenes for wet weather cover. If studio sets are not an option, then a location that is required for more than a couple of days shoot might be negotiated for holdover days for wet weather cover, a house interior location for instance. It is best to schedule exteriors that have their own wet weather cover first, and then to follow with the remaining exteriors, holding the studio sets as cover. Each film has its own set of problems and sometimes there is no 'best' solution. Sometimes there is no cover. The two major problems of wet weather cover are possible additional cost of cast held, and the additional cost of studio hire if held as cover. This is a decision for the producer. As with all insurance it has its costs, but a schedule should offer the producer this option.

✳ **Time of day.** A director of photography (DOP) may have a preference for some scenes to be shot at a specific time of day. A common desire is to shoot all exteriors in the late afternoon. The ability of a schedule to service these wishes exists, but is usually limited if locations and sets are to remain grouped. If 'time of day' requirements are given priority over locations and cast, then the producer and director must be involved as there will be production trade-offs. These may include reduced dramatic continuity, lost shooting time due to more movement between sets or travel time between locations, increased location costs due to return visits or longer stay and increased shoot days for cast.

194

*   **Children.** The limited shooting time available with children can override every one of these categories. The younger the child the more restricted the shooting time. For example, a child who can only work four hours per day may cause location or set moves to make up a day's work. The relevant state Department of Community Services (children's employment unit) will supply current regulations for film work with children. These regulations are periodically revised.

*   **Extras.** If a large number of extras are called, then they start to become a scheduling cost, just like principal cast days. This is compounded for 'period' extras because of the additional work time and cost required to dress and make them up.

*   **Art department.** For the art department to deliver the sets as scheduled, it has a construction, dressing and striking schedule all of its own. If all constructed sets are scheduled in the first week, then this puts enormous pressure and expense on the art department and it makes sense to reschedule to even out the workload.

*   **Wardrobe.** This department needs to be considered if casting is late. Late casting can mean that an actor's wardrobe will not be ready until sometime into the shoot. If the producer can foresee a casting problem, then this contingency can be anticipated. If there are repeated big extra days with period wardrobe on different locations then the wardrobe will need time to regroup or hire extra staff to cope. It is usually possible to spread these days to allow all departments to work smoothly.

*   **Expecting the unexpected.** When the runner sneezes the cast catches a cold. A schedule should allow for some human error and frailty. It is wise to schedule at the end of a shoot or before a location move, scenes which will be the least expensive to reshoot or that can be cheated to another location. If the laboratory has scratched the negative and the crew have wrapped or travelled, it is good not to have a night scene to reshoot or to have expensive travel back to a distant location. If the scene is big or a potential problem, it should be scheduled in the body of the shoot, so that any difficulties or possible reshoots can be absorbed within the schedule.

Summary

When all these requirements are taken into account, the schedule usually reveals a logic of its own that dictates the order of shooting. It is crucial to be aware of each department's requirements so they can be included in the schedule. A preliminary schedule is normally discussed at a production meeting with each head of department present. This meeting allows for conflicts to be discussed or new information to be added. A new schedule will result and be presented at the next meeting and so on, as a work in progress. The schedule may have problems that cannot be worked around, be it cast availability or too many locations on one day. The solution for the cast problem may be to recast or drop cast from a particular scene. With locations, it may mean finding a new location that can contain two sets, or rationalising the sets in the script.

The Length Of The Schedule

When the schedule order is established, the shoot days can be allocated and the length of the schedule determined. The following is a guide to different factors affecting the speed of shooting and can be generally taken as cumulative in difficulty and time. The categories are not exhaustive, but might warn you off trying to do an action adventure with kids and animals on a boat in a storm at night!

* **Director's style.** Some directors go for a minimalist shooting style and like to rehearse with the cast on set. Others prefer to rehearse in pre-production and to shoot extensive or complicated coverage. It is of paramount importance to have an idea of how the director wishes to shoot the film, scene by scene. What reads as complex may be simple and what looks simple may be complex. Budget and production schedules are often, but not ideally, prepared before the director is confirmed. A shooting schedule must be done hand in hand with the director to reflect their style and priorities, within the constraints that the producer can afford.

* **Director of photography.** Producers employ DOPs because they bring to the picture a certain cinematic 'look'. The amount of lighting time necessary to achieve this 'look' can be a contentious issue and requires agreement between the director, producer and DOP about shooting expectations and what lighting time is reasonable. Frequently, this is not done and the first assistant director (1st AD) is left during the shoot with the difficult job of finding a workable solution between the director and DOP while trying to keep the shoot on schedule. If a producer's expectations require a lot of lighting time then the schedule must reflect this or an explicit arrangement made with the director to restrict their shooting time to accommodate the necessary lighting. This will usually mean a reduction in the amount of coverage possible.

* **Big scenes.** Actors, like anyone on the crew, get tired. There is a limit to what an actor can be asked to do in a shooting day while still expecting a spirited performance. Actors are troopers and will go on until they drop, but film is unforgiving and so is an audience. It's wise to quit when you're ahead.

* **Studio dialogue.** This is the most straightforward filming and, in terms of screen time, the quickest to shoot.

* **Day exterior dialogue.** Can be as fast as studio as there is usually little lighting required. However, it can be affected by weather conditions like cloud and rain, location sound problems like aircraft and motorbikes, and general location hassles like drunks and fed-up residents.

* **Night exterior dialogue.** Has to be lit extensively, plus all the problems for day exteriors and cast/crew fatigue.

* **Action.** Needs a lot of coverage, frequently over an extended area. In combination with other variables can be extremely time consuming.

* **Montage.** Sequences that involve many images to tell the story. Often scripted in many locations or with the same cast but with different looks. Very deceptive on paper as frequently the images required are not made explicit in the script.

* **Fights.** Need extensive rehearsal which is best done in pre-production but this is not always possible. May need many shots to make the hits look convincing. Cannot be rushed or injuries will result.

* **Crowded public areas.** Can be very slow to work as it only takes one mug waving at the camera or even just looking to blow the shot. Filming at night with lights can draw a big crowd. Areas where drunks collect are bad news for fast filming.

* **Children.** Limited call time, sometimes difficult to get a performance from them, and subject to fatigue and occasional off days.

* **Cars.** Travelling car shots – car to car, car rigs or low loaders – are time consuming. Best left to second unit or reduced unit if at all possible. Usually not.

* **Dancing.** In the video age needs a lot of coverage. If strenuous, cannot be repeated forever. Needs to be broken up into shots.

* **Animals.** Must be well trained. As for children, but worse.

* **Aerials.** Time consuming and affected by turbulence, which is usually least in the morning and late afternoon. Potentially lethal and must not be rushed.

* **Boats/water.** Depending on the water and the size of the boat, this category can increase in difficulty by a factor of ten. This is one area where experts will always save time and money and make for successful and safe filming.

* **Trains.** Slow and usually hedged with restrictions.

* **Stunts/special effects.** Take time to set up and co-ordinate. Cannot and must not be rushed. Potentially lethal if not executed by experts.

* **Rain.** Can be time consuming to do well.

* **Wind machines.** As wind is made more visible with dust this is usually included as well. Time consuming to set up and reposition. Noisy and dirty to work with.

* **Extremes of climate or terrain.** Snow or deserts, mountains or tidal flats, sand (beaches), windy or wet. All slow filming.

* **Locations with difficult access.** Usually force gear either to be carried or transported on four-wheel drives. Difficult to service unit. Examples are beaches, waterfalls or even rooftop pools, as lifts rarely go to the roof.

* **Prosthetic make-up.** Very long make-up time and particular lighting requirements.

SUMMARY

It is clear that the script content will radically affect the time it takes to shoot a project. A producer's desired budget will normally determine the length of the schedule. Sometimes, due to the content of the film, it cannot be shot in the time allocated. Either the shoot must be extended or the script modified. A producer can commission a schedule in the development period from a 1st AD or production manager. They can be contacted through the technicians' agencies. When in production, the 1st AD normally schedules the script. A preliminary schedule, discussed at a production meeting with all heads of departments at the first opportunity, will ensure that all schedule requirements are accounted for.

SCHEDULING ON STRIPBOARDS AND COMPUTERS

STRIPBOARDS

Stripboards are used to manually schedule the script. A board consists of six or eight panels into which fit thin strips of coloured card. There are nine colours, including white. Each strip represents a scene or a series of scenes that share common sets and cast. Reading down a strip, each will have the scene number, day or night, Int (interior) or Ext (exterior), location and set and the characters required in the scene. Each character is given a unique number on a large white card called the header board that slots into the left hand side of the first panel. Reading down the strip you will come to the number representing the character which can be read off the header board.

The strips contain four variables (Sc No, D/N, Ext/Int, Loc/Set) plus all the variables of the cast. The nine colours allow nine more variables to be added or some of the above to be made more explicit. For instance, certain locales could be given a uniform colour, or a colour could be used for a location, or day exteriors, and night exteriors and so on. On reading the script, it is usually clear which variables are going to be the most important to the schedule. The colours are then allocated to highlight these variables and make them easier to schedule by grouping the same coloured strips, or mixing them in a set way, for instance, half day shooting and half night shooting.

The scheduler will reorder the strips (which presumably have been broken down in script order) according to the variables discussed above, and then divide them into days – using black and white day divider strips – and weeks – using all black dividers. From the stripboard, the cast crossplot is drawn up which shows on which days of the shoot each member of the cast is working. It is from this that the contracts are drawn up, taking into account any additional days required for weather cover. From the order of the stripboard, a full schedule will be written up which will detail the scene and its cast, extras, props, special requirements and a one-line synopsis of the scene. All departments work from this. Its late delivery in pre-production will badly hamper the production.

COMPUTERS

A computer program is based on the same principles as the stripboard. Its main advantage is that once the information is broken down from the script and typed into the program, changes can then be printed out very quickly. Schedules typed on word processors can be changed quickly, but are prone to typographical errors unlike a dedicated schedule program.

If a production manager or 1st AD is not familiar with computers, they should allow some extra time for the schedule preparation as they climb the learning curve! Computers in some hands seem to make work, not get rid of it. If the production has someone who is fast on a word processor and no one who is confident with a scheduling program then the production will be better served staying with a stripboard. Computers come into their own on bigger productions.

There are two areas of confusion with computer scheduling programs. Much of the software comes from the US. The American Screen Actors Guild contract with producers allows for an actor to be contracted for a given number of days, then if they do not work for some time on the picture, to be 'Dropped' and then 'Picked Up' again after which they remain employed until they finish work. They can only be dropped once. The contract can only fall into two parts, each of continuous employment, made up of Days Worked and Days Held between Days Worked. In Australia we can contract so many days spread over a given period. If you like, we have multiple Drops and Pickups with no limits. For an American cast contract to contain a Drop and Pickup, the Drop must be for at least ten days. This can vary but ten days is standard. In the computer crossplot that is called the Day out of Days, the Drop/Pickup can be varied. If set to zero it stops working and will configure to our standards. You can get rid of the Drop/Pickup/Hold terminology and just get it to print days worked.

The second area of confusion is 'Banners'. They are a device to separate scenes with a note like 'Travel'. They do not behave in a consistent way. If you find the schedule is not printing as you expected, or the Day out of Days is doing something odd, delete Banners and use breakdown strips with the Banner headings, and see if it comes right.

Scheduling software does have bugs. If you have consulted the manual and still have a problem, ring someone who is familiar with the program or ring the company help line.

SUMMARY

The successful use of the stripboard or computer lies in the identification and clear marking of the variables that most affect the schedule so that scenes can be intelligently ordered.

CONCLUSION

A good schedule resolves the sometimes conflicting interests of the different departments to the betterment of the whole film. It is a realistic blueprint of how the film is going to be made, from which the crew and cast can reliably plan. It's up to the 1st AD, the production manager, the producer and director to make sure that it is realistic. A head in the sand 'she'll

199

be right' pre-production will only postpone hard decisions. A shoot that consistently falls behind is depressing to work on and hard to get back on schedule when the crew is tired. Schedules that are not adhered to make planning impossible. Constant changes are difficult and expensive and soon wear professional relationships thin. A production that fails to stay on schedule will ultimately involve the financial backers stepping in and imposing conditions to bring it back on budget.

Production Accountancy

Penny Carl

Financial control and management accounting is an integral part of film making because of rising budgets and the requirements of the funding bodies, whether they be government, private investment organisations or individual investors. The producer must therefore be aware of how a film accountancy system should operate, what is expected of production accounts and what should be expected from an accountant. The accounting service must provide a clear picture of all expenditure and estimates to complete, measured against the budget, in a format that can be readily understood by the producer. It then becomes a management tool, used for decision making during the production period. The system must also provide a complete audit trail for the security of the investors and for tax purposes.

Each production must be considered as a business project, and the budget is the financial blueprint against which all reports must be monitored.

Setting Up The System

* **The budget.** Finalise the budget: all known factors should be taken into consideration before locking it off for reporting purposes (preferably 5–6 weeks before shoot). Each budget category is allocated a computer code, and each cost component within the category has a sub-code. This becomes the chart of accounts which is personalised for the production. All expenditure is then posted to that code as part of the general ledger system. Establish non-deductible components of budget if funded under Section 10BA.

* **Cash flow.** Prepare a cash flow. Break down the budget into the periods in which it is anticipated that the funds will be committed, taking into consideration laboratory, equipment and other deposits, bonds, etc.

* **Order book.** Establish an order book system incorporating the Sales Tax Exemption Certificate declaration relating to the First Schedule of the *Sales Tax (Exemption Classifications) Act 1992*. Each person authorised to commit expenditure should use a triplicate order form: one copy to the supplier, one for the accountant, and one fixed copy for their own reference. This order must give a fixed price or estimate and this amount will be accrued as a sundry creditor or known liability of the company.

* **Bank accounts.** Open bank accounts in accordance with the investment agreement. It is normal to have a cash management account through which all the investors' funds will flow, and a production account. All cheques should require two signatures. Arrange cashing facilities at a local branch for cash floats and wages. If the production is funded

under Section 10BA, it will also be necessary to open a 'non-deductible' account to isolate that expenditure.

* **Group/payroll tax.** Apply for group tax and payroll tax registration in the name of the production company. Numbers will be allocated for monthly returns. Note that, as the employer, a producer is responsible for deducting tax from employees. It is strongly recommended that the Certificate of Incorporation and workers' compensation documents of sub-contractors should be sighted to determine whether PAYE tax should be applied. Payroll tax is a state levy, and must be applied to the gross earnings including allowances and per diems. It is applicable in each state in which wages are paid, and therefore more than one registration may be necessary. Group tax is a federal levy.

* **Petty cash.** Issue petty cash floats to authorised personnel. These floats must be monitored weekly, and only reimbursed as authorised by approved expenditure. If a float does not turn over within a ten-day period, it should be reduced.

* **Wages.** Obtain copies of contracts for all crew and cast. Wages records should be established with an individual record for each person, who must be paid in accordance with their contract. Any overtime should be a separate claim by each individual, and authorised by the department head. Knowledge of the relevant awards, particularly those with the Media, Entertainment and Arts Alliance, is essential, and loadings/rights must be established. Writers, producers, directors, and others who may have special contracts also should be paid as per their contracts. If **tax is not to be deducted,** the appropriate company or taxation department exemptions must be obtained (refer to group tax, above). This also applies to all casual labour, including extras.

* **Insurance covers** must be taken out upon commencement of pre-production, including film producer's, negative, public liability and money insurance. Workers' compensation or Workcare is also a state levy, and must be taken out in each state where the production will be employing staff. The rate varies, and will be based on the gross wages paid to crew and cast. An estimate should be given to the insurance company at the commencement of the production, and this will be adjusted on the final audited figures.

* **Files.** Set up files for all paperwork including: accounts for payment, paid accounts (A–Z is preferable), petty cash, wages records, contracts and production information.

* **Accounting records.** If computerised establish a chart of accounts. If not, open a cash book, journal and ledger. Apart from expense accounts, the records must include the private ledger accounts, e.g., bank accounts, investors, sundry creditors & debtors, floats, and so on. It is essential to work on a double entry system. The cost report should always be accompanied by a statement of investors' funds.

* **Bonds & deposits.** Record all bonds and deposits individually.

* **Production information.** Open a file for all production information, including copies of the schedule, daily call sheets, and production progress reports. This information is essential to the accountant to establish weekly costs estimates for cast and crew

overtime, laboratory developing and printing, sound transfers, catering, special equipment, transport, personnel (all of which should have been covered by orders), and the cost trends reflected by the daily shooting ratios and minutes shot.

* **Invoices.** All invoices should be sighted and approved by the producer or production manager and matched with the relevant orders before payment.

* **Superannuation.** Register the production company for the JEST and STA superannuation schemes for cast and crew, respectively. Allow the current percentage of gross wages for budget purposes. JEST and STA will send out monthly returns to be completed and sent back to them.

Crew should give you their STA number. Occasionally a crew member may belong to a different superannuation scheme. Check that the scheme is a 'complying fund' under the Superannuation Guarantee legislation before making any payments.

The Audit

In most cases the investment agreement will require that an audit of the film's production costs be carried out. The producer should therefore be aware that the auditor will require the following information and records to be made available:

* written confirmation of appointment to the auditor defining the scope of the audit, and to whom they are to report;

* copy of the film prospectus or offer document, together with a copy of the detailed budget and timetable of the production periods of the film;

* details of all production bank accounts;

* copies of contracts with investors, producers, directors, scriptwriters (including rights or options), principal cast, principal crew, insurance company, completion guarantor, brokerage recipients, investors' representative;

* all accounting records;

* final statements of cost of production, and investors' funds;

* details of any contingent liabilities, including any matters pending of a legal nature, or relating to taxation.

A Day In The Life
Of A Drama Production

Damien Parer

The Daily Paper War

Every production runs on paper. The following requirements are essential and critical to the smooth running of the production. During any one day you may have to create, refer to or use each or all of them. Keep them properly filed, and handy:

* the relevant portion of the script

* strip board

* shooting schedule

* location survey report

* location design sketch plan

* location agreement

* letter to residents near location

* map(s) of area(s) clearly indicating locations

* scene breakdown sheet

* cast cross plot

* safety report

* design/props requirements

* wardrobe requirements

* SFX requirements

* call sheet

* movement order

* continuity sheets, marked up script

✳   camera report sheets

✳   sound report sheets

✳   film stock reconciliation

✳   second assistant director's daily report sheet

✳   artists' worksheet

✳   daily artists' salary voucher

✳   crew time sheet

✳   accident report

✳   daily production progress report

✳   weekly cost report

On the following pages are examples of some of these daily paper requirements.

SAMPLE PORTION OF SCRIPT

MATTHEW AND SON

Written by

Christine Schofield

and

Marcus Cole

TELEVISION HOUSE FILMS LTD
229 Lennox Street
RICHMOND VIC 3121

MATTHEW AND SON

1. Ext. Disco. Night.

Kids hanging around entrance to disco. It's a lonely, hungry sort of feel. We hear the sound of the band tuning up over this. Testing equipment … The twang of guitars and amplifiers … Drums being tuned. The screech of feedback. All these discordant sounds over the shots of the kids outside lit by harsh street lighting, flashing neons. Their laughter and ad lib chatter under the band's preparations. Directly after this image of the joint, we see an older (late twenties), distinctive looking guy moving through the crowd. We'll call him Max. There's a hard edge to him, even when he smiles. He's a predator. As he enters the disco we hear the sound of the lead singer counting 1-2-3-4 and into a driving, harsh, raunchy number.

2. Int. Disco. Night.

(Opening titles during this scene.)

A big crowd of teenagers dancing and surging to deafening music. The band is on a raised stage at one end of the large room giving it their all, coloured lights flash on and off - standard spots, ultra violet, lasers even – a full-bodied assault on all the senses.

A glass false ceiling hangs above the revellers, it is a patchwork of pulsating, flashing colours and designs, the disco is multi-level: stairs leading to a bar on one floor, an area with tables and chairs on another. Upstairs you can look over the railing and see the complex lighting rig playing through the glass ceiling piece onto the dancers below. The place is really jumping, everyone into it – except Max. He is sitting quietly at a table in a shadowy corner near the bar. He has a drink – tomato juice – and is alone. He doesn't respond to the music or the dancing. He just waits and watches.

A hip-looking eighteen year old boy is approaching him. He sits down beside Max, they nod hello – they know each other, but only as dealer and client, the kid leans forward and speaks over the din – a brief dialogue. Very carefully Max passes a small silver-paper wrapped something under the table to the kid. There is a rolled note in the kid's hand. The exchange is made. The kid stands and moves away goes into the men's lavatory. Max drinks some juice.

Downstairs the dancing is building to fever pitch. The band really tearing it up. Time has passed …

We become aware that the young guy is now grooving along on the edges of the crowd watching the dancers. There's a loose, chaotic feel to the way he's moving – 'out of it' – glazed eyes – head lolling – he appears also to be shivering, his forehead is sweaty – he bumps into the people standing near him - his balance is off – he staggers – there's a second – he shudders

– and his movements become exaggerated – extreme it's as if he's dancing in some excessive way twisting, writhing, throwing himself around the kids standing near him nudge each other to watch him laughing because his dancing is so bad he lurches into a group falling against a girl her boyfriend reacts pushing the guy who turns on him, and give him an almighty shove the laughter turns to alarm girls squeal the bouncers shoulder their way through the crowd a bouncer grabs the guy who shoves him away into the crowd. The kid violently pushes people aside as he rusher for the stairs. The band rocks on.

The bouncers pursue him as he heads upstairs. The kid doesn't know where he is or where he's going. He's off his face. He tips tables over in his haste, people scatter. Girls shriek. We see the table in the corner where Max was, tomato juice still there, but he is gone. The bouncers descend on the kid once more and both grab him.

Downstairs the band still rocks on. The kid struggles like mad. He has herculean strength. A chaotic scene. Using all his frenzied strength the kid suddenly pulls free, but he is too close to the safety railing and the impetus of his pull free carries him over the railing and crashing onto the lighting rig and glass ceiling. Glass shatters, sparks fly, the lighting goes crazy, the kid screams.

Below, the band stop playing and people scatter girls scream as glass and sparks rain down. The kid is seen jerking convulsively in silhouette through the lighted glass panes still unbroken.

3. Ext. Disco. Night.

Matt pulls up outside the disco. A police car there. An ambulance. Ambulance men giving first aid to several people cut by glass. A fairly big crowd out front mainly dancers who were inside earlier: shocked, chattering, not wanting to go home yet.

Matt moves through the kids, carrying his medical bag. He is surprised how young some of them are.

SAMPLE LOCATION SURVEY

DATE	*21 March*
SCENE NO	*1,2,3,4,5,6*
DAY/NIGHT	*Both*
INT/EXT	*Both*
BRIEF DESCRIPTION	*Crazed drug addict*
	Arrival of Matt Caine
DETAILS OF LOCATION	*Operating discotheque/restaurant*
ADDRESS OF LOCATION	*22 Regal Street, City*
DIRECTIONS	*See Melway's street directory*
MELWAY'S MAP REF	*49 G9*
DIRECTION SIGNS	*Required*
ACCESS ROAD	*Scotland Lane*
CONTACT AT LOCATION	*Gina Smith (621 6921)*
TELEPHONE AT LOCATION	*In office*
AMENITIES	*Electricity on site*
	Generator for filming purposes
LAVATORY/WATER	*Inside location*
PARKING	*Scotland Lane*
	Space booked with city council
USE OF TELEPHONE	*Yes. Company to meet costs*
CATERING FACILITIES	*Kitchen of restaurant to cater on the day.*
SOUND	*Interior neutral*
DIRECTION OF SUN	*Not applicable*
CAMERA DEPT NOTES	
TIME RESTRICTIONS	*Location opens for business 9pm.*
SAFETY SURVEY NOTES	*Stunt to be choreographed and supervised by stunt coordinator*
SECURITY ARRANGEMENTS	*Special area of location to be set aside for o'night storage of the gear.*
OWNER	*Brian Smith*
ADDRESS OF OWNER	*Phone 621 6921*
LOCATION FEE OR CREDIT	*Personnel costs, catering charge, screen credit*
GENERAL NOTES	*Main meal break to be called at the same time as restaurant's lunch to minimise clash.*
	See also time restrictions.

209

SAMPLE SCENE BREAKDOWN

DATE   4 June

SCENE	EXT/INT	TIME OF DAY	PAGE
Sc 2	Int	Night	1-3

WARDROBE: DAY/NIGHT NUMBER	LOCATION/STUDIO
night/1	Disco

SCENE DESCRIPTION	SCRIPT TIME	SHOOT TIME	PAGE LENGTH
Drug deal Addict jumps to death	2.54min	8 hours	

CAST	EXTRAS		
Max	Barman	X 2	
Addict	Musicians	X 5	
Stunt bouncer X 2	Dancers	X 28	

PROPS & DRESSING	VEHICLES	SFX & STUNTS
Flashing lighting grid Tomato juice Drinks Drug deal & money Band eqp		Flashing, lighting grid Addict runs and falls

SPECIAL REQUIREMENTS & SAFETY; EXTRA EQP

Stunt coordinator, safety officer, nurse, special fx coordinator, dance coordinator

NOTES

Multi-cam setup
Sound playback

SAMPLE SHOOTING SCHEDULE

DATE: 4 June
DAY 7
WEEK 2

SCENE PAGE	EXT/INT	DAY/NIGHT	LOCATION	SYNOPSIS	CAST	EXTRAS	PROPS & VEHICLES	REQUIREMENTS/SAFETY/SFX
2/1	Int	Night	Disco	Drug deal. Addict jumps to death	Max. Addict (stuntman). 2 bouncers. 3 stunt dancers	33 good dancers 5 musicians. 2 Barmen.	Flashing light grid, Tomato drink, Silver drug deal, Table & chairs, Paper money, Soft drinks, Band equip.	SFX: Flashing light grid. Exploding lights. STUNTS Struggle and chase with bouncers. Fall through light grid onto dancefloor. REQUIREMENTS: Safety officer. Nurse. Stunt coordinator. Band to prerecord playback req. Louma crane. Multicam. Prelight.
			TRAVEL TO DISCO EXT. LOCATION					
1/1	Ext	Night	Disco	Max turns up at disco.	Max	10 kids	Joints Flashing neons. Harsh lights.	Prelight. Wet down.

SAMPLE LOCATION AGREEMENT

DATED: 31 May

NAME OF OWNER/AGENT: Melbourne Subterranean Restaurant PL

ADDRESS: 22 Regal Street, Melbourne 3000

LOCATION ADDRESS: 22 Regal Street Melbourne

AGREED SHOOT DATES: Monday 4 June–Tuesday 5 June

LOCATION FEE: $

I/We being the Owner/Agent of the Premises specified above do hereby agree to the conditions as stated on the following page:

For and on Behalf of   For and on behalf of

....

....

(Title)   (Title)

....

(Date)   (Date)

Location Agreement for MATTHEW AND SON

1   To give Television House Films ('the Producer'), its employees and/ or nominee permission to pictorially represent the Premises and to make such use of this as the Producer may require, for the purpose of filming the feature film currently entitled 'Matthew and Son'. Use of the Premises shall include the right to park vehicles at or near the Premises, to bring personnel and equipment (including props and temporary sets) onto the Premises and the obligation to remove the same and all rubbish after completion of work.

2   The permission to use the Premises is granted for the period specified above, or longer as may be necessary, subject to change in case of changes in the production schedule or weather conditions, and continuing until completion of all scenes or work required, including retakes or adds scenes, if any. Should additional shooting time be required, permission will be granted at a pro rata rate.

3   The Producer shall have the right to pictorially represent the Premises under any name whether real or fictional according to the requirements of the feature film. I/We do hereby also agree to allow the Producer to incorporate the representation of the Premises in the feature film (and all off-cuts) either as a sequence on its own or preceded, interlaced or followed by such other representations as the Producer may require (including scenes of studio sets representing for the purposes of the feature film, the interior/exterior of the premises).

4   To allow the Producer or its nominee to exploit in every manner the feature film, still photographs and sound recordings with or without the Premises pictorially represented. Neither I/we nor any other tenant or party now or hereafter having an interest in the Premises shall have any right of action against the Producer or any other party arising out of any use of the Premises whether or not such use is or may claim to be defamatory, untrue or censorable in nature.

5   In consideration of permission being granted to allow filming facilities at the Premises, the Producer hereby agrees that it will hereby indemnify me/us for any liability, loss, claim or proceeding in respect of the personal injury or death of any person and the loss or damage to the Premises or any property connected thereto caused by negligence or wilful act of omission by the Producer, its agents and servants.

5(a) In relation to any loss or damage to the Premises, I/we agree to notify the Producer in writing within seven (7) days of completion of the Producer's use of the Premises, any damage claimed to have arisen from the Producer's use of the Premises and to allow the Producer and its representatives access to the Premises to assess, and, where appropriate, rectify any such damage.

5(b) Failure by me/us to notify the Producer in writing within seven (7)

SAMPLE LOCATION AGREEMENT

days, under Clause 5(a) shall relieve the Producer of all responsibility in respect of damage claimed to have arisen from the Producer's use of the Premises.

6   I/We warrant and represent that I/we have the full right and authority to enter into this Agreement concerning the Premises and the consent or permission of no other person, firm/body/agency or incorporation is or will be necessary in order to enable the Producer to exercise and enjoy fully the rights herein granted and I/we indemnify and agree to hold the Producer and its licensee, successors and assigns free and harmless from and against any and all loss, costs, liability, damages or claims of any nature arising from or concerning a breach of the warranties and representations in this clause.

7   Subject to the Producer's obligations continuing hereunder, the Producer may assign the rights granted in this Agreement. This Agreement shall be binding upon and inure to the benefits of the successors, licensee and assigns of the parties hereto.

8   In consideration of the permission to use the Premises and all other rights granted in the Agreement, the Producer shall pay to me/us as total remuneration, the location fee specified above.

In the event that the Producer is unable to use the Premises for any reason or that the use by the Producer is interrupted for any reason beyond the control of the Producer, then the Producer shall only be obliged to pay me/us for that period for which the premises were so used, calculated on a pro rata basis.

TRAFFIC CONTROL

1. Traffic Control requires the use of:

    STOP/SLOW SIGNS

    Illuminated vests for operators of these signs

    Witches hats for surround of film crew in hazardous filming areas such as a main road approach, pass and rear shots

    The display of "A" boards to approaching traffic to warn of film crew ahead.

2. All drivers of vehicles to hold current driving licences.

3. Lead or rear cover vehicles to hold current driving licences.

4. Some form of warning (red flag or flashing orange light) on all camera mounts protruding from travelling vehicles.

5. Difficult or hazardous driving scenes to be arranged in conjunction with stunt co-ordinator.

6. Stunt co-ordinator to select stunt double for hazardous driving, both driver and passenger if required.

7. Vehicles to be used in driving scene to be selected and checked by stunt co-ordinator before being used for stunt driving.

FIRE PRECAUTIONS

The following fire extinguishers are to be carried by the unit at all times and should always be readily accessible to people on the set –

> 2 x 9 kg stored water extinguishers, suitable for paper, wood, etc. fires.

> 1 x 6 kg CO_2 extinguishers for electric fires.

> 1 x 9 kg BCF and 1 x 4.5 kg BCF dry chemical extinguishers for larger fires and flammable liquids. Note that by preferably these extinguishers should not be used on sensitive equipment, and certainly not on personnel.

This list of fire extinguishers are only a minimum requirement and more should be provided if necessary.

SAMPLE CALL SHEET

Day:	7
Date:	Mon 4 June
Location:	Disco – Melbourne Subterranean Restaurant 22 Regal Street, Melbourne Melways Map Ref: 49 G9
Contact:	Gina Smith (03) 621 6921
Weather:	Fine & sunny but with some cloud cover. Expected top: 18°C. Expected low: 8°C. Sunrise: 0728. Sunset: 1709.
Call times:	Crew 08.00 Wardrobe 08.30 Makeup/hair 08.30 Art Dept/SFX 06.00

Scene No: 2   **Int/Ext:** Int   **Day/night:** N1   **Set:** Disco

Action: Dancing. Drug deal. Death dive.

Characters:	Artists:	Pick Up:	W/r M/u:	On set:
Max	J Mannering	Own transport	09.00	10.00
Addict	M Hennessy	"	08.00	10.00
Stunt bouncer	R Roordink	"	09.30	10.00
Stunt bouncer	C Hargraves	"	09.30	10.00
Barmen x 2		"	08.30	10.00
Musicians x 5		"	08.30	10.00
Dancers x 28		"	08.30	10.00

Scene No: 1   **Int/Ext:** Ext   **Day/night:** N1   **Set:** Disco

Action: Max turns up at disco.

Characters:	Artists:	Pick Up:	W/r M/u:	On set:
Max	J Mannering			Called
10 kids (dancers)				Called

Sample Second Assistant Director's Daily Report Sheet

Production Day: 7

Date: 4 June

Department	Called	Meal Break	Wrap Called	Department from Location
ADs & Continuity	08.00	13.15	20.20	22.00
Camera	08.00	+0		22.00
Sound	08.00	14.00		21.45
Grips	08.00			21.45
Electrics	08.00			20.15
Makeup	08.00			20.15
Wardrobe	08.00			20.15
Stills	present			
Art Department	07.30			21.15
Other				

Catering Numbers

Morning Tea   85

Lunch   85

Afternoon Tea   85

S Stephens

....

Caterer

Requests for Equipment, Expendibles etc

Comments on Weather, Delays, Late Arrivals etc

1. Mr Kewle, states that all departments worked with speed and were efficient and productive.

2. Delay caused by complex preparation of electrics and SPX on lighting grid for disco dancing effects and explosive effects.

B Reynolds

....

2nd Assistant Director

SAMPLE ARTISTS' WORKSHEET

Day:	7
Date:	Mon 4 June
Location:	Int/ext disco

Name/character	Call Time	Finish Time	Meal Break (hrs)	Total Hours Worked	Signature
Actors agency					
Jack Dobbs / Waiter	08.30	21.00	3/4	11 3/4	J. Dobbs
Seiko M'ment		-	-	-	
Frank Tolsen / Waiter	08.30	21.00	3/4	11 3/4	Frank Tolsen
A & J		-	-	-	
Maria Watson / Dancer	08.30	20.15	3/4	11	Maria Watson
Laurel Teffs / Dancer	08.30	20.15	3/4	11	Laurel Teffs
Sandy Tully / Dancer	08.30	20.15	3/4	11	S Tully
L Thompson / Dancer	08.30	20.15	3/4	11	L Thompson
Di Gardiner / Dancer	08.30	20.15	3/4	11	Di Gardiner
F Ormond / Dancer	08.30	20.15	3/4	11	F Ormond
R Tellegrino / Dancer	08.30	20.15	3/4	11	R Tellegrino
Lisa Windows / Dancer	08.30	20.15	3/4	11	L Windows
M Chadwick / Dancer	08.30	no show		-	
P Robertson / Dancer	08.30	20.15	3/4	11	P. Robertson
Steve Canter / Dancer	08.30	20.15	3/4	11	Steve Canter
Gomez Tangier / Dancer	08.30	21.15	3/4	11	G Tangier
Richard Dom / Dancer	08.30	20.15	3/4	11	R. Dom
Tracey Allens / Dancer	08.30	20.15	3/4	11	Tracey Allens
Melb M'ment					
Mick Niss / Dancer	08.30	21.00	3/4	11 3/4	MICK NISS
BMA					
Laurel Craig / Dancer	08.30	21.00	3/4	11 3/4	Laurel Craig
M Kellog / Dancer	08.30	21.00	3/4	11 3/4	M Kellog
Liz Davey / Dancer	08.30	21.00	3/4	11 3/4	Liz Davey
Chris Ariel / Dancer	08.30	20.15	3/4	11	Chris Ariel

SAMPLE DAILY ARTIST'S SALARY VOUCHER

DATE   *4 June*

ARTIST'S NAME: *Maria Watson*

ADDRESS: *999 Timber Street*
                        Balmaine Vic 3030

AGENCY: *A&J*

CONDITIONS:

The person engaged must at all times observe the directions of the Production Company and its representatives.

The fee referred to herein is the full and the only amount payable by the Production Company.

I hereby give and grant to you the right to photograph my physical likeness in any manner you desire and/or the right to reproduce and record my voice and other sound effects made by me, and any reproductions of my voice and other sound effects, by you, your licensees, successors and assigns, in advertising and exploitation and/or other use of any of the photoplay, and/or otherwise. I agree that the voice of the Artist may be dubbed in any languages as desired except English.

I agree that my engagement is subject to the conditions above, all of which I agree to observe.

....
Passed by Assistant Director

....
Signature of the Artist

POST-PRODUCTION

FILM POST-PRODUCTION

KERRY REGAN

FILM POST-PRODUCTION FLOW CHART

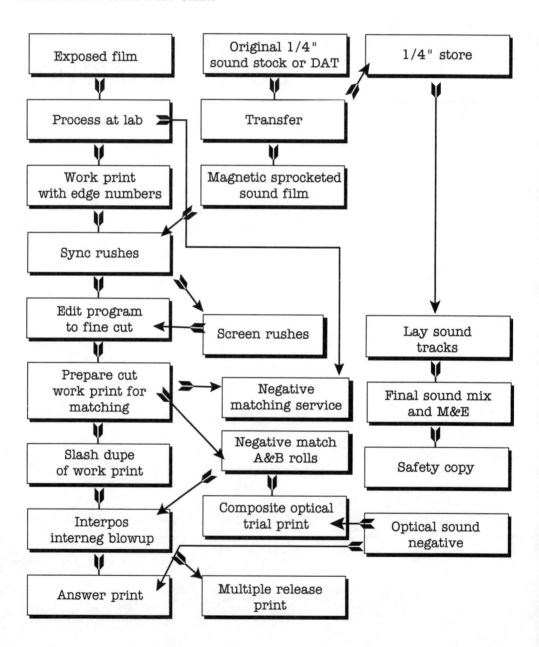

This chapter provides an outline of the system and procedures if you are post-producing entirely on film. More often than not these days, non-linear systems are used which are described by Stephen Smith (see pp. 229–237). Whichever way you choose to go, it is important that you:

*   pick qualified people;

*   bring them in early;

*   let them set your scheduling;

*   give them authority;

*   let them have a budget that won't be cut short by problems created by the shoot.

The last stages of the production are not the areas to cut short. After spending millions of dollars to produce a film there is not reason to throw it away in its last stages.

INITIAL PROCESSING

THE FILM

From the location or studio, the film is delivered to the lab for processing. A report on the condition of the negative is made and a copy sent directly to the production office. An overseas actor might need to fly home, a costly set might need to be dismantled or the crew might be moving to a distant location. Whatever the reason, that report must be delivered as soon as possible.

A contact work-print which carries through the edge numbers from the original negative is made. This is then processed and the positive image work print is sent to the editing department or, in some cases, if the organisation is large enough, to a quality control person. The print is also screened on either a high-speed or normal projector before it leaves the lab, and a report is made to the production office – usually only if there is a problem.

After the quality control, the film is delivered to the editor's assistant, where it is logged in and broken down ready for syncing.

THE SOUND

Let's assume the lab is handling the sound transfers also. The ¼" tapes arrive from location and are sent directly to the sound department for transfer. As film has a number of formats, so does the sound. The compatible format is nearly always the one to go for: 16 mm film = transfer to 16 mm magnetic film. In Australia we still do have 17.5 mm option (usually due to budget) which is 35 mm magnetic film cut in half: 35 mm film = transfer to 35 mm or 17.5 mm magnetic film. The sound transfer is monitored and any problems reported to the production office. Like the film, the original ¼" master tape should be stored separately from its copy as a safety precaution, for example, in case of fire. The transferred sound is then sent directly to the editor's assistant, where again it is logged and broken down in preparation for syncing.

SYNCING THE RUSHES

Rushes, or dailies, are prepared by the editor's assistant. The preparation of the dailies for the evening's (or morning's) screening is a relatively simple task. The main thing is to try and sync the rushes in ascending numerical order, which is usually the way they were shot during the previous day. This is not always possible on account of multi-camera shooting, second unit or out-of-sequence shooting. The director might ask to see the footage in a different format.

'Roll camera, Speed, I.D., Scene 1, Shot 1, Take 1 and a Clap' are heard. The assistant rolls the picture through until he or she sees the closing face of the clapper board meet and then marks this frame. The sound is run through also to this point and the first frame on which the sound of the clap is heard is marked. This task of 'marking up' can either be done simultaneously or separately. The syncing process now only requires that these two points (the marked frame on picture and sound) be synchronised and made into rolls up to 1000 feet. Mute slates are filled in on the sound roll with unused magnetic film or 'junk' spacing. After the syncing has been completed on the bench, a check screening should be carried out on an editing machine to look for any further possible problems and to ensure that the syncing is correct. This is, of course, possible only if the assistant has the time. The answers to all the problems found in that day's rushes should have been found or at least reported, before the screening so as to limit the number of distracting surprises.

THE EDIT

During the shoot the editor has been kept busy editing the scenes as they come in. As a run of scenes becomes available he/she will assemble them in order of script and probably adjust them, having now seen them in a run, for timing. The director might want a periodic look at these scenes to see how they're going, and that the editor is going in the right direction. Protocol at this stage should enable the director and editor to arrive at 'the director's cut' with as little interference as possible from anyone, including the producer. There are a number of reasons for this. By the time they have finished their edit, the director and editor are ready for an objective view, which will possibly throw some fresh light on some rather clouded scenes. Or they might have missed an important point by being too close to the material. Whatever the reason, the fact is that it's better for the producer to see the film as one run and with as few interruptions or stops as possible, in order to be clear-minded and constructive, and to get an overall 'feel' for the film. The producer's screening should cover the following:

*   Does the film work?

*   Does it run to time?

*   How is the structure, including flow?

*   How are the actors' performances?

*   Does the film require more cutting?

224

*   Sound, music, FX?

These are some of the questions that need to be answered. Usually no matter how good a film is on the first cut, it may be necessary to have a second, third or even fourth and fifth cut. However, it should be noted that re-editing for its own sake is costly and demoralising. There comes a time when fiddling must stop and the continuation of post-production must proceed. The schedule should be an indication of this.

SOUND EDIT

Upon the final approval of the fine cut, the editor must prepare for the sound edit and print preparation (negative matching). To enable the sound editor to start, and the negative matching to proceed, a slash dupe of the program from the cutting copy is made in colour. Because the slash is a carbon copy of the cut image, it will allow the sound editor to start work.

Usually the dialogue tracks are the first to be split and extensions of atmosphere added to help the mixer meet their mark of excellence. Everything that the sound editor does from here is to make the mix easier and faster so as to allow the mixer more time to finish the job well. If the tracks are laid up professionally, this will lead to a more economical sound mix. It pays to employ a good sound editor. If the production is pushed for time or has the budget, FX and music editors and an assistant for each editor will be employed. The post-production supervisor would oversee the operation and book all facilities, as well as constantly keep tabs on the day-to-day running of the post-production process.

The first meeting the director has with the sound editing staff is as soon as possible after, or during, the fine cut. This may also include the composer, who at this stage has been informed of the progress and told of any changes to schedule or concept. However, it is advisable to have a separate spotting session with the composer so that everyone can concentrate entirely on music requirements during the session.

Assuming that there is a staff of editors including dialogue, FX and music, the meeting with the director could be a long one, covering everything from post-sync dialogue to spot FX. The producer need not be there unless he or she feels that they can be of some assistance. The dialogue editor should be at any further recording of post-sync dialogue or voice over. The post-sync session consists of artists, director, producer, studio technical director, editor and assistant editor. The film can be set up in a number of difference ways, so a check with the studio where the work is to be done would be advisable. Post-sync FX are very much a professional job. These FX, when played back, can add so much to a film that they should be considered a must for all drama and some documentaries. They add dimension to the program and are used to fill spaces in the music and effects (M & Es). Some countries are very particular about the M & E quality, and rejects can be costly.

OPTICAL FX AND TITLES

During the sound editing, the vision side of the business carries on. The negative matcher should have marked up the cut work print and logged the same numbers, checking that he or she has all rolls of film from the shoot, including all pick-ups and opticals made during the cut. The first job is to remove the negative that is required for opticals. This list of shots and edge numbers is prepared by the editor, who simultaneously marks all the dissolves, using

225

a grease pencil, on the work print. The optical make-up is prepared by the negative matcher and sent to the optical house to be shot.

Meanwhile the negative matching proceeds. This process is a relatively simple one of matching the edge numbers from the cut work print to the same on the negative. Each consecutive shot on 16 mm is placed on an alternate roll with black spacing filling the hole on the opposite reel. This is called A and B rolling. This is to allow for grading changes to be triggered mechanically and simple opticals, such as dissolves, to happen during the printing of the answer print. The splices are made by a heated cement splicer carefully checked before the job to ensure correct alignment so as not to cause jumping in the printing. The opticals, when completed, can be dripped into spaces kept in the A and B rolls. Firstly, though, they must be checked on a projector to ensure their correctness and quality. The post-production supervisor must go to this screening.

During all this, art work for the titles needs to be made. Deciding on the type of lettering and style of setting becomes a time-consuming task, as is the checking of spelling. It must be right! There are a number of graphics houses that will make this job a little easier. They will arrange all the previous matters and present the credits in scroll form for approval and a final spelling check. They then shoot the titles or graphics and send the printing materials to the optical house for printing.

The Grading At The Lab

Upon completion of the negative matching, after the negative has been cleaned and reasonably tightly rewound to ensure no movement during shipment, the rolls are sent to the lab for first answer print. Upon their arrival, the A and B rolls are sent to the grading department. The grader usually grades from a video screen connected to a computer, calibrated to lighting changes, e.g. red, green and blue, and runs a reel at a time to balance or correct to the director of photography's requirements. The post-production supervisor should be involved here also, to represent the interests of the production, and act as quality control officer.

The Mix

After the tracks have been laid and checked to ensure no breakages will occur during the mix and that everything is in sync, a track run should be carried out to ensure that the director is happy with the lay-up. This should happen a couple of days before the scheduled final mix to allow the editor sufficient time to do fix-ups at the director's request. In the case of drama, it might be necessary to do a dialogue pre-mix, an FX pre-mix, and any other pre-mixing that will lessen the time required for the director and producer to be present in the mixing room. Some directors – even producers – might want to be present during all mixing sessions. The final mix is a collaborative exercise and requires judicious guidance from the producer. The proverb 'too many cooks spoil the broth' applies to the mixing theatre. The mixer is hired for his or her skills and should be allowed to use them, provided they fall in line with the slant of the program. In some cases it may be necessary to have three mixers on the desk at the same time for maximum efficiency.

However, it should be noted that the producer (and director) may wish to be present at the pre-mixes to ensure that there are no 'surprises' during the final mix itself, and it is going to sound as agreed to or intended.

The mix is usually recorded onto 35 mm three or four stripe master. Each track has been allocated either music, FX, dialogue or M & E. These combinations vary from place to place and film to film. However, if you have an overseas sale, it will be essential to have a music and FX track free of voice over or dialogue, so that the country supplied can lay in its own language. The music and FX can be mixed or separate: some countries require that they be separated, some not. There is a cost consideration also in stock and extra transfer, and maybe mixing time. Your distribution contract may list these requirements. If not, you should consult a marketing company for current requirements.

Last of all you must make a copy mix as soon as possible. Due to the current quality of noise reduction, it will be possible to use the copy for further sound dubbing work. The dub and master should be kept separate at all times. It might be necessary to do a ¼" centre time-coded dub for an overseas sale.

OPTICAL SOUND NEGATIVE

The final mix is sent to the lab and turned from an electrical magnetic sound track to a visual chemical sound track, the optical sound negative. As the A and B rolls are negative, so must be the sound. The same gauge sound negative is used as the film, i.e. 16 mm sound = 16 mm image. You can have an A wind negative or a B wind negative depending on the state of your printing.

THE PRINT

The graded A and B rolls plus the sound negative are ready for printing into one film. This print is regarded as the 'com/opt', that is, composite optical print. The process is simple but time-consuming. Each roll of film has to be printed separately and the optical sound also run separately. The result is the first answer print. If this print is good enough it can be used as a release print, but more often than not it will be rejected for many reasons, not least the grading. Subsequent prints will be charged for, provided the lab is not at fault with problems. The post-production supervisor, director of photography, the director and producer should be present for the screening of the first answer print. Subsequent prints can be checked by the post-production supervisor if changes are small.

The next step is to provide safety materials for the program, so as to protect them from possible damage. The A and B rolls will be printed on a positive based fine grain stock and then from that a dupe negative will be produced. A print is then run off and checked by the post-production supervisor and a report made to the producer. The quality of this print will not be the same as the print from the original A and B rolls. It will have less definition and the grain will be more obvious, but the film stocks available these days have ensured that the loss of quality is minimal. Subsequent prints may be run from the dupe negative until such time as the film is damaged and then a new dupe negative can be made from

227

the interpositive. Grading can change during the safety process but it is unlikely. Sound quality should not change at all.

Wrapping Up

With the film completed and all staff finished with, it is now up to the post-production supervisor to wrap up. All materials *must* be labelled clearly, boxed and safely stored in a film vault. Some legal requirements insist that all components be kept for a minimum of seven years, others for life. A complete and comprehensive list *must* be made of all copies delivered to all parties, e.g., production company, producer, vault, distributor, TV station, broker or completion guarantor. Notes referring to the state of the program – when completed – will save many hours later when components for trailers, or such things as cut downs are to be made.

Captions For The Deaf

In 1983 the Supertext Subtitle Service was set up to give access to television to a million Australians whose deafness or hearing impairment had deprived them of the major communications medium of our time.

This service allows subtitles to be transmitted in a hidden part of the television signal. They are viewed by receiving the signal through a teletext decoder. These titles are boxed in a single coloured background and their colouring and positioning identifies individual speakers in dialogue.

This hidden signal can be transmitted by the ABC, the three major commercial networks and many regional stations.

Procedures

To subtitle a program the captioner requires a video tape copy with visual time code – Audio 2 (*matching the master*). A script is helpful where there is unusual vocabulary.

The subtitles are created and recorded on a floppy disc. This is sent with the master to a television station for encoding (Channels 7 and 9 in Sydney have encoding facilities, Channel 10 in Melbourne). This encoded master is now ready for broadcasting by any television station.

When copies are required, the encoded master can be sent to any production house for dubbing. The message remains on the subtitled master for all dubs thereafter.

Open subtitled copies can also be produced from this.

This process of creating the subtitles takes one week. It is wise to allow a further few days for the encoding process.

Non-Linear Post-Production

Stephen F Smith

The modern introduction of non-linear post-production has changed for good some of the traditional post-production methods. Many procedures have been greatly simplified. This chapter will look at the changes which have been brought about by the new technology, as well as some of the consequences and areas of concern.

We will look at the following areas:

* tape shoot – tape finish

* 25 FPS (frames per second) film shoot – tape finish

* 24 FPS film shoot – tape finish

Tape Shoot – Tape Finish

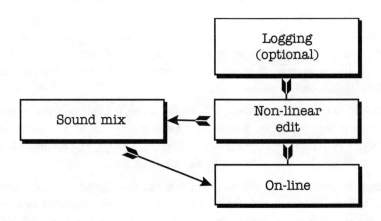

A non-linear edit of tape shoot and tape finish is not dissimilar to a traditional linear off-line edit. Because non-linear systems all have powerful databases for keeping track of footage, it is a good idea to take full advantage of this feature.

Logging Of Footage

Usually logging can be done with a small Powerbook or Laptop computer and a nine-pin serial interface VTR (i.e. SVHS and Beta SP). Accurate logging can save a lot of time when it comes to the actual edit. The computer controls the VTR while tracking frame accurately, all time code information.

The logging process, particularly for bigger projects, allows you not only to screen your footage, but fully organise the edit even before digitising (i.e., dubbing sound and vision on to disc drives) any footage. In traditional terms, logging is a very sophisticated 'paper cut' resulting in a highly organised database which can be used to easily sort material during the non-linear edit.

Most logging software allows you to make up any criteria in the creation of the footage database. These criteria can be headings such as Scene, Description, Comments, Soundrolls, Character, Subject, etc., as well as time code, source reels and other information required for the final EDL (edit decision list). Once the information is in the database, the process of finding shots becomes quite easy. For example, you may want to find all the shots in Scene 1, described as MCU (medium close up) of Joe Bloggs, which, in Comments are described as 'OK takes'. Simply 'sift' through the database or bin using the above criteria and the computer will do the rest. Remember, the database is only as good as the information you input, so be organised and consistent. If you type in 'MCU' as a description, don't change halfway through the logging to 'medium close up'.

DIGITISING FOOTAGE

As mentioned earlier, digitising is the process of dubbing sound and vision onto disc drives to be used in the edit, i.e., converting an analogue image to a digital one.

Non-linear systems vary in the amount of 'on-line' storage capacity. The varying factors include picture and sound resolution, storage size and number of disc drives. Simply put, the higher the picture and sound resolution, the more storage required. A general rule of thumb is, 1 Gb (gigabyte) of disc storage holds approximately one hour of VHSquality picture and two channels of full digital quality sound.

Although digitising is a real time process, you should allow for tape changes, spooling time, etc. The benchmark here would be a ratio of approximately 1.5 to 1, depending on how quick the VTR is. In other words, for every 1 hour of footage to be digitised, allow 1.5 to 2 hours of assistant's or editor's time to do the job.

Using the logged information, the editor or assistant can sort through all the 'bins' created, organising the footage in source reel order to help minimise the digitising process. During the course of the edit, the editor can easily sift through the bins using the database created at the logging stage to find the appropriate shot.

Once picture lock off has been completed, an EDL is created for the on-line session.

25 FPS FILM SHOOT – TAPE FINISH

FINISH FIRST

This may sound a bit like putting the cart before the horse, but there are actually three different methods of finishing on tape. The method you choose will affect the process you use to transfer your rushes. So let's first look at how you may want to finish.

TAPE FINISH #1

Pull NG (no good) takes (optional) and transfer print takes to tape. This would be a 'one light' transfer only to analog tape, i.e., SVHS or Beta SP. The negative, after telecine transfer, is sent to the negative matcher where it is logged into their computer system. Upon completion of the non-linear edit and picture lock off, an EDL is generated based on time codes or key codes, depending upon the non-linear system you are working with. Using this EDL, the neg matcher pulls takes from the camera stop to camera stop and assembles them in shot order. The negative is then graded and transferred to Beta SP or other broadcast tape format. A new EDL containing the new source time code numbers is computed by the neg matcher for the final on-line.

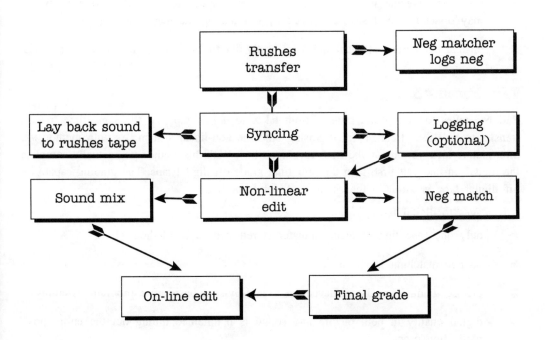

Advantages:

∗   all shots are graded in program order using a high-end telecine for the grade;

∗   rushes are transferred using a less expensive telecine by the operator only, not requiring attendance by director or DOP;

∗   the final on-line edit is faster due to fewer source reel changes.

Tape Finish #2

Pull NG takes (optional) and transfer print takes to tape. All grading takes place at the initial telecine transfer and recorded to Beta SP or other broadcast format. After the non-linear edit is completed and you have picture lock off, an EDL is created and you head straight to on-line.

Advantages:

∗   no neg matcher is required, meaning less handling of film and less number crunching;

∗   there is no need for a second telecine transfer, providing some cost savings.

Disadvantages:

∗   since footage is not graded in shot order, there may be extra grading required of some shots at a later date, depending on how they match up when cut together;

∗   a highend telecine and grader are required for a much longer period up front, which may offset any cost savings gained by eliminating the neg matching;

∗   on-line will be less efficient and more costly due to the greater amount of source reels.

Tape Finish #3

Pull NG takes (optional) and transfer print takes to *digital* tape. At the same time, record transfer to SVHS or Beta SP for digitising onto the non-linear system. As with method #2, after picture lock off, output and EDL for the on-line. With this method you actually complete the digital on-line edit first, then do your final grade off digital tape. The grading capability off digital tape is virtually the same as direct from film.

Advantages to digital tape:

∗   only one 'one light' telecine transfer is required as in Method #1;

∗   no neg matching is required;

∗   precise grading can be achieved on a shot-by-shot basis after program assembly;

∗   digital quality in both picture and sound is maintained throughout the entire post-production process.

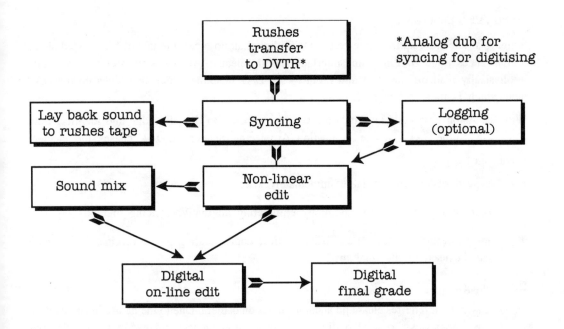

Disadvantages to digital tape:

*   digital tape stock is more expensive than analogue stock. Again, this may offset some initial cost savings;

*   a Digital Edit Suite is currently about twice the hourly rate of a conventional analog suite. As well, there is still the lack of efficiency in the edit suite due to the greater number of source reels;

*   to take full advantage of digital technology, a digital telecine should be used recording straight to a digital VTR. This will cost you more money for rushes transfer.

SYNCING

There are three options available for syncing of rushes:

*   sync at telecine during transfer of rushes;

*   sync rushes tape to tape using an edit controller device such as Shot Lister;

*   sync rushes on the non-linear system or assistant's work station.

SYNC AT TELECINE

Syncing at telecine requires time-coded DAT (digital audio tape), the use of time coded slates ('smart slates') and DAT machine interlocked with telecine. At rushes transfer the time code is physically read off the slate and input to the DAT machine which then cues up the DAT tape which is then locked to telecine.

With the Aston time code system, time code is burned into the film edge and identical time code is fed to the DAT machine on location. At telecine transfer the DAT 'chases' the telecine.

Advantages:

∗   synced rushes are available immediately after rushes transfer;

∗   there is a possible cost saving by eliminating alternative syncing methods;

∗   most telecine logs can 'trace back' to time codes relating to the original DAT which can be used in the final mix.

Disadvantages:

∗   this method requires clear and accurate slates on camera. Due to the nature of production, this is not always possible, particularly with action sequences and documentaries. Without clear slates it becomes a matter of trial and error which takes up expensive telecine time, possibly offsetting any cost savings;

∗   accuracy and technical quality of time code on the DAT is a must. Again, this may not be possible due to the rigours of location production.

SYNC TAPE TO TAPE

This method requires an edit controller such as 'Shot Lister'. Using a time-coded DAT machine and Beta SP or SVHS, the rushes are synced directly to the rushes tape. This tape is then used for digitising and/or rushes screening. After the edit, a trace back to the original DAT time code is done and a new sound EDL is given to the mixing facility.

Advantage:

∗   at the digitising stage, sound and picture can be digitised simultaneously. This is a requirement for some non-linear systems as they are limited to only tracking one time code source.

Disadvantages:

∗   tape to tape is time consuming as it requires the traditional method of not only finding sync, although time code slates speed up this process, but then recording the track real time to tape;

∗   once you have picture lock off, a lot of number crunching must take place to trace back to the original DAT time code using yet another computer;

∗   once the footage is digitised, there is still the process of breaking the slates and footage down and placing shots into respective 'Bins' or 'Picture Galleries'.

SYNC – NON-LINEAR

Both Avid and Lightworks are now providing smaller systems for use by the assistant editor at an assistant's work station. These systems can be used for syncing and logging of rushes which will greatly simplify and streamline the whole process. The picture and sound are digitised separately; this is a real time process. After syncing the rushes, the audio is laid back onto the rushes tape for screening.

Advantages:

* syncing non-linear is a much faster process. Unlike conventional tape to tape methods where each slate has to be recorded in full, after finding the in and out points on non-linear simply click the mouse and the entire slate is laid down and you are ready to move onto the next;

* since the footage has already been digitised, it is a simple process to break down the slates into appropriate 'Bins' or 'Picture Galleries' and transfer files to the main editing system;

* both Avid and Lightworks have the ability to track picture and sound time code and output as a separate EDL for each.

24 FPS FILM SHOOT – FILM FINISH

You will be pleased to know that this process has been greatly simplified with non-linear editing. In the past, if you were cutting 24 FPS on tape, there was always the conversion problem from 25 FPS to 24 FPS. Just to give a brief overview of 25 FPS/24 FPS: on tape there exists a 25-frame 'hole' which needs to be filled. With 24 FPS, there are only 24 frames to fill it, therefore you need an extra frame. (For the purists, this equates to one field every twelve frames.) When playing back video which has recorded film transferred at 24 FPS, you will see what appears to be a jump or duplicate frame every second. This is particularly noticeable on long pans and zooms or tracking shots. Likewise, there was always the problem for the editor to determine what frame was actually being cut. Then there was always the negative matching problem in determining which was the actual duplicate field or frame. Now, fortunately, all of this is behind us.

Both Avid and Lightworks have standardised a method which deals effectively with 24 FPS. The film shot at 24 FPS is actually transferred at telecine at the video rate of 25 FPS. This means there are no duplicate frames and the time code is frame accurate. The film is now running on tape at the faster rate of 25 FPS. Once the rushes have been digitised, the non-linear system plays back at the original speed of 24 FPS. The editor is now working at 24 FPS for the entire cut.

SYNCING

The simplest method of syncing rushes is on the non-linear system. Sound is digitised from DAT at speed. The DAT, recorded at 24 FPS, runs at speed with the film played back at 24 FPS. Syncing and logging are completed (refer to the section above entitled 'Sync – non-linear'). The next step is the lay back of sync sound to the rushes tape. The non-linear system actually speeds the sound up to 25 FPS matching the telecine rate on the rushes tape, giving

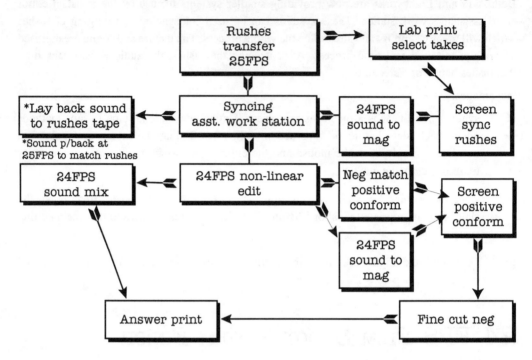

you sync rushes for screening. You also have the option of outputting sound at original 24 FPS to DAT for transfer to mag for screening of workprint sync rushes or positive conform for double head screening of cut film (more about this later).

TO PRINT OR NOT TO PRINT WORKPRINT

Since the introduction of non-linear editing, workprint has become an option in the budget. Recently there has been a lot of discussion regarding this. The general consensus, with which I am in full agreement, is that, at minimum, the cost of selected workprint and a positive conform should be included in the budget. There has been some movement on behalf of the labs to reduce the price of workprint, which makes this more palatable. To explain further, select workprint would be workprinting certain set ups or any takes which may be of concern to the director or DOP. A positive conform would consist of pulling full takes (stop to stop) based on the final EDL, printing and cutting the print. This can easily be done by the neg matcher and should be included in their quote. The sound, as explained before, can be taken directly from the non-linear system at 24 FPS, dubbed to mag and synced for a double head screening (either workprint or positive conform). If changes to the cut are required, re-cut on non-linear, output a change list, and re-conform the workprint. Although computers today are reliable, they are only as good as the information fed to them. A positive conform should be looked upon as an insurance policy, allowing all concerned to see the film as it was intended, on the big screen. You will also sleep better at night and just think how much money you will save on Valium!

Sound

Some non-linear systems have more sound capability than others to include, for example, audio dissolves, level control, EQ and multi-track. All non-linear systems are capable of digitising at full digital broadcast quality (44.1 kHz or 48 kHz sampling rate).

Sound for all projects can be handled in three ways:

1. The final tracks can be transferred from the Avid to time-coded DAT. This can then go to the audio facility and can be used in the final mix.

2. A separate EDL can be generated for the sound which relates to the original video source tapes. Using the EDL, the sound facility can do an 'auto track lay' from the source tapes nominating various tracks for final mixing.

3. Audio and picture files can be taken in digital form directly from Avid using OMFI (open media format interchange). Some non-linear track lay systems such as Avid's Audio/Vision support this format and can accept files directly from the Avid without having to re-lay dialogue or effects tracks used in the picture edit.

MARKETING AND DISTRIBUTION

Marketing And Distribution

Damien Parer

Audience Questionnaire

Q.1 Did you like the film...   A LOT..................☐
    (PLEASE TICK ONE BOX)   A LITTLE...................☐
                                                                                    NOT AT ALL...................☐

Q.2 What did you most like about the film? (PLEASE WRITE IN)

....

....

Q.3 And what did you least like about the film? (PLEASE WRITE IN)

....

....

Q.4 Which of the following statements most applies to you? PLEASE TICK ONE
    BOX

I WOULD RECOMMEND IT TO ALL MY FRIENDS.............................☐
I WOULD RECOMMEND IT TO MOST OF MY FRIENDS.......................☐
I WOULD RECOMMEND IT TO SOME OF MY FRIENDS.......................☐
I WOULDN'T RECOMMEND IT,
BUT I WOULDN'T TELL THEM NOT TO SEE IT.................................☐
I WOULD TELL THEM NOT TO SEE IT..☐

Q.5 Which of the following words or phrases do you feel best describe your reactions
    to the film? (YOU MAY TICK AS MANY AS YOU WISH)

EXCITING.................................☐	UNBELIEVABLE............................☐
FRIGHTENING...........................☐	WELL ACTED..............................☐
FAST MOVING.........................☐	CONFUSING.................................☐
POORLY ACTED.........................☐	UNCOMFORTABLE TO WATCH........☐
BORING...................................☐	SATIRICAL...................................☐
REALISTIC................................☐	INVOLVING..................................☐
EASY TO WATCH......................☐	ENJOYABLE...............................☐
SLOW MOVING.........................☐	SERIOUS.....................................☐
AMUSING................................☐	Any other comments...................☐
THREATENING.........................☐	....

Q.6 YOUR AGE: Years
Q.7 YOUR SEX: MALE   FEMALE

Marketing is as much a part of the producer's role as making the program in the first place.

Success for the film or TV program is not wholly dependent on its quality or topicality. We have all seen films which drew us in on a promise, only to be disappointed. Similarly, many fine films have died because of a bad campaign.

Selling films is an expert's job but you can assist the experts do their job better. Film making is a collaborative art form and the publicist, distributor, sales agent or TV programmer need to understand the film or program from the producer/ writer/ director's point of view so that the potential audience for the film is targeted and encouraged to attend or view it. In this way maximum revenue can be generated.

Publicists meet with distributors and exhibitors regularly to maximise returns. Campaigns can be changed, venues altered, screening times swapped. You, as the producer, need to be involved as much as you can both to learn and to help.

The best advertising in the world is personal recommendation. Therefore, good 'word-of-mouth' advertising is one of the strongest ways of building a successful cinema release.

THE TOOLS OF MARKETING

Much of the following work will become the responsibility of the distributor's or TV network's publicity or marketing department. However, it is important for you, as producer, to understand the processes. If you are making a low budget movie, you may have to carry out many of the following tasks yourself.

RESEARCH

The preferences and tastes of audiences are constantly changing. The composition of audiences is varying all the time. Different territories have different attendance and viewing patterns. The skill of turning research into valuable information is in the interpretation. Mixed with intuition and lateral thinking, research can make a huge difference to profitability.

Before you take the film or program into production, you must develop a clear idea of the target audience. You'll need to do this even before your raise the finance for the project. And you'll need to develop at least a draft marketing plan to convince your potential investors that you have thought about marketing the film, and have ideas about how to maximise its revenue.

To design a successful marketing plan you'll need to:

* identify the principal audience for the film;

* ascertain the genre: what other films can be compared to it in a marketing sense?

* develop strategies for publicity and promotion;

* ask whether the critics like the film;

* determine how fast the potential audience response to good word-of-mouth recommendations will be;

241

* estimate what revenue can be generated from each of the market segments, i.e., from cinema, TV and home video.

Once the film is finished, the distributor or TV network will be keen to test the film with an audience. This is an important factor in refining their marketing campaign.

PUBLICITY

Publicity is anything which promotes the film but is not paid for directly. Publicity starts in pre-production and continues through the life of a film until the investors, the producer or distributor feel that no further revenue can be obtained. It is most effective just before the major release. To maximise publicity's effect you should plan to:

* Employ a unit publicist during the production. Make sure you keep them informed about progress and work with them closely.

* Release a film or television program nationally rather than regionally to maximise the more widespread forms of promotion, e.g., TV programs which are broadcast in all states, magazines which are sold nationally.

* Ensure that good production stills are taken by the stills photographer for black and white and colour release. Find out what the unit publicist needs. Ensure that all major moments of the story are covered; portraits of the lead actors in character are very useful to have too.

* Press releases – tell the trade press early and keep potential sources of publicity informed. They get tired of chasing you and may not be as co-operative as you want when you want them.

* Seek out new angles for stories.

* Keep the press kit up to date.

* The distributor will usually arrange press screenings for critics and other people like radio announcers.

* Clips from the film or TV program should be available for use in promotional situations, e.g., TV interviews.

* Enter the film in appropriate film and TV festivals. It may be useful for stars, director and producer to attend.

* Run preview screenings to selected audiences or members of the public to test audience reaction and to accelerate word-of-mouth advertising.

* Ensure that merchandising is available at the release date.

* Music from the film can be released before the opening and will help promote the film.

* Cinema trailers need to be made, in consultation with the distributor.

* Posters and day bills also need to be designed.

* Study guides can be a useful publicity and marketing tool.

ADVERTISING

This is paid promotion and should be in proportion to box office returns. The film's profitability is dependent on spending decisions. Too little and you jeopardise the film's chances; too much and you waste money. Early agreement needs to be reached with the distributor about the level of expenditure on paid advertising.

Advertising budgets should be 10-25 per cent of gross box office returns.

Some types of advertising are:

* television and radio commercials

* newspaper advertisements

* billboards

* competitions and promotions

CAMPAIGN

A carefully planned campaign will have the following elements:

* Press kit containing synopsis, film running time, list of cast and crew, their biogs, selected photographs with suitable captions, favourable reviews and awards.

* Poster. An invitation to see the film. Contains title and graphic design of lettering, lead line under the title, contracted credits of lead cast and crew.

* Cinema trailer.

* Television and radio commercials.

* Artwork for press ads.

* Video film clips for talk shows and TV promotion.

* Production stills, captioned with a brief description of the scene and the character names and actors in it. The title of the film and the producer and director should also be included in the captions.

* Press screenings.

* Promotional screenings – premiers or previews specially targeted at the film's audience demographic.

✱ Press releases pre-planned to coincide with magazine and newspaper run-up time.

✱ Market research may be undertaken into the effectiveness of the various marketing items, e.g. the poster, the trailer and maybe even the film itself.

The *Trade Practices Act*

Section 52 of the Act states: 'A corporation shall not, in trade or commerce, engage in conduct that is misleading or deceptive or is likely to mislead or deceive'.

Here are some areas to be aware of:

• Trailers and advertisements cannot show scenes or photographs which are not in the program.

• Promises must be fulfilled. Claims must match the program content.

• Care should be taken with susceptible audiences, e.g., children can be easily fooled by advertising and the Act is designed to protect them. Programs made for a more sophisticated audience may be allowed a little more latitude.

DELIVERY ITEMS REQUIRED BY THE DISTRIBUTOR

FILM & VIDEO MATERIALS

35 mm feature
internegative
textless background neg. of main and end titles and any superimposition within the film
magnetic sub master – 3 track separate mixed dialogue, separate mixed music and separate mixed sound effects
mixed music and effects track
optical sound track
magnetic tape (15 ips) of music composed and recorded for the film
release print

35 mm trailer
interneg textless background magnetic sub master
music & effects track release print

video
1" PAL & NTSC sub master with sound track cassettes

promo reel 1" PAL & NTSC sub master with sound track cassettes
television commercials 1" PAL & NTSC sub master with sound track cassettes

NOTE

If the cinema, television or home video tapes vary in content then printing or duplicating materials must be made available for each version.

DOCUMENTATION

* Copies of all agreements in relation to the underlying rights chain of title. This must include any licence or agreement allowing the production company to make the film and sell the rights.

* Copies of all agreements with the director and the starring artists in the film, and other relevant cast and crew, showing:

  - contracted advertising or screen credit obligations for cast and crew;

  - extra payments to be made in the future (including any share in the revenues);

  - any approvals which the director or lead cast have.

* Title report usually through Brylawski, Cleary & Komen, in Washington, DC.

* Clearances for stock shots or library footage used in the film.

* Final screenplay.

* Post-production or release script.

* Music cue sheets.

* Composer's contract, publishing agreement or relevant licences confirming rights to synchronisation or performance of all music in the film.

* Current errors & omissions insurance policy with distributor and/or sales agent named as additional insureds.

* Laboratory access letter allowing the distributor to order prints and other necessary material. Letter should state that the producer is not liable for lab costs incurred by the distributor.

* Certificate of origin.

* Certificate of nationality.

* Certificate of authorship for the screenplay (for France).

✻   Censorship clearances and rating.

✻   Colour and black and white still photograph contact sheets.

✻   A variety of colour and black and white production stills, clearly captioned.

✻   Necessary materials for stills duplication, e.g. negatives, transparencies.

✻   Press kit. Lead cast and crew list and biographies, synopsis, production notes, press items and reviews.

✻   Merchandising. Any book, record or other tie-ins.

✻   Complete set of posters, day bills and samples of any other promotional or advertising material, including key artwork if available.

✻   Film length at 24 and 25 FPS.

WHEN DO YOU INVOLVE THE DISTRIBUTOR OR BROADCASTER?

You should involve the distributor or broadcaster in marketing your film as early as possible – that is, after you have developed the package consisting of a satisfactory, working script, a director and maybe one or two lead actors.

You'll need to speak to a distributor or sales agent early on because most film investment packages require a pre-sale or minimum distribution guarantee to reassure investors of the financial viability of the deal. In this case the producer should try to leave as much 'blue sky' as possible. A pre-sale backed by an irrevocable letter of credit from a bank can, of course, be cashed at a bank to provide investment funds.

After production has commenced you or your sales agent can stimulate further sales in unsold territories by providing a promotional or show reel of various scenes, together with press kits.

Sales can also be achieved when the film is completed and promotional and advertising materials are available.

If you have been unable to pre-sell the film at all (e.g., perhaps it is a low-budget film or feature documentary) you can speak to exhibitors about 'four-walling' the film. You will probably need to guarantee the total cost of exhibition, e.g., 'house nut' and advertising costs.

NEGOTIATING A DISTRIBUTION CONTRACT

Of course you would consult your lawyer before and during these negotiations. A guide to elements to be found in most contracts:

* description of the product;

* rights granted – they may include theatrical, non-theatrical, broadcast, television and video. You may wish to retain rights to pay TV, US network and merchandising rights;

* publicity and promotional material to be supplied including trailer, posters and press kits;

* territory – a geographic description of the area in which the distributor is licensed to market the film, e.g., North America, Australasia, Africa, UK or Europe;

* term of the contract;

* definition of distribution rights over the film – Can you sell it off outright?

* accounting – producer's right to audit the film returns from the books of the distributor and the exhibitor;

* definition of terms like 'film rental', 'distribution expenses', 'gross receipts';

* calculation of royalties – a definition of 'royalties' and how they are calculated;

* advance payments, buy-out or minimum distribution guarantee; time frame of payments;

* exploitation obligation 'windows';

* censorship – contract could become void if the film is rejected by censor;

* delivery dates – when do you have to deliver the picture by?

* warranties:

  – copyright

  – no defamation or obscenity

  – debts, etc

* minimum and maximum length of the film;
* income split distributor/producer;
* standard delivery items – a guide to the items usually required by the distributor.

EXPORT INCENTIVES

The following information has been provided by Jennifer Huby, Tress, Cocks and Maddox.

The Export Market Development Grants Scheme is available to film producers to assist and encourage them in marketing their films overseas, through the provision of cash grants.

WHO IS ELIGIBLE FOR A GRANT?

To be eligible for a grant you must firstly, be either an Australian resident, a company incorporated or carrying on business in Australia, or a partnership carrying on business in Australia. Secondly, you must have incurred 'eligible expenditure' during the grant year (July–June) of $30,000 or more.

WHAT IS ELIGIBLE EXPENDITURE?

To qualify as 'eligible expenditure', the expenditure must:

* be incurred by the person making the claim;

* be primarily for the purpose of creating or seeking opportunities for, or increasing demand for, Australian goods and services in overseas countries; and

* be comprised of certain types of expenses, such as the following:

    – expenses of an overseas agent for the purpose of market research, advertising or seeking out business;

    – expenses associated with providing free samples outside Australia;

    – expenses for packaging and labelling of goods;

    – expenses for foreign language training;

    – expenses for foreign registrations and insurance of Australian inventions, trademarks, copyrights and designs, and

    – expenses for hotels, meals and entertainment on overseas visits for you or your agent (but not a sales representative).

THE FILM AND MUSIC INDUSTRIES

In the film industry, grants are payable in respect of certain expenditure including that incurred in promoting or seeking out opportunities for the sale (or intended sale) of rights in an Australian film to overseas distributors or TV networks who will further exploit those rights.

Similarly, in the music industry, promotional expenditure may qualify for grant entitlement if it comes within the distinct categories specified in the legislation and is for the purpose of creating or increasing demand for the export sale of goods (records, cassettes, discs) or the sale of copyright and associated rights in the songs and sound recordings to people overseas.

To be eligible to make a claim you must hold the rights in the film or music as owner or exclusive licensee but not as an agent.

How Much Can You Claim?

If your expenditure is approved as eligible expenditure then you are entitled to receive a grant equal to 50 per cent of that expenditure over $15,000, subject to a maximum of $250,000 in any one year. After you have received two grants, further entitlements are subject to your level of export earnings and generally you cannot claim more than eight times.

Handling Hollywood

So you have decided to take the plunge into the shark-infested waters of Los Angeles. Movie deals are done there every minute of the day. No, they don't seem to sleep - well, they do with each other but that's funding your film the hard way.

Be very enthusiastic! Get your act together. Until you know clearly what you want to achieve by the visit, then you will achieve very little.

Do the groundwork before your arrival. Are you seeking pre-sales, selling a completed film or just having an initial look around?

You will need to contact and see quite different people for each of your film projects. There are hundreds of companies in LA. Often they have found a niche and make their money in their own specialised area. You need to identify the best ones for your films.

The Australian Film Commission, friends, associates and former pilgrims will assist you to draw up a short list of people and corporations most likely to be able to help you. Write to them in advance of your arrival. Articulate clearly what you want from them and inform them of your arrival date and hotel. Don't tell them your departure date, it's useful as a negotiating tool later. Don't forget to pack lots of NTSC copies of the film, brochures and your CV.

Now, if it's important enough for you to go to the Land of the Free to seek the golden fleece (that is, you fleece them more than they fleece you), then you should look, feel and act the part. My hero, David O Selznick, says 'There are only two classes, first class and no class'. They didn't have business class then but then DOS knew a thing or two about making movies. Stay in a hotel that answers the phone with the name of the establishment, rather than 'hello' or 'YMCA'. Be comfortable and stay in the area where the action is. LA is a Sydney sprawled six times. Which leads me to ground transport.

Taxis are difficult to get and expensive, but hiring a car is not. Stretch limos are abundant but you may have to wait until your second visit to the dream factory when the results of this trip have paid off.

So there you are, newly arrived, bright-eyed and bushy-tailed in the smog. Get on the phone as soon as possible and start making those appointments, including breakfast. A lot of business is done at that time of day.

Those readers who have persevered with this piece will now be rewarded. The key to having the movie capital of the world work for you is to understand how they work for themselves. Al Daff, an Australian who was a US studio chief, said 'They will kiss you out the door'.

Pauline Kael, the movie critic, put it another way: 'In Hollywood one can die from encouragement'. Executives in the film industry in the USA have perfected the art of hedging their bets. They will rarely say 'yes', and never say 'no'. They are the most courteous, witty and warm people in the world.

The truth is that selling films is difficult and competitive. Your deal needs to be so tempting and full of potential advancement for them personally, that they can't keep their hands off it. Otherwise you will be 'kissed out the door', feel warm and loved, and have no deal in place.

And that's show biz.

Between appointments you may wish to avail yourself of the amusing side of LA. Don't miss the tour of Universal Studios, it's on every day. Stand on the corner of Hollywood and Vine where they discovered all the stars, and while you're down there, call in to Larry Edmunds Cinema Bookshop, the biggest and best in the world. Stay enthusiastic, keep repeating your mantra, stay off the nose candy, and have faith in yourself.

And remember, as you sip your coffee looking out on Rodeo Drive, that the good-looking waitress who served you is one of 50,000 actors in LA who are hopeful of making it, and if they think it's worth a try, why shouldn't you?

MAJOR FESTIVALS AND MARKETS

American Film Institute International Film Festival

2021 N Western Avenue
Los Angeles CA 90027
USA

Tel: (1) 213 856 7707
Fax: (1) 213 462 4049

American Film Market

10850 Wiltshire Boulevarde
9th Floor
Los Angeles CA 90024
USA

Tel: (1) 310 446 1000
Fax: (1) 310 446 1600

American Film & Video Festival
(educational films only)

8050 Milwaukee Avenue
Niles Illinois 60648
USA

Tel: (1) 708 698 6440
Fax: (1) 708 823 1561

Annecy International Animation Film Festival (Alternate years)

2, boulevard du Lycee
74013 Annecy
France

Tel: (33) 50 574 172
Fax: (33) 50 678 195

Berlin International Film Festival
(includes Panorama, Youth Film Festival)

Budapester Strasse 50
D-1000 Berlin 30
Germany

Tel: (49) 30 254 890
Fax: (49) 30 254 89249

Cannes International Film Festival
(includes Film Market, Directors' Fortnight, Critics Week)

71 Rue Faubourg St Honoré
75008 Paris
France

Tel: (33) 1 42 669 220
Fax: (33) 1 42 666 885

'Cinema Giovani': Turin International Festival of Young Cinema

Piazza San Carlo 161
10123 Turin
Italy

Tel: (39) 11 562 3309
Fax: (39) 11 562 9796

MIPCOM – Cannes

179 Avenue Victor Hugo
75116 Paris
France

Tel: (33) 1 44 344 444
Fax: (33) 1 44 344 400

Chicago International Film Festival

415 North Dearborn Street
Chicago Illinois 60610
USA

Tel: (1)   312 644 3400
Fax: (1) 312 644 0784

Cork Film Festival

Hatfield House
Tobin Street
Cork
Ireland

Tel: (353) 21 271 711
Fax: (353) 21 275 945

'Films de Femmes': Créteil International Women's Film Festival

Maison des Arts
Place Salvador Allende
94000 Créteil
France

Tel: (33) 1 49 803 898
Fax: (33) 1 49 990 410

Edinburgh International Film Festival

Film House
88 Lothian Road
Edinburgh EH3 9BZ
UK

Tel: (441) 31 228 4051
Fax: (441) 31 229 5501

Festival dei Popoli

Via Castellani 8
50122 Florence
Italy

Tel: (39) 55 294 353
Fax: (39) 55 213 698

Hof International Film Days

Lothstrasse 28
D-8000 Munich 2
Germany

Tel: (49) 89 129 7422
Fax: (49) 89 123 6868

Hong Kong International Film Festival

Level 7, Administration Building
Hong Kong Cultural Centre
10 Salisbury Road
Tsim Sha Tsui
Kowloon
Hong Kong

Tel: (852) 2734 2900
Fax: (852) 2366 5206

India International Film Festival

Directorate of Film Festivals
Lok Nayak Bhavan
4th Floor Khan Market
New Delhi 110003
India

Tel: (91) 11 615 953
Fax: (91) 11 694 920

International Documentary Film Festival

PO Box 98
CH-1260 Nyon
Switzerland

Tel: (41) 22 361 6060
Fax: (22) 361 7071

International Film Festival of Mannheim-Heidelberg

Collini Center Galerie
68161 Mannheim
Germany

Tel: (49) 621 102 943
Fax: (49) 621 921 564

Karlovy Vary International Film Festival

Valdstejnska 1
118 11 Prague 1
Czech Republic

Tel: (+42) 2 513 2473
Fax: (+42) 2 537 055

Locarno International Film Festival

Via della Posta 6
CH-6600 Locarno
Switzerland

Tel: (41) 93 310 232
Fax: (41) 93 317 465

251

London Film Festival

National Film Theatre
South Bank, Waterloo
London SE1 8XT
United Kingdom

Tel: (441) 71 815 1323
Fax: (441) 71 633 0786

Melbourne International Film Festival

PO Box 2206
Fitzroy Mail Centre
Fitzroy Vic 3065
Australia

Tel: (03) 417 2011
Fax: (03) 417 3804

MIFED Italy

Largo Domodossola 1
20145 Milan
Italy

Tel: (39) 2 480 12912
Fax: (39) 2 499 77020

MIP-TV

Maidem Organisation
179 Avenue Victor Hugo
75116 Paris
France

Tel:(33) 1 44 344 444
Fax: (33) 1 44 344 400

Monte Carlo Television Market

CCA7 boulevard Louis II
98000 Monte Carlo
Monaco

Tel: (33) 93 304 944
Fax: (33) 93 507 014

Montreal International Festival of New Cinema and Video

3726 boulevard St-Laurent
Montreal Quebec
Canada H2X 2V8

Tel: (1) 514 843 4725
Fax: (1) 514 843 4631

Montreal World Film Festival

1455 boulevard Maisonneuve Ouest
Montreal Quebec
Canada H3G 1M8

Tel: (1) 514 848 3883
Fax: (1) 514 848 3886

Moscow International Film Festival

(Alternate years)

Interfilm
10 Khokhlovsky Pereulok
109028 Moscow
Russia

Tel: (+7) 095 227 8924
Fax: (+7) 095 227 0107
(the 0 in 095 is correct, do not omit)

New Directors-New Films

Film Society of Lincoln Center
165 West 65th Street
New York NY 10023-6595
USA

Tel: (1) 212 875 5628
Fax: (1) 212 875 5636

New York Film Festival

140 West 65th Street
New York NY 10023
USA

Tel: (1) 212 875 5628
Fax: (1) 212 875 5636

Oberhausen International Short Film Festival

Grillostrasse 34,
46042 Oberhausen
Germany

Tel: (49) 208 807 008
Fax: (49) 208 825 5413

Rotterdam Film Festival

PO Box 21696
Rotterdam   3001 AR
The Netherlands

Tel: (31) 10 41 18080
Fax: (31) 10 41 35132

San Francisco International Film Festival

San Francisco Film Society
1521 Eddy Street
San Francisco CA 94115-4102
USA

Tel: (1) 415 567 4641
Fax: (1) 415 921 5032

San Sebastian International Film Festival

Apartado Correos 397
20080 San Sebastian
Spain

Tel: (34) 43 481 212
Fax: (34) 43 481 218

Seattle International Film Festival

Egyptian Theater
801 E Pine Street
Seattle WA 98122
USA

Tel: (1) 206 324 9996
Fax: (1) 206 324 9998

Sydney Film Festival

PO Box 25
Glebe NSW 2037
Australia

Tel: (02) 660 3844
Fax: (02) 692 8793

Taormina Film Festival

Via Pirandello 31
98039 Taormina
Italy

Tel: (39) 942 21142
Fax: (39) 942 23348

Telluride Film Festival

Box B1156
Hanover NH   03755
USA

Tel: (1) 603 643 1255
Fax: (1) 603 643 5938

Tokyo International Film Festival

4F Landic Ginza Building, II
1-6-5 Ginza
Chuo-ku
Tokyo 104
Japan

Tel: (81) 3 3563 6305
Fax: (81) 3 3563 6310

Toronto Festival of Festivals

c/- Cinemateque Ontario
70 Carlton Street
Toronto Ontario
Canada M5B 1L7

Tel: (1) 416 967 7371
Fax: (1) 416 967 9477

Venice International Film Festival

Ca'Guistinian 1364A
San Marco
30124 Venice
Italy

Tel: (39) 41 521 8711
Fax: (39) 41 522 7539

'Women in Film' International Film Festival

6464 Sunset Boulevard
Suite 530
Hollywood CA 90028
USA

Tel: (1) 213 463 6040
Fax: (1) 213 463 0963

**World Festival of Animated Films –
Animafest Zagreb**

(Alternate years)

Festa
Zagreb Concert Management
Kneza Mislavi 18
41000 Zagreb
Croatia

Tel: (385) 41 410 131
Fax: (385) 41 443 022

NOTE

The AFC's Marketing Branch can provide further details of festivals and markets.

The *BFI Guide to International Film and Video Festivals* is available from the British Council in Sydney.

Lists are also published regularly in *Movie & TV Marketing*.

MARKETING BUDGET

PRELIMINARY/FINAL

FILM TITLE

_____

PRODUCTION COMPANY

_____

PRODUCER

_____

DATE

_____

SAMPLE MARKETING BUDGET

BUDGET SUMMARY

CODE	DETAILS	$
A	PRINTING MATERIALS	
B	PUBLICITY MATERIALS	
C	PROMOTION MATERIALS	
D	AUDITIONS & EVENTS MATERIALS	
E	ADVERTISING	
F	ADMINISTRATION	
G	MISCELLANEOUS	
	TOTAL $	

PRINTING MATERIALS

A   FEATURE $

1 x 35 mm Composite Colour Release Print

1 x 35 mm Magnetic Final Mix Sound Track (Master)

1 x 35 mm Inter Negative

1 x 35 mm Background – Main & End Titles

1 x 35 mm Magnetic Music & Effects Track

1 x 16 mm Composite Colour Release Print

1 x 16 mm Magnetic Final Mix Sound Track (Master)

1 x 16 mm Inter Negative

1 x 16 mm Inter Negative (For TV Printing)

1 x 16 mm Background – Main & End Titles

1 x 16 mm Magnetic Music & Effects Track

Production Costs Mixing/Transfers 16/35

International Sound Track

TRAILER

1 x 35 mm Composite Colour Release Print

1 x 35 mm Magnetic Final Mix Sound Track (Master)

1 x 35 mm Inter Negative

1 x 35 mm Background – Titles

1 x 35 mm Magnetic Music & Effects Track

1 x 16 mm Composite Colour Release Print

1 x 16 mm Magnetic Final Mix Sound Track (Master)

1 x 16 mm Inter Negative

1 x 16 mm Background – Titles

1 x 16 mm Magnetic Music & Effects Track

Production Costs Mixing/Transfers 16/35

International Sound Track

Freights

Customs

Insurances

Censorship Clearances

TOTAL $

PUBLICITY MATERIALS

B   Release Scripts Feature $

            35 mm Footage

            16 mm Footage

Release Scripts Trailer

            35 mm Footage

            16 mm Footage

Production Costs

Printing Costs ...... copies @ ......

Press Kits (including Biographies, Synopses,
        Running Time, Complete Credits,
        Advertising Examples)

Black & White Publicity Stills ..... size ..... sets @

Colour Publicity Stills .....size .....sets @

Colour brochures (English/Multilingual)

Posters:

        Day bills

        One Sheeters

        Handbills

Freight

Customs

Insurance

                            TOTAL $

PROMOTIONAL MATERIALS

C Sample Merchandising Materials $

        T-Shirts

        Badges

        Coasters

        Toys

        Books

        Records/CDS

        Other

Educational Promotion Kits

Festival Printings

Direct Mail Postage/Couriers

Freight

Customs

Insurance

Censorship Clearance

Subtitling Costs

Translation Costs

                        TOTAL $

SAMPLE MARKETING BUDGET

AUDITIONS & EVENTS

D $

35 mm Viewing Prints – Feature

35 mm Viewing Prints – Trailer

Master Video Tape Recording 1" or 2"

Pan & Scanned Master Video Tape Recording 1" or 2".

Sony U-Matic Cassettes

PAL No.....@....

NTSC No....@....

Secam No...@....

Entertainment – Media/Agents/Distributors

Invitations

Business Cards

Hand Bills

Front of House

Radio Commercials:

        Safety Copy Radio Commercial Mixing Elements

        Sample Set Radio Commercials – 1/4" Tape

TV Commercials:

        Safety Copy TC Commercial Mixing Elements

             16 mm Film/Video Tape

        Sample Set TV commercials –

             16 mm Film/Video Tape

Freights

Customs

Insurance

Censorship Clearance

Hire of Screening Theatres

Hire of Video Equipment

                                   TOTAL $

259

SAMPLE MARKETING BUDGET

ADVERTISING

E $

Cinema Papers (Cannes Edition)

Le Bulletin

Variety

Screen International

Television Business International

Hollywood Reporter

Festival Magazines

Other

Publicist Fee

Creation of Press Advertisements

Artwork

Brochures

TOTAL $

SAMPLE MARKETING BUDGET

ADMINISTRATION

F $

Unit Costs:

Telephone/Fax

Postage

Interpreters

Translators

Travel

Accommodation

Expenses (Miscellaneous)

Transport

Home Base

Cannes

London

New York

Los Angeles

Unit Salaries

Accounting Fees

Audit Fees

Legal Fees

TOTAL $

MISCELLANEOUS

G

$

TOTAL $

Marketing The Shorter Film

Frank Heimans

Marketing is a most complex and fascinating aspect of film making. It is the producer's responsibility and it involves research, promotion, distribution and exhibition. The role begins well before production commences and continues long after the answer print has been delivered.

The First Steps: Examine Your Motives

Before marketing begins, it is important for the producer to have thoroughly researched the marketplace. What are the chances of success in selling the film? Factors to be considered and questions the producer should ask him/herself are:

* How many films already exist on the subject of the proposed film? Who am I competing against?

* Is there a definite need for a film on this particular subject? Who will see it and where? Is it suitable for television, theatre, home video or only one or two of these media?

* Why is it so important that this film should be made? What do I hope to achieve?

* What age group and socioeconomic group am I aiming at?

* How long will the subject matter and theme of the film be current? A month, a year, a decade? What is its 'shelf life'? Will people still want to see it five or ten years from now? Will its value increase or decrease with age?

* What is the marketing budget for the film?

If these questions can be successfully answered, then the producer can begin to look at the marketplace.

Television — Australia

Australian television is the major area of sales for the shorter film and the way to reach millions of viewers to communicate your story. Being the most lucrative market, it is also the most difficult to penetrate. Television is structured into program formats and time slots. Program managers, who do most of the buying, need a program to fit into an existing format, for example, wildlife, travel or a general documentary series. These are mostly one-hour slots but the program must not exceed 48 minutes in length if one is dealing with a commercial network. Then there are time slots for drama programs (usually one hour and usually only on ABC-TV), children's programs (these can be anything from 25 minutes to 48 minutes in length), and so on. It is important to aim the film at a particular program format, however exceptional it may be.

Television program managers and network managers have the very responsible job of deciding whether or not to purchase a particular program. Naturally they are interested in concepts that treat subject matter in a different and refreshing way and in programs that entertain. They try to determine how well the film will 'rate', because high ratings increase advertising revenues. They will also take into account the promotable features of the film that they are buying. Program managers watch a lot of film and television and they are hard-nosed, commercially oriented people. They will only buy a fraction of material offered, because the criteria they use for deciding whether to purchase a program are:

* interest and appeal of the subject matter

* entertainment value

* standard of production, technically and artistically

* promotable features

* cost

* competing and similar programs on other channels

When selling a program to television in Australia, the producer always sells the exclusive right for a television network to screen that program a certain number of times over a specified period. A normal arrangement is to license the television network to screen the material twice over a three-year period. But if the price is high, the producer may have to settle for unlimited runs over seven years, or three runs over four years. It depends on the deal negotiated. Today, it has become necessary for producers to arrange a 'pre-sale' for their projects. A pre-sale is an arrangement whereby a television network will agree to purchase a program upon completion of the film on the condition that the program will be of a sufficiently high standard to meet Australian Broadcasting Tribunal standards, and if the film is completed by a particular date. A contract or letter of agreement is signed between the producer and the network and the producer can then use this conditional pre-sale to raise investment funds.

When selling television rights, be sure to engage a good lawyer to handle contracts. Never sell *all* television rights, because cable TV, satellite, subscription TV and home video rights can all be exploited separately.

Prices for a one-hour program in Australia can vary between $25,000 and $80,000 an hour, depending on type and quality for documentaries. Drama programs can achieve much higher prices.

In an ideal world, a producer should receive about 50 per cent of the production budget from domestic television sales. In practice, however, 30–35 per cent is more commonly achieved, leaving the greater part of the budget to be returned from overseas distribution.

TELEVISION – USA

The United States is the largest market, comprising the big three networks – NBC, ABC, CBS – an educational network, Public Broadcasting Service (PBS), and numerous pay/cable and radiated subscription television services.

The large networks offer the best return – between $100,000 and $200,000 per hour, but they rarely buy programs that they do not make or commission themselves. Very little foreign product is screened by these networks, for reasons perhaps only known to themselves. But if the product is exceptional enough, you may find a market. However, they are more likely to buy your film for stock footage use in their magazine-type programs at the usual rate of between $1,000–$3,000 per minute.

PBS television is more receptive and accessible, and quite a number of Australian productions have been sold and screened on PBS. Generally, their program standards are very high and they will only buy the best. The central buying office is in Washington, but they also have regional networks throughout the US which buy by voting on product. The more votes, the larger the area and the more is paid to the producer.

Cable and subscription television is a good and fast growing market. Home Box Office, Showtime, the Discovery Channel and others are challenging the commercial networks and provide real competition for the three giants. National Geographic started a documentary cable network late in 1984, and there are many cable companies specialising in sports, ethnic minority programming, R-rated movies, and all kinds of instructional and educational material. They have an insatiable appetite for material and some of them operate on a 24-hours-a-day basis. The subscriber pays a monthly fee and is fed material directly into the home. To the cable operators, ratings are not as important as viewer satisfaction and it is a case where television is not dealing with advertising agencies, but directly with the consumer. Here the consumer, not the networks, dictate the choice of programming.

Another way of distributing television programs is by syndication. This is a system whereby the program is sold city to city by salesmen employed by the syndication company. The process is time-consuming and it normally takes fully three years to penetrate the market, but the returns can be lucrative. Viacom is one such organisation that handles syndication, selling to non-network and network affiliates throughout the country.

TELEVISION – THE REST OF THE WORLD

Most of Europe is interested in high-quality drama and documentaries and good sales figures can be chalked up there if one has a good agent. In the box below you will find prices paid by most countries for 50-minute long documentaries. Drama programs can achieve up to 50 per cent more than the figures quoted.

Normally, the network will buy the English language version and make their own translation from the script. They will also do their own dubbing at their cost. All networks need at least the following materials:

* 16 mm colour print with the English soundtrack in optical sound, or a 1" or SP Betacam video master of the completed program in either PAL, SECAM or NTSC format;

* a script of all dialogue and narration in the program, with timings;

* a music cue sheet of all music used in the program, with clearances for use in their territory;

* an M & E track (mimed sound track with music and effects and excluding narration);

* publicity stills, a synopsis of the program, and press clippings or reviews.

Promotion At An International Film Market

One of the best ways to sell to television is to attend one of the international film fairs such as MIP-TV or MIPCOM in France, or the American Film Market in the US. It is a place where many buyers come to seek product. They rarely sign contracts on the spot, but many sales often materialise in the months following. The Australian Film Commission usually has a stand at the major film markets, and individual producers may share facilities to screen their product. Individual space can be hired, and expenditure could be eligible for a rebate under the Export Development Grants Scheme.

You will need to send at least two video cassettes of your program a month before the film market begins. The Australian Film Commission can usually arrange shipment. A good brochure is also a vital tool to promote the program. The brochure should give a clear indication of the subject matter of the film, the producer's name and address, technical details of the film, length, censorship classification and cast and crew details.

It is also usual to make a 'promo' or trailer of the film to show to buyers who are short of time. Usually about four to five minutes in length, a promo is an invaluable tool. The promo should be designed as an attention-grabber and should give a clear indication of what the film is about.

Naturally, you will need a marketing budget and this should have been included in the original production budget of the film. A typical marketing budget* for a person going to MIP-TV in Cannes, France, would be as follows:

1.	printing of 2,000 single sheet brochures including costs of artwork, lettering, typesetting, photographic colour plate(s) and printing	$3,500
2.	air fares and accommodation and living expenses for the producer to attend MIP-TV film market for one week approximately	$6,200
3.	cost of producing five video cassettes from master videotape	$ 350
4.	freight and customs charges, carnets, etc	$ 350
5.	miscellaneous expenses advertising, publicity, costs of hire of facilities at AFC stand	$2,000
	TOTAL	$12,400

* Based on costs for a 50-minute production, as at October 1994.

The marketplace for documentaries
(Average price per 50 minutes)

	($US)		($US)
African countries	4,000–6,000	New Zealand	1,000–2,000
Argentina	2,000–3,000	Norway	1,000–2,000
Australia	15,000–80,000	Pakistan	500
Austria	2,000–3,000	Philippines	1,000
Belgium	3,000	Poland	500
Brazil	5,000	Portugal	400–600
Canada CBC	20,000–30,000	Rumania	600
CBC French	8,000–14,000	Scotland	5,000
China	NA	Singapore	2,000
CATV	20,000–30,000	South Africa	1,000–1,750
Czechoslovak TV	1,000	Spain	2,000–3,000
Denmark	2,000–3,000	Sweden	5,000–8,000
Egypt	1,000	Switzerland	2,000–10,000
Finland	3,000–4,500	Taiwan	500
France	12,000–20,000	Thailand	2,500
Germany TV rights	8,000–10,000	Turkey	500
all rights TV & tape package	5,000–30,000	United States of America single station sale up to	30,000
Greece	1,200–1,400		
Hong Kong	2000–5,000	United Kingdom the BBC	8,000–40,000
Hungary	1,000	Uruguay	400
India	1,000	Venezuela	1,000
Indonesia	1,000	West Indies	400
Iran	800	Yugoslavia	NA
Ireland	2,000–3,500		
Israel	1,000		
Italy	4,000–6,000		
Japan	3,000–35,000		
Korea	1,000		
Mexico	2,600		
Middle East (other than Egypt, Iran, Israel)	2,000–,5000		
Netherlands	5,000–10,000		

The prices quoted are only intended as a guide, as they can vary from television network to television network, and are also dependent on quality, demand and whether they are single episodes or series. The figures quoted are also, in most cases, *gross* figures, i.e., before distributor commissions are deducted.

There are also hire markets, such as the American and Australian film hire markets and the international and Australian home video hire markets. The hire markets return a continual flow of small amounts over the years.

267

Appointing A Sales Agent

If all this is too much trouble, it would be wise to appoint a sales agent. The sales agent's job is to sell your product efficiently and quickly. Agents are useful in that they know network executives personally, they should know who is looking for what, and which network is likely to buy. They may include your film in a package of similar films and be able to make deals that you could not make yourself. Agents love series and will normally make a greater effort in selling packages than 'one-offs'.

An agent will want you to sign an exclusive contract to represent your film in a particular territory, and for a specified period. Commissions on sales vary from 10 to 40 per cent of the gross returns. The agent must, of course, pay all expenses and travelling in promoting your film and these expenses are not deductible from sales figures. However, you will have to supply brochures, stills, video cassettes and a promo if you want your agent to work effectively for you.

Agents may sub-license the film to other agents who specialise in a particular territory. In this case, the sub-agent's fees must be paid by the agent out of the total commission payable by the producer, and must not be an additional charge to the producer.

Sales agents' fees vary considerably; a typical scale of fees is given below.

Sales agent's commission as a percentage of gross sales

US network	10 per cent
BS TV (US)	25 per cent
Cable TV, RSTV	30–35 per cent
Syndication (US)	35 per cent
Non-theatrical	20–25 per cent
Australia & rest of world, television	25–35 per cent (negotiable)

It is usual when granting rights to an agent to specify exactly the territory and the media the agent is to exploit. Agents have particular expertise in certain areas: for instance, it doesn't often happen that an agent who has good television prospects will also have the same connections in the non-theatrical market. As the rights to non-theatrical distribution are separately exploitable, it would make more sense to give these particular rights to an agent or distributor who specialises in that field.

Deals are also done with territories: for instance, an agent who has good connections in France may also want the rights for French-speaking Canada, or the German rights may include those to Austria and German-speaking Switzerland.

Contracts With Agents

A contract specifies clearly the agent's territory, term and media of distribution – whether television, cable TV, etc. There should also be an option to renew at the end of the term for a further term.

It is a good idea to include a performance clause: this is a clause in the contract where the agent has to chalk up a certain sales figure in the first year of distribution. If the target figure is not met, a new agent can be appointed by the producer. The contract should also clearly state what materials will be supplied to the agent and who pays for these. All sales should be approved by the producer in order to stop an agent selling films at prices well below market for a quick sale.

The agent must remit all moneys received from the sales of films within a certain period to the producer – the best contracts specify quarterly returns, accompanied by full details of the sale price, the buyer, gross sales, net receipts and commissions deducted.

The producer should retain the right of inspection of the books kept by the agent at any time and the contract should, of course, include the right for both parties to cancel on default, either by producer or agent.

NON-THEATRICAL DISTRIBUTION

Films for schools and colleges must usually be no longer than 20 minutes. This usually means editing a shorter version designed specifically for the non-theatrical market.

Films for libraries can usually be sold in their original length. In Australia, State Film Libraries pay an average of about $30 per minute for 16 mm prints. Once the film is sold to a State Library, any registered borrower may use the film for non-profit screenings. Prices paid for video cassettes average about $2 to $3 per minute for $1/_2$" cassettes.

There are various ways for a distributor to publicise the film: inclusion in the catalogue and exposure in film festivals that cater specifically for non-theatrical distribution, such as the annual American Film Festival, held in New York.

The non-theatrical distribution area includes sales of prints/cassettes to ships at sea, remote communities, the armed forces, cruise ships, clubs and other specialised uses, including the right to sell stock footage to television program producers.

In America, the campus circuit is a lucrative area if you have the right film. There are thousands of universities and colleges in the US which are looking for programs on cultural, social and political themes, and a distributor can achieve very good returns from this market if it is properly exploited.

There are also lecture tours on which a producer can embark. Certain American organisations will arrange for a filmmaker to take his/her film on the college circuit and screen at selected universities throughout the country. Each screening is at an agreed fee and travelling expenses are the producer's responsibility. A lecture tour can be an exhausting affair, but if you have the time it can be a way of seeing the US in 'eighty days'.

THEATRICAL DISTRIBUTION

The shorter film did once have a place in mainstream theatrical distribution as a supporting film to the main feature. It was also a way to showcase independent filmmakers' work and perhaps the only way that new talents were able to emerge and test their films on cinema audiences. However, this is a shrinking market and very little opportunity remains in Australia and the US, as cinema exhibitors are precluding 'shorts'. They are packing more cinema sessions in a single day and the practice of screening supporting films has all but disappeared.

HOME VIDEO

Among the fastest-growing markets is home video. With sales and rentals in the millions of dollars, it must be a serious challenge to all other forms of distribution. Short films and non-fiction have so far not participated in this boom. The few selected subjects included in catalogues are mostly sporting events. The 'how to do it' category – golf, tennis, carpentry and home maintenance – will also probably grow in the future.

A final word on marketing: most of it is planning, careful research, and access to information. Then follows the hard work of screening, travelling and following up contracts and sales. And it is all made much easier if you have a good film or video to sell.

APPENDIXES

Profiles Of Useful Organisations

Arts Law Centre Of Australia

The Gunnery
43 Cowper Wharf Road
Woolloomooloo NSW 2011
Telephone: (02) 356 2566 or (1800) 221 457

The Arts Law Centre of Australia is a community legal centre which provides legal and accounting advice and information on arts-related issues to artists and organisations throughout Australia.

Legal And Accounting Services

The Centre provides information and advice on arts-related legal and accounting matters including contracts, copyright, insurance, defamation, business structures, employment and taxation. Initial telephone advice is free and available to callers outside Sydney on the Centre's toll-free number.

The Centre is an advice and resource centre and does not litigate matters, draft documents or conduct negotiations. If these services are required it is referred to the Centre's panel of referral lawyers or accountants. Where mediation is more appropriate, the Centre's Mediation Service provides referrals to mediators experienced in the arts industry.

Subscription

For ongoing advice and to take full advantage of the Centre's services, artists and organisations can subscribe. Annual subscription rates depend on whether the client is a full-time student, individual, non-profit organisation or commercial enterprise.

The benefits of subscription include:

* ongoing legal and accounting advice;

* discounts to seminars and conferences on topical issues affecting the arts industry;

* access to the Centre's Legal Advice Night Service (available in Sydney, Adelaide, Perth, Hobart and anticipated for Melbourne by mid-1995);

* referrals to arts and entertainment lawyers, mediators and accountants;

* quarterly newsletter;

* a wide range of discounted publications.

EDUCATION

The Arts Law Centre offers a range of arts law workshops, lectures, seminars and publications. The Centre is happy to liaise with organisers of educational events or to devise specific educational programs. An annual seminar series and occasional conferences are conducted on topical arts law issues in which papers are presented by industry experts. During 1994 seminars included: *Auteur or Author? Moral Rights and the Film Industry* and *Understanding Film Production and Investment Contracts*. The Centre also held a conference on *Multimedia and the Law*. Contact the Centre for a list of available papers.

The Centre publishes sample contracts, information sheets, handbooks and publications. Some useful publications for the film industry include information sheets on *Protecting Your Ideas, Partnership Checklist, Film Funding* and *Sample Letter of Demand*, and sample contracts such as a *Performer's Release, Interviewee's Release, Location Release, Option and Purchase Agreement, Music Commission Agreement* and community broadcasting contracts.

AUSTRALIAN INTERACTIVE MULTIMEDIA INDUSTRY ASSOCIATION (AIMIA)

PO Box 148
Collaroy Beach NSW 2097
Telephone/Fax: (02) 972 2066

AIMIA was established to provide an Association for individual professionals working in the context of interactive multimedia; which reflects in a balanced way all sectors of the interactive multimedia industry; and which reflects equally all regional (in Australia 'state') interests.

AIMIA's objectives are to:

* represent the interactive multimedia industry in its relationships with customer groups, Government and suppliers;

* provide industry practitioners with the opportunity to contribute to the development of the interactive multimedia industry;

* promote, within the Australian region, a wider understanding of the benefits offered by the utilisation of interactive multimedia and establish supportive alliances;

* represent Australian interactive multimedia interests in relevant world forums;

* promote professional standards in ethics and business for the interactive multimedia industry and to communicate and monitor these as widely as possible;

* provide a forum for the exchange of views amongst members;

* provide a forum for special interest groups;

* provide services to members and to the industry to support their growth;

* research and develop further markets for interactive multimedia.

MEMBERSHIP STRUCTURE

Two membership categories have been created:

A   INDIVIDUAL MEMBERSHIP
Individual membership is available to persons who wish to make a contribution to the interactive multimedia industry through participating in AIMIA.

B   CORPORATE MEMBERSHIP
Corporate membership is available to all organisations operating in the field of multimedia which consider that a major part of their business focuses in the area of interactive multimedia.

AUSTRALASIAN MECHANICAL COPYRIGHT OWNERS SOCIETY LIMITED (AMCOS)

14th Floor, 56 Berry Street
North Sydney NSW 2060
Private Box 2135
North Sydney NSW 2059
Telephone: (02) 954 3655; Fax: (02) 954 3664

AMCOS represents virtually all music publishers based in Australia and New Zealand and, by way of reciprocal arrangements, with equivalent international societies, the vast majority of the world's composers, writers and music publishers.

As the licensing arm of the Australian Music Publishers Association Limited (AMPAL), AMCOS collects and distributes royalties on the reproduction and synchronisation of musical works where it would be impossible, impractical or uneconomic for individual members to do so. It acts as a central clearing house for users, enabling the recording of music to be authorised swiftly, efficiently and economically – without the need to enter into the labyrinth of copyright clearance, involving costly and time-consuming telephone calls and correspondence.

Whilst the synchronisation of commercially released published musical works into films made for theatrical release requires the direct negotiation between the filmmaker and the music publisher (this is not done through AMCOS) AMCOS is the exclusive licensee in Australia and New Zealand for a large number of Production Music Libraries controlled by AMCOS publisher–members. Production Music provides a high quality but inexpensive means of providing music for film and video production.

AMCOS has a comprehensive database listing the copyright owners of over 500,000 recorded musical works. It offers a service where details of the copyright owners of synchronisation and/or print rights are provided to film production companies, advertising agencies and other users of music. All that is required is the forwarding to AMCOS of a completed Copyright Ownership Research Application. The client is charged on a monthly basis for information provided.

AUSTRALASIAN PERFORMING RIGHT ASSOCIATION LIMITED (APRA)

1A Eden Street
Crows Nest NSW 2065
PO Box 567, Crows Nest NSW 2065
Telephone: (02) 922 6422, Fax: (02) 925 0314

The Australasian Performing Right Association Limited, incorporated in 1926, is a non-profit association of Australian, New Zealand and Fijian composers, authors, music publishers and other parties interested in the so-called 'performing rights' in copyright musical works and the words that form part of them. These performing rights encompass the rights to perform the works in public, to broadcast and telecast the works, and to transmit the works to subscribers to a diffusion service (i.e., 'cablecasting'). Members assign to APRA, for the latter's administration, their performing rights.

Similarly constituted performing right societies exist throughout the world, with which APRA has reciprocal agreements, essentially providing that the performing rights in the works of the members of one society are administered in the other's territory by that other society. The result of all these arrangements is that, for APRA's territory, it controls the performing rights in what are, in practice, all copyright musical works and associated words in use throughout the community.

APRA administers these performing rights through a range of licence schemes, each one of which is designed to provide comprehensive permission for different circumstances and methods of performing right music usage. These licence schemes bear a common element of authorising the usage, as envisaged by the licence, of any and all works within APRA's repertoire in return for the payment of licence fees.

All the licence fees APRA collects are distributed, together with investment and other revenues generated pending distribution, to APRA's members and to affiliated societies for distribution, to their members in accordance with the reported usage of their works, less only administration expenses.

In so far as the producers of films and television programs are concerned, they are generally required to obtain permission in the form of a licence to authorise the synchronisation of copyright musical works and associated words into the production soundtrack, a type of reproduction or 'mechanical' right licence.

Naturally, it will be envisaged that the production will be performed in cinemas, broadcast on television and,'or transmitted on cable systems. When this occurs, the music on the soundtrack will be likewise performed in public, broadcast and/or cablecast, as the case may be. However, arrangements concerning these performing right uses of the music are met as between the cinema, telecaster and/or cablecaster and the local performing right society as a matter of course, and the producer need not be directly involved.

As performing right societies, including APRA, require details of music usage in order to effect distribution of revenues, information as to music incorporated into audio-visual productions is gained by way of 'cue sheets', a listing of the relevant titles and their respective durations. The supply of cue-sheets is a normal condition of synchronisation licences, and they are usually supplied to APRA as a matter of course.

AUSTRALIAN BROADCASTING AUTHORITY (ABA)

Head Office

Level 15 Darling Park
201 Sussex Street
Sydney NSW 2000
PO Box Q500
Queen Victoria Building
NSW 2000
Telephone: (02) 334 7700; Fax: (02) 334 7799

The Australian Broadcasting Authority is the broadcasting regulator for radio and television in Australia. As well as planning the availability of segments of the broadcasting services bands (VHF/UHF television, FM and AM radio) the ABA has the power to allocate, renew, suspend and cancel licences and collect any fees payable for those licences. The ABA is also empowered to assist broadcasting service providers (licensees) develop codes of practice, conduct research into community attitudes on programming matters, develop program standards relating to broadcasting in Australia and monitor and investigate complaints about licensees. The ABA determines and monitors the suitability of licensees to ensure compliance with the ownership and control provisions of the Act. In addition the ABA is required to inform itself and the Minister about advances and trends in broadcasting technology.

The ABA has been given a range of powers and functions to be used to produce stable and predictable regulatory arrangements. The ABA is also directed to use its powers to deal effectively with breaches of the *Broadcasting Services Act 1992* in a way that balances the broadcasting needs of the Australian community with the interests of the broadcasting industry.

The ABA was created in October 1992 under the Broadcasting Services Act, replacing the Australian Broadcasting Tribunal. The Act is aimed at reducing the amount of regulation needed to achieve Government objectives and promote economic and administrative efficiency.

PROGRAM STANDARDS AND CODES

The primary responsibility for ensuring that programs reflect community standards rests with radio and television stations themselves. The ABA sets compulsory program standards for Australian content on television and children's television only.

Industry groups representing commercial television and radio have produced codes of practice governing all other aspects of program content. Codes of practice for other sectors of the industry are being produced. The ABA registers the code if it meets the requirements under the Act.

COMPLAINTS

Complaints about aspects of programs on radio and television stations which are covered by an industry code of practice, must first be made to the broadcaster concerned. Codes cover matters such as violence, language, sex and nudity, racial vilification and the amount of advertising. A person can complain directly to the ABA if a station fails to answer a written complaint within 60 days, or the response is considered unsatisfactory. The ABA can accept direct complaints for matters relating to the standards for children's television or Australian content on television.

THE AUSTRALIAN CHILDREN'S TELEVISION FOUNDATION

199 Grattan Street
Carlton VIC 3053
Telephone: (03) 348 1144; Fax: (03) 347 4194

See page 128 for full details

AUSTRALIAN COPYRIGHT COUNCIL

3/245 Chalmers Street
Redfern NSW 2016
Telephone: (02) 318 1788; Fax: (02) 698 3536

The Australian Copyright Council is a non profit company, which is largely funded by the Australia Council and the Australian Film Commission. The Copyright Council's objectives are to raise awareness and promote acceptance of copyright, and to seek legal and other changes which will benefit owners of copyright, creators and performers.

The Council has four staff lawyers who provide free legal advice about copyright to members of the public. In addition, the Council conducts a series of seminars each year, and produces a series of publications. *Film and Copyright* is available from the Council for $16.

The Council also makes submissions and representations on law reform and policy issues which affect copyright.

AUSTRALIAN FILM COMMISSION

Head Office:

Level 4, 150 William Street
Woolloomooloo NSW 2011
GPO Box 3984
Sydney NSW 2001
Telephone: (02) 321 6444; Toll Free: 008 22 6615
Fax: (02) 357 3737

Melbourne Office:

120 Clarendon Street
South Melbourne VIC 3205
PO Box 404, South Melbourne VIC 3205
Telephone: (03) 279 3400; Toll Free: 008 33 8430
Fax: (03 696 1476

London Office:

2nd Floor, Victory House
99-101 Regent Street
London W1R 7HB
Telephone: 441 71 734 9389; Fax: 441 71 434 0170

See pp. 131–133 for full details

AUSTRALIAN FILM FINANCE CORPORATION PTY LIMITED

Sydney Office:

Level 12, 130 Elizabeth Street
Sydney NSW 2000
GPO Box 3886, Sydney NSW 2001
Telephone: (02) 268 2555; Toll Free: 008 251 061
Fax: (02) 264 8551

Melbourne Office:

221a Bay Street
Port Melbourne VIC 3207
Telephone: (03) 646 8399; Toll Free: 008 333 655
Fax: (03) 646 2933; Toll Free: 008 808 426

See pp. 131–135 for full details

AUSTRALIAN FILM INSTITUTE (AFI)

National Office:

49 Eastern Road
South Melbourne VIC 3000
Telephone: (03) 696 1844; Fax: (03) 696 7972

Sydney Office:

Sydney Film Centre
Paddington Town Hall
Cnr Oxford Street and Oatley Road
Paddington NSW 2010
Telephone: (02) 332 2111; Fax: (02) 332 2299

The Australian Film Institute is the national film culture organisation. Established in Melbourne in 1958 as an independent, non-profit organisation, the AFI offers a range of services and activities to filmmakers and the wider community.

AFI AWARDS

The annual AFI Awards are the film and television industry's most prestigious recognition of achievement in film making. Entries are invited each April for features and non features, telemovies and mini-series. During August and September, AFI members are entitled to view all nominated films and to register their votes. The films are shown during the Australian Film Festival in seven capital cities and are open to all registered AFI members. These screenings are a unique opportunity to view the year's production output. The Awards are presented late October/early November each year, in a ceremony which is the highlight of the film year.

TOURING EXHIBITIONS

The AFI packages, promotes and distributes specially curated seasons aimed to foster appreciation and knowledge of cinema. The season offers Australia's filmmakers and audiences the chance to familiarise themselves with contemporary developments in local and international cinema through comprehensive seasons and to re-appraise the heritage of world cinema. The AFI is one of the few exhibitors to release non-mainstream Australian shorts, documentaries and low budget features.

The National Cinematheque, co-ordinated by the AFI in partnership with the Melbourne Cinematheque, offers weekly screenings in each of seven capital cities.

DISTRIBUTION

AFI Distribution markets an extensive collection of Australasian shorts, documentaries, animation and feature films and is committed to disseminating its collection throughout Australia and New Zealand.

Its films and video tapes are marketed to cinemas, home video and to television. AFI Distribution is also a specialist in the non-theatrical market and promotes titles widely to schools, community groups and other organisations and institutions.

RESEARCH AND INFORMATION

The AFI Research and Information Centre is located in Melbourne. It houses an extensive collection of literature focusing on film theory, history and criticism; Australian television and video are also covered.

SERVICES

The services offered by the Centre include:

*   research on any aspect of Australian or international cinema via CINESEARCH;

279

* CINEDOSSIER, a comprehensive weekly compilation of film, television, video and new technology press coverage in an indexed booklet, available by subscription;

* CINEDEX, a research database of distributors of films on theatrical release in Australia;

* online access to a comprehensive international film industry database.

* THE MOVING IMAGE series of monographs published by the AFI.

MEMBERSHIP

Membership of the AFI is open to everyone with an interest in film. The Institute's membership consists of people who work in film and those who are film lovers. Benefits include:

* cinema discounts;

* quarterly newsletter;

* discounted entry to AFI's weekly Cinematheque program;

* discounted subscriptions to Encore and Cinema Paper magazines;

* opportunity to register and attend Awards screenings during the Australian Film Festival and vote for the AFI Awards;

* access to special membership events including film previews and Conversations on Film.

CINEMAS

The AFI operates the State Cinema in Hobart, and manages the cinemas at the Sydney Film Centre, Paddington, in conjunction with commercial operators. AFI programs are released through independent and publicly funded cinemas Australia-wide.

THE AUSTRALIAN FILM, TELEVISION & RADIO SCHOOL (AFTRS)

Cnr Epping and Balaclava Roads
North Ryde NSW 2113
PO Box 126, North Ryde NSW 2113
Student Services: Telephone: (02) 805 6444; Fax (02) 887 1030

Melbourne Office

1st Floor, 45 Whiteman Street
South Melbourne VIC 3205
PO Box 1008, South Melbourne VIC 3205
Telephone: (03) 690 7111; Fax: (03) 690 1283

STATE REPRESENTATIVES

Queensland

Unit 1A, 92-96 Methyr Road
New Farm QLD 4005
Telephone: (07) 254 0212; Fax: (07) 358 1592

South Australia

20 Princess Street
Adelaide SA 5000
Telephone: (08) 232 4266; Fax: (08) 232 4210

Tasmania

77 Salamanca Place
Hobart TAS 7000
Telephone/Fax: (002) 238 703
Mobile Tel 61 018 125 688

Western Australia

C/- Reel Images
4/24 Thorogood Street
Victoria Park WA 6100
Telephone: (09) 470 5330; Fax: (09) 362 5500

AFTRS is the national centre of excellence for education and professional training in film, television and radio production. The primary focus of the School is on the cultural development role giving its students the skills, confidence and professional standard of practice to prepare and sustain them for leading creative roles. The AFTRS' production-based training programs have a strong industry-related vocational emphasis, integrating creative development with new technologies, professional skills and business practice. The School offers full-time training as well as a large number of short and part-time courses.

The School was established in 1973 as part of the Commonwealth government's strategy to expand training in the arts and the media and contributes to the government's cultural and economic objectives by fostering creative and professional development. Since that time there has been an outstanding growth in the production and distribution of Australian film and television programs and in radio broadcasting.

AFTRS has played a key role in that development with hundreds of aspiring and practising makers of the film and broadcasting industries attending courses conducted by the AFTRS. Productions by its students have won some five hundred national and international awards. Former students can be found in all areas of the industry: in commercial radio and television, in government and independent production houses, in arts and media administration.

The School has strong links with the film and broadcasting industries. Leading industry professionals are members of its governing council. Its teaching staff and lecturers are also drawn from experienced industry practitioners.

COURSES AT AFTRS

The AFTRS approach to training is twofold: to develop new and emerging talent and to provide working professionals with opportunities to gain additional skills.

The education and training programs are designed around the particular needs and interests of students and of the industry.

Available courses are:

* a three-year degree program leading to the award of **Bachelor of Arts (Film and Television)**;

* **specialist extension courses** from six months to one year in scriptwriting, production design, editing, sound, production, cinematography, and title design;

* a twenty-week course in **commercial radio**;

* **industry short courses** and workshops in a variety of specialist subjects.

Permanent Australian residents from all states are accepted for full-time training at the School's Sydney base. Industry courses are conducted in all capital cities and some country areas.

BACHELOR OF ARTS (FILM AND TELEVISION)

The Bachelor of Arts (Film and Television) is a full-time course providing specialist craft training in key creative areas rather than training generalist program makers. These are: scriptwriting, production, production design, sound, editing, direction, and cinematography.

The BA is conducted over three years. Each training year begins in February and is divided into two semesters.

Most units in the curriculum combine theory, analysis and practical, hands-on experience.

The first year, known as **Foundation Year**, provides students with introductory training in all craft skills offered as specialisations in the following years. Students also complete units in documentary, screen studies and industry and cultural studies.

In the second or **Specialist Year**, students concentrate on the development of skills in the specialised craft they have chosen. This is achieved through direct instruction, working on their own film or television project and crewing on projects by other students. Second-year students undertake short attachments to professional film and television organisations to gain work experience. Students are also required to complete a major research project on a topic of relevance to the Australian film and television industry.

The third year is known as the **Production Year**. It focuses on the completion of a major film or television production. This may be a project designed and implemented by the student or take the form of specialist crewing for other students' major productions. Further intensive training is undertaken in some specialisations. Students also complete professional attachments as in the Specialist Year.

No fees are payable for the degree course, but all students are liable for the Commonwealth Government's **Higher Education Contribution Scheme** charge.

SPECIALIST EXTENSION COURSES

Extension courses are aimed at professionals already working in a particular specialisation who wish to enhance and expand their skills through intensive training. Extension courses are available in cinematography, editing, producing, production design, scriptwriting and sound. Extension courses are currently not available in directing.

The extension courses are defined by the formal requirements of the syllabus and also the potential for individual creative development (primarily through involvement in the production slate). This creative potential is, by definition, specialised (generally limited to the chosen craft specialisation) and limited by the restricted time frame of the course.

Extension courses are usually two semesters, with some exceptions in cinematography, editing and sound where students may, in consultation with their Head of Department, elect to study for the period of time that suits their needs.

Extension course students don't have a production budget allocated to them.

COMMERCIAL RADIO COURSE

A twenty-six week, full-time course in commercial radio is run each year. Training is provided in all aspects of commercial radio, including the techniques of announcing, copywriting, interviewing, studio and production skills, sales and marketing, programming, talk-back, drama and sound.

Students are required to complete a series of written and practical assignments. All students spend four weeks in attachments at regional radio stations to gain work experience.

SHORT COURSE PROGRAM

AFTRS short courses are offered nationwide through its state offices in a large number of specialist subjects. These courses are aimed at practitioners already working in the industry who wish to broaden their skills without undertaking full time study.

The short course program includes industry conferences, seminars, forums, masterclasses and courses ranging from one evening to ten days.

Short courses and seminars fall into the following categories:

1   courses for recognised film, television and radio industry practitioners who are upgrading skills or reskilling;

2   courses for industry professionals aimed at providing breadth of vision, understanding of technology and its implications;

3   transition courses for professionals working in allied fields who wish to enter the film, television or radio industries, such as writers and theatre directors;

4   courses associated with professional development or research activities of tertiary educators, critics, media commentators and other sectors of the film and broadcast industry.

283

Examples of courses include: doing business with funding bodies, production management and accountancy, television direction, television production management, video post-production, script editing, radio copywriting, new technology workshops, documentary cinema, marketing, 16 mm editing, corporate video, multimedia workshops, graphics and animation.

While the AFTRS highly subsidises the costs of these courses, nominal fees are charged.

SummerSkill Program

Success in the film and broadcasting industries depends to a large extent upon the individual's unique combination of creative and technical skills in the art of visual and/or audio communication. The AFTRS SummerSkill program provides the opportunity for those preparing for a career in film, television or radio to develop these skills.

A range of seminars aimed at providing a greater understanding of the production process are conducted over the summer period for fee paying students.

Specialist Client Training

The AFTRS also provides assistance and courses for specialist clients. In 1994 sixteen students graduated from the Indigenous Video Training Course and the Industry Fund for Women provided sponsored, on-the-job and short course training for women fulfilling the selection criteria. The School conducts the Technical Trainee Scheme which combines supervised, on-the-job training in television operations or maintenance with part-time TAFE study.

In addition, the AFTRS offers the expertise of its staff and top industry practitioners to employers who wish to provide tailor-made training programs for their own staff and freelancers.

International Training

For many years, the School has offered a range of short courses in the Asia-Pacific region including seminars, masterclasses and workshops. A new international program based in Australia of intensive production-based training will begin in 1995 for selected international industry practitioners.

In addition, the School aims to provide attachments and exchanges that give Australian practitioners and students the opportunity to develop strategic relationships in order to further professional skills to produce and market programs in other territories.

Applications

Applications for all AFTRS courses are highly competitive because places are limited. Applicants for all courses will generally have to demonstrate some pre-existing knowledge or experience as well as clear training objectives.

Applications for all courses must be made on the official forms available from the Student Centre.

BACHELOR OF ARTS (FILM AND TELEVISION)

The degree course accepts a maximum of twelve students. The minimum age for applicants is generally 22 years. Applications are taken up to 12 July each year for the following year's course.

All applications must be accompanied by examples of work such as a script, short film or videotape and a statement outlining professional objectives and views on the industry. Short-listed applicants proceed to an interview, after which a final selection is made.

There is a non-refundable processing fee for all applications for the degree course.

SPECIALIST EXTENSION COURSES

Specialist extension course applications close 23 August.

All applications must be accompanied by examples of work such as a script, short film or videotape and a statement outlining professional objectives and views on the industry. Short-listed applicants proceed to an interview, after which a final selection is made.

There is a non-refundable processing fee for all applications for extension courses.

COMMERCIAL RADIO COURSE

The commercial radio course is limited to twelve students. The minimum age on admission is generally 21 years, with a maximum of 29 years.

Applications must include a statement outlining personal objectives and experience in broadcasting or public performance. Short-listed applicants are required to submit an audition tape to a given format. From there, applicants are chosen for interview, after which the final selection is made.

Applications for the course close in September of the preceding year.

SHORT COURSES

Attendance in short courses is generally limited to between eight and twelve participants. Applicants for courses need to supply their curriculum vitae and a statement outlining how the skills gained from the course will be used.

As far as possible applicants for each course are matched in terms of experience and levels of competence.

Inquiries for short courses can be directed to Student Services at the Sydney Base or to the state representatives.

FINANCIAL ASSISTANCE

Students accepted into any course of six months or longer may be eligible for Austudy. An AFTRS allowance may be available to those who are ineligible.

NSW country and interstate full-time students may also be eligible for reimbursement of initial travel costs and a contribution towards relocation and establishment.

EDUCATIONAL RESOURCES

THE JERZY TOEPLITZ LIBRARY

The only library in Australia to specialise in this area, the Jerzy Toeplitz Library contains an extensive collection of material relating to the collaborative crafts of film making and broadcast production.

Apart from over 17,000 books and periodicals there are 5600 film and video titles, hundreds of scripts and screenplays, CD-ROMs and newspaper clippings. In addition to publishing regular AFTRS bibliographies, the library puts out a monthly *New Technology Update* which lists new articles, reports and books on multimedia, the digital revolution and the rapidly changing television industry.

The library is open to the film and broadcasting industry, educational institutions and the general public.

PUBLISHING

The AFTRS Publishing Unit has a comprehensive publishing program which includes training manuals, handbooks, research documents and reports, commercial and corporate publications and the highly regarded international quarterly media journal, *Media Information Australia*. AFTRS books are available though AFTRS Direct Sales and selected book stores.

EDUCATIONAL MEDIA

This Unit produces film, video and computer based training resources to support the training needs of the AFTRS curriculum and the film and broadcasting industries. Topics covered in programs range from basic skills to the latest industry developments, from new technologies to filmmaker interviews. AFTRS training videos are available through AFTRS Direct Sales and selected distributors.

FACILITIES

The building has 10,500 m² of space over two levels. The upper level includes a 240-seat projection theatre, seminar rooms, writing studio, library and offices. The lower level accommodates most of the specialised technical facilities, including two television studios, a sound stage, set storage and construction, OB garage and stores, radio studios, editing booths and a camera workshop.

The new premises have been fitted out with a comprehensive range of up-to-date, professional electronic and technical equipment.

AUSTRALIAN RECORD
INDUSTRY ASSOCIATION (ARIA)

9th Floor,
263 Clarence Street
Sydney NSW 2000
PO Box Q20
Queen Victoria Building
Telephone: (02) 267 7996; Fax: (02) 264 5589

ARIA is the only representative body of the record industry and manufacturers in Australia. Therefore, ARIA has direct and active relationships with federal and state government departments and politicians, as well as affiliations with the international record industry and with trade associations representing the music industry in Australia.

In the past seven years, ARIA's successful campaigns, activities and achievements have included:

* discouragement of radio and TV advertising suggesting home taping;

* campaign to eradicate commercial piracy from Australia;

* retention of the quota for Australian product to be broadcast on commercial radio;

* the governing body of the Australian Record Industry Awards, the 'ARIAs';

* the institution of a national Top 50 sales chart and 'ARIA Report';

* the institution of an industry catalogue and the 'AEROS' electronic retail ordering system;

* the compilation of industry statistics, which are available to members;

* ARIA is allied to the Recording Industry Association of America (RIAA), the Recording Industry Association of New Zealand (RIANZ), the British Phonographic Industry (BPI), the Japanese Phonographic Industry (JPI), and an affiliate of the International Federation of the Producers of Phonograms and Videograms (IFPI).

ARIA's significant tasks in the immediate future are:

* continued high-profile relationship with government departments on importation, piracy, performers' rights, protection of small business, and new rights needed for the 'superhighway' use of recorded music;

* to provide a central negotiating body for industrial awards with singers and musicians;

* protection of copyright from violation by new technology;

* to represent the record industry at various inquiries by means of submissions and/or appearances;

* to conduct and/or advise members of seminars pertinent to the interests of the industry;

287

* introduction and administration of Blank Tape Royalty Scheme;

* maintain an equitable mechanical royalty rate with music publishers;

* establishment of Export Music Australia;

* negotiation of bi-lateral copyright agreement with the Australian government and Indonesia, Thailand and Singapore.

ARIA, in conjunction with AMCOS and the Australian Film Commission, has entered into a licence agreement whereby the incidental use of music and sound recordings in film are licensed. The usages covered are, for example, the inadvertent reproduction of songs playing on a radio during a scene. Further details about this agreement are available from the AFC together with a recently released brochure covering the use of music in films.

AUSTRALIAN SCREEN DIRECTORS' ASSOCIATION LIMITED (ASDA)

PO Box 211
Rozelle NSW 2039
Telephone: (02) 555 7045; Fax: (02) 555 7086

The Australian Screen Directors' Association (ASDA) was established in 1980 to represent the interests of film and television directors. Its membership base has recently been extended to independent producers. ASDA is proud to represent the key creative personnel of the film and video making community. Its membership of over 350 currently includes feature film and television drama directors, documentary filmmakers, independent producers, and directors of a range of other genres including animation, short experimental film and video, music video, TV news, current affairs and sports, and commercials.

ASDA aims to give its membership a professional, industrial and creative identity at the centre of the production process and to represent their interests, through its broader objectives of:

* supporting the professional and creative endeavours of its members and of the industry as a whole;

* creating an environment that fosters open debate, analysis, criticism, innovation and cultural diversity among its members;

* developing initiatives that recognise the work and value of its members and further their professional growth;

* developing professional relationships with other industry bodies and guilds; and of

* actively engaging in the continuing development of industry policy.

ASDA, in its planning, programs and activities and in its dealings with its members and with the film/television industries, values:

*   artistic and craft excellence

*   ethical behaviour

*   collaboration

*   screen culture

*   diversity in an Australian cultural identity and expression

*   professional development

ASDA is managed and run by its members. Its main services are the provision of standard contracts, professional and legal advice and referral, a regular newsletter, and a wide range of cutting edge screen culture and craft events, screenings and discussions, industry information meetings, policy debates, and lobbying on issues of importance to its members.

THE AUSTRALIAN WRITERS' GUILD LIMITED

60 Kellett Street
Kings Cross NSW 2011
Telephone: (02) 357 7888; Fax: (02) 357 7776

Victorian Office:

310 Rathdowne Street
North Carlton VIC 3054
Telephone: (03) 347 9294; Fax: (03) 347 0539

Monday to Friday, 10am–3pm

Queensland Office:

535 Wickham Terrace (PO Box 596)
Spring Hill QLD 4004
Telephone/Fax: (07) 839 8373

Tuesday, Wednesday, 10.30am–4pm

South Australian Office:

The Writers' Centre
187 Rundle Street
Adelaide SA 5000
Telephone: (08) 232 6852; Fax: (08) 232 3994

Tuesday and Thursday, 9am–1pm

Western Australian Office:

1 Museum Street
Perth WA 6000
Telephone: (09) 227 6938; Fax: (09) 227 5306

Tuesday to Thursday, 10am–4pm

289

The Australian Writers' Guild Ltd is a professional association for writers in the area of television, radio, screen, stage and video. Its aims and objectives are to promote and protect professional interests in Australia or originators and adaptors of written material for media.

The Australian Writers' Guild Ltd is an organisation run by its members, who elect a National Council (the supreme governing body of the Guild, which has representation from each state on a proportional basis) every two years, and a National Committee of Management each year. All full members of the Guild are eligible to vote and are also eligible for election. Committees elected in Victoria, South Australia, Western Australia and Queensland report regularly to the Management Committee, which is based in Sydney. Interstate representatives attend National Council meetings and Management Committee meetings in Sydney on a regular basis.

In addition, further members are regularly co-opted to service on various Guild sub-committees covering specific areas such as stage, television, feature films, negotiations, disputes and other areas as required.

While the Guild has dealings with government bodies and has policies on legislative issues concerning writers, the Guild is non-party political. It has no association with any political party and generally does not involve itself in political issues. The Guild is a body of writers, individuals all, but united in the common cause of regulating the conditions under which writers work and are paid and of correcting abuses in matters affecting its members. The Guild maintains a permanent secretariat and office in Sydney and offices in Melbourne, Brisbane, Adelaide and Perth.

Ongoing activities and services to members are:

* negotiation of minimum basic writers agreements with major producers of television, radio and stage productions;

* drafting of model writers' agreements for feature film, documentary film, television and audio-visual work, telemovies, theatre-in-education and assorted other work;

* recommendation of minimum fees for writers where negotiated agreements do not exist, e.g., script editing, amateur theatre, translation and research;

* credit arbitration service in event of disputes over writer credits and dissemination of information concerning standard credit;

* legal and copyright advice service to writers and assistance with disputes, including advice re individual contracts. The Australian Writers' Guild has a Legal Officer and a Writer's Contract Service for this purpose;

* *Viewpoint* – published monthly except January. *Viewpoint* is the Guild's major means of communication with its Australia-wide membership. Members are kept abreast of industry news and developments and informed about forthcoming meetings and courses in their States;

* AWGIE Awards – first presented in 1967, the AWGIE Awards recognise excellence in scripts for stage, film, radio and television produced in the previous year, and are the only Australian writers' awards judged solely by writers.

DEPARTMENT OF COMMUNICATIONS AND THE ARTS

GPO Box 2154
Canberra ACT 2601
Telephone: (06) 279 1000; Fax: (06) 279 1515

The Film Branch in the Department co-ordinates the provision of policy advice relating to film and television production to the Minister for Communications and the Arts and the government. It complements specific policy advice provided by other film agencies, such as the Australian Film Commission.

The Branch is involved in the development and implementation of policy proposals requiring central co-ordination and liaison with film bodies.

The Branch also recommends to the Minister which films should be considered qualifying Australian films under Division 10BA of the *Income Tax Assessment Act.* (The Australian Film Finance Corporation Pty Ltd is required to sight a certificate that a film is a qualifying Australian film before making a decision to invest in that project.)

FILM AUSTRALIA PTY LIMITED

101 Eton Road
Lindfield NSW 2076
Telephone: (02) 413 8777; Fax: (02) 416 5672

Film Australia Pty Ltd is an incorporated company wholly-owned by the federal government. Film Australia is housed in an extensive film studio facility at Lindfield, a northern suburb of Sydney, NSW. It currently employs 70 regular staff (period contract and permanent) and issued some 600 short-term employment contracts to the independent production section for the 1993-94 year.

The Company's annual turnover is approximately $17 million, a third of which ($6 m) is derived from a Commonwealth contract to produce Film Australia's National Interest Program.

THE NATIONAL INTEREST PROGRAM

The National Interest Program is a four-year contract provided by the federal government to Film Australia to devise, produce and distribute at least 80 programs which examine matters of national concern and which illustrate and interpret the lives and experiences of Australians. It is required that the programs achieve the greatest possible public exhibition and use at home and abroad. Although the National Interest Program now represents a minority of Film Australia's financial operations, this Program remains the heart of the enterprise.

Film Australia employs no writers, producers nor technical production crews on staff. All of its productions, including National Interest Programs, are produced with independent freelancers from the private production industry around Australia.

THE ARCHIVE

Eighty years of film making on behalf of the Australian government is archived at the Lindfield studios. This collection includes more than 2500 titles, approximately seven and a half million feet of stock footage and a stills photography and sound effects library. This national resource is made available to local and overseas producers on a commercial basis.

FACILITIES

Film Australia maintains as an active production studio the extensive facilities created in 1962 for the former government film unit, Commonwealth Film Unit (CFU). This complex contains many unique facilities which no company could afford to build today. Three private companies are currently exploiting this valuable resource on a rental basis. This private sector activity is in addition to Film Australia's maintaining a full range of post-production services for independent filmmakers as well as meeting its own production needs.

MARKETING AND DISTRIBUTION

From the basic requirement to maximise exhibition of its National Interest Program, Film Australia has built a global marketing and distribution enterprise. In 1993, Film Australia distributed programs on film, videotape and disc to appropriate theatrical, non-theatrical, rental and consumer video, broadcast, cable and satellite television systems in more than 60 countries. This service has been offered to independent producers. This expanded catalogue contributes significant cost efficiencies to the task of creating the highest possible profile for National Interest Program programs around the world as well as expanding Australia's profile overseas.

Film Australia continues its community service tradition of ensuring the broadest possible non-theatrical distribution of Australian titles to local communities via schools, libraries and special interest groups.

FILM AUSTRALIA COMMUNICATIONS

As a business strategy Film Australia has broadened its services in this communication field and established a new unit called Film Australia Communications (FAC). The unit has its head office in Forrest, Canberra, has expanded its market to include the corporate sector and extended the services beyond production and distribution to include training, project management and presentation services.

Earlier R & D by Film Australia has enabled FAC to offer the production of interactive videodisc as a very cost effective medium of training and automated enquiry response service.

THE INVESTOR FINANCED PROGRAM

As a creative studio, Film Australia develops theatrical and television drama projects which are financed with pre-sales, private investment and, when required, top up investment from the Australian Film Finance Corporation.

Major theatrical drama production improves the viability of the facilities complex. It also increases Film Australia's profile with local audiences and enhances our reputation in international markets.

The Investor Financed Program, combined with the activities of:

* running a facilities operation

* providing marketing and distribution services

* producing programs within the two distinctive streams of the National Interest Program and commissioned work provides the company with annual sales of approximately $17 million.

FILM AND TELEVISION INSTITUTE (WA) INC.

92 Adelaide Street
Fremantle WA 6160
PO Box 579,
Fremantle WA 6160
Telephone: (09) 335 1055; Fax: (09) 335 1283

The Film and Television Institute (WA) primarily acts as a resource centre for independent filmmakers in Western Australia. It has a wide range of activities planned to support independent film and video production (described below).

EXHIBITION

Two cinemas in Fremantle showing the Perth Cinematheque, the WA Film and Video Festival, as well as on-going specific exhibition, and two cinemas in Perth at the Lumiere, showing the Jump Cut Film Festival, the Queer Film Festival and on-going general exhibition.

Every year the Institute holds the WA Film and Video Festival, which has Showcase and Competitive categories.

PUBLICATIONS

A quarterly magazine, *In The Picture*, and bi-monthly FTI Members Newsletter.

LIBRARY AND RESOURCE CENTRE

Holding a collection of periodicals and books of special interest. The centre is staffed part-time and is designed to complement other collections.

PRODUCTION SERVICES

Consultants are available to independent filmmakers for advice on scripting, budgeting, methods of production and funding application procedures. FTI services cover the film making support area, which includes: training courses, production, production support, equipment hire, facility hire.

The FTI is a unique facility in Australia in the way it combines film cultural activities with a production support base. As well as the structured list of services outlined above, the FTI can also be of assistance through use of its staff expertise.

FILM QUEENSLAND

Level 16, 111 George Street
Brisbane QLD 4000
PO Box 1436
Brisbane QLD 4001
Telephone: (07) 224 4536; Fax: (07) 224 4077

See pp. 135–136 for details

FILM VICTORIA

4th Floor, 49 Spring Street
Melbourne VIC 3000
PO Box 4361
Melbourne VIC 3001
Telephone: (03) 651 4089; Fax (03) 651 4090

See pp. 136–137 for details

INTERNATIONAL TELEVISION ASSOCIATION AUSTRALIA (ITVA)

1/204 Spit Road
Mosman NSW 2088
PO Box 380
Spit Junction NSW 2088
Telephone: (02) 969 1400; Fax: (02) 969 2856

The International Television Association of Australia is the professional association representing the interests and needs of the corporate video communicator, user and supplier.

The International Television Association (ITVA) Australia is a member of an international affiliation with members in the USA, UK, Germany, Spain, Austria, Canada, The Netherlands, New Zealand, Denmark, Japan and Ireland.

ITVA strives to advance the standing and recognition of the industry and its practitioners and to promote the use of the corporate video communications to potential users.

Recognising corporate video as a specialised field of endeavour, ITVA provides an open channel of communication among practitioners and those companies that supply video equipment, materials and services.

Each year in October ITVA Australia conducts its annual MOBIE Awards to recognise the best corporate video productions in a number of categories such as: Internal Communications, Regular Employee Communications, Training, Sales of Products and Services, Corporate Image and Public Relations, Public Welfare and Community Service, Video Publishing for Sell Thru and Student Productions.

Winners of the Australian Awards are entered in the International Awards where Australia has an enviable record of taking off the major prizes.

Entries for the awards may be in video format, multimedia or teleconferencing.

When and where possible ITVA conducts seminars, conferences and training programs relating specifically to corporate video.

The aims and objectives of ITVA are:

* to widely promote the recognition of corporate video communications as a specialised field of endeavour;

* to promote professionalism among the practitioners in the field;

* to develop appropriate standards for corporate video, and to disseminate information relevant to those standards to practitioners, manufacturers, suppliers and users;

* to provide liaison between professional video communicators and others of like interest both within the video communications field and in allied and associated fields.

ITVA elects a voluntary committee each year which employs the secretarial services of AGENDA to run an official office for the association.

NATIONAL FILM AND SOUND ARCHIVE

Headquarters:

McCoy Circuit
Acton ACT 2601
GPO Box 2002,
Canberra ACT 2601
Telephone: (06) 209 3111; Fax: (06) 209 3165

Melbourne:

223 Park Street
South Melbourne VIC 3205
Telephone: (03) 690 1400; Fax: (03) 699 4874

Sydney:

84 Alexander Street
Crows Nest NSW 2065
Telephone: (02) 438 1477; (02) 436 4178

NATIONAL COLLECTION

The Australian national collection dates from the 1890s to the present day and consists of more than one million items including discs, audio and video tapes, films, phonographs, cylinders, piano rolls and artefacts and a further million items of documentation such as photographs, scripts, publicity items, posters and newspaper clippings.

In building its collection the Archive gives priority to material of Australian origin or association which is endangered, unique or rare material of high heritage value, and material not acquired by other institutions. The Archive uses a well-developed and systematic selection policy to identify and secure material of enduring Australian cultural significance.

PRESERVATION

Preservation work at the Archive focuses on duplicating, conserving and restoring collection materials and providing technical support for access to the collection. The national collection of recorded sound and moving image material is maintained in secure and controlled storage environments.

ACCESS

The core purpose of the Archive as a heritage collecting institution is to provide access to its collection both now and in the future. Access to the national collection is provided to researchers, program makers, special interest groups and the general public through client access services, educational presentations, exhibitions and the release of collection-based products.

Services include: on-site viewing and auditioning facilities; research and information services; access to film, sound and documentation material; video, film and audio duplication; and loans from the access collection.

NSW FILM AND TELEVISION OFFICE

Level 6, 1 Francis Street
East Sydney NSW 2010
GPO Box 1744
Sydney NSW 2001
Telephone: (02) 380 5599; Fax: (02) 360 1090

See pp. 137–138 for full details

NORTHERN TERRITORY

For information and assistance contact:

Department of Industries and Development
76 The Esplanade
Darwin NT 0800
GPO Box 4160
Darwin NT 0801
Telephone: (089) 895 210/(089) 895 333; Fax: (089) 811 240
Public Relations Manager: (089) 895 384

or:

Office of the Arts and Cultural Affairs
(Department of the Chief Minister)
8 Cavanagh Street, Sasco House,
Darwin NT 0800
GPO Box 1774, Darwin NT 0801
Telephone: (089) 897 375; Fax: (089) 896 836

OFFICE OF FILM & LITERATURE CLASSIFICATION (OFLC)

1st Floor, 255 Elizabeth Street
Sydney NSW 2000
Telephone: (02) 581 7000; Fax: (02) 581 7001

Melbourne Office:

26th Floor, 200 Queen Street
Melbourne VIC 3000
Telephone: (03) 606 1222; Fax: (03) 670 2939

The OFLC examines and classifies local and imported films and video tapes for home use, as well as printed matter. There is a single classification system for film, video and television. The range of media subject to government intervention and regulation is growing.

The OFLC also handles complaints about recorded telephone information services. The OFLC is developing guidelines for computer games and computer generated images.

While every effort is made to interpret the guidelines consistently and to make classification assessments objectively, there must always be a degree of latitude to take into consideration such things as the intent of the filmmaker (is the film serious, or purely an entertainment – perhaps a comedy, a musical, or aimed at kick-boxing fans?) and the integrity with which it is made (is it making a statement about the human condition; do the love scenes have relevance to the plot, or are they exploitative, there simply to titillate?). Classification laws also direct that consideration be given to the literary, artistic or educational merit of a film.

It is in considerations such as these that views will differ. In arriving at each decision all these conflicting views must be balanced and a classification applied which will give potential viewers a clear indication of what they can expect to see and hear.

A word of caution: the classification of a film should not be seen as a recommendation for viewing by a particular audience; adult films like *Driving Miss Daisy* and *Howard's End* have been classified 'G', yet are clearly not intended for children; likewise some films intended by their makers for young children have been classified 'PG' or 'M'.

Properly used the classifications and consumer advice will allow parents in particular, but also anyone who is cautious of what films they see, to make suitable choices for themselves and their families.

Why a movie is rated:

G   General (suitable for all ages)

Parents should feel confident that children may view material in this classification without supervision, knowing that no distress or harm is likely to be caused.

Language:	The mildest expletives, but only if infrequent and used in exceptional and justifiable circumstances.
Sex:	Very discreet verbal references or implications, provided they are justified by the narrative or other context.
Violence:	Minimal, mild and incidental depictions, provided they are justified by the context.

PG   Parental Guidance (parental guidance recommended for persons under 15 years)

Films in this classification may contain themes or concepts which, when viewed by those under 15 years, require the guidance of a parent or guardian.

Language:	Low level coarse language is acceptable, provided its use is not excessive.
Sex:	Discreet verbal and/or visual depictions, references to sexual matters.
Violence:	Depictions of violence must be mild in their impact and/or presented in a stylised or theatrical fashion, or in an historical context.
Other:	Discreet informational and/or anti-drug references. Mild supernatural or 'horror' themes may warrant 'PG'. Minimal nudity if in a justifiable context.

M 15+   Mature (recommended for mature audiences 15 years and over)

Material which is considered likely to disturb, harm or offend those under 15 years to the extent that it is recommended for viewing by those 15 years and over will be classified 'M'. Most adult themes may be dealt with, though the degree of explicitness and intensity of treatment will be an important factor.

Language: Crude language may be used but not if overly frequent or impactful.

Sex: Sexual intercourse or other sexual activity may be discreetly implied.

Violence: Realistic violence of low intensity may be depicted if contextually justified.

Other: Drug use may be discreetly depicted but not in an advocatory manner. Supernatural and 'horror' special effects may be depicted, but not if graphic or impactful.

MA 15+ **Mature Accompanied (restrictions apply to persons under the age of 15 years)***

Material which contains coarse language or depictions of sex or violence or any combination of elements likely to disturb, harm or offend those under 15 years to the extent that it should be restricted to those 15 years and over, will be classified 'MA'.

Language: Crude language may be used, but not when it is excessive, unduly assaultative or sexually explicit.

Sex: Sexual intercourse or other sexual activity may be discreetly implied or simulated.

Violence: Realistic violence of medium intensity may be depicted, but violent depictions with a high degree of realism or impact are acceptable only if contextually justified.

Other: Drug use may be depicted, but not in an advocatory manner. Supernatural and 'horror' special effects usually warrant an 'MA' classification, but not if overly graphic or impactful.

*Children under 15 years will not be admitted to cinemas unless accompanied by a parent or guardian; video material restricted to persons 15 years and over.

R 18+   **Restricted (restricted to adults 18 years and over)**

Material considered likely to be harmful to those under 18 years and/or possibly offensive to some sections of the adult community warrants an 'R' classification.

Language: There are virtually no restrictions on language in 'R' films.

Sex: Sexual intercourse or other sexual activity may be realistically implied or simulated.

Violence: Highly realistic and explicit depictions of violence may be shown, but not if unduly detailed, relished or cruel. Depictions of sexual violence are acceptable only to the extent that they are necessary to the narrative and not exploitative.

Other: Drug abuse may be depicted, but not in an advocatory manner. Extreme 'horror' special effects usually warrant an 'R'.

X 18+ Contains sexually explicit material (restricted to adults 18 years and over)

The classification and guidelines for video are the same as those for cinema except that for video there is an extra classification, 'X', which is defined as follows:

No depiction of sexual violence, coercion or non-consent of any kind is permitted in this classification. Material which can be accommodated in this classification includes explicit depictions of sexual acts between consenting adults and mild non-violent fetishes.

REFUSED CLASSIFICATION

Any film or video which includes any of the following will be refused classification:

(a)   depiction of child sexual abuse, bestiality, sexual acts accompanied by offensive fetishes, or exploitative incest fantasies;

(b)   unduly detailed and/or relished acts of extreme violence or cruelty; explicit or unjustifiable depictions of sexual violence against non-consenting persons;

(c)   detailed instructions or encouragement in:

    (i)   matters of crime or violence

    (ii)   the abuse of proscribed drugs

SCREEN PRODUCERS' ASSOCIATION OF AUSTRALIA (SPAA)

Suite 2, 144 Riley Street
East Sydney NSW 2010
Telephone: (02) 360 4900; Fax: (02) 360 7106

SPAA is the industry association of the Australian independent film and television production industry. It represents the interests of all producers on issues which reflect the business of film making.

SPAA's members include independent film and television producers and production companies, post production houses and studio facilities, entertainment lawyers and accountants, completion guarantors, equipment and material suppliers.

SPAA's aim is to create the environment and conditions under which a vigorous and independent production industry can thrive in Australia and to provide members with the means to have an effective say in government decisions and industrial relations. SPAA negotiates industrial reform, advocates the needs of the industry to governments and statutory authorities and develops industry policies that promote commercial viability.

By consolidating IR employment advice and representations to government on behalf of all members, SPAA is able to provide these services at a fraction of the cost to individuals. The results are much more effective when the industry speaks with one voice.

SPAA's national office is in Sydney with a full time professional secretariat who are always available to answer queries or requests from members. Chapters in each state keep the national office informed of the concerns of members.

SPAA's Stance

Television Broadcasting

SPAA monitors the operation of the Australian content standard to television programs and advocates greater use by broadcasters (including the ABC) of independently-produced Australian programs.

SPAA actively responds to the developments of new technology; it makes representations to Government and the Opposition to ensure local content on pay tv, it is supportive of increased budget allocation to SBS for further investment in Australian independent production.

Economic Analysis Of The Production Industry

SPAA jointly commissioned a report, with the AFC and DAAS, on the economic structure of the industry by the South Australian Centre for Economic Studies. Copies of the publication *The Economics of Film & Television in Australia*, are available from the AFC and SPAA offices.

International Trade

SPAA ensures that the Australian industry's interests are not neglected at international trade negotiations.

Australian Film Finance Corporation

Representing its members' views, SPAA liaises with the FFC on funding guidelines, the terms of contracts and the form of legal documents; member's concerns are addressed at regular meetings. SPAA will assist members in making representations to the FFC.

Industrial Relations

In the best interests of independent film and television producers in Australia, SPAA delivers employee relations advice and industrial relations services to its members. This includes:

* representation in Industrial Tribunals;

* negotiations with relevant unions and associations;

* updated award rates, standard contracts and industry OHS developments.

ANNUAL SPAA CONFERENCE

SPAA's annual conference is a non-profit venture which provides a crucial meeting point for the film making community and representatives from government and key industry figures from Australia and overseas.

It is the largest and most comprehensive gathering of the industry in Australia, connecting producers, broadcasters, directors and scriptwriters with financiers, programmers, distributors, academics and advertisers to examine the issues facing the industry. It attracts key government figures who recognise the opportunity to deliver policy statements to an influential group of delegates.

The conference strives to celebrate and promote audio visual production in this country and is a forum for established and emerging filmmakers to share their knowledge, experience and ideas.

Members receive discounted rates for the conference.

MEMBERSHIP RATES

Members pay a yearly membership fee and a levy on productions, with rates scaled to reflect the level of activity.

SCREEN WEST

Suite 4, 420 Hay Street
(PO Box 1308)
Subiaco WA 6008
Telephone: (09) 382 2500; Fax (09) 381 2848

See pp. 138–139 for full details.

SOUTH AUSTRALIAN FILM CORPORATION

3 Butler Drive
Hendon Common
Hendon SA 5014
Telephone: (08) 348 9300; Fax: (08) 347 0385

See page 139 for full details

Tasmania

For filming and general assistance contact:

Associated Filmmakers – Tasmania, Inc.
PO Box 589
Hobart TAS 7002
Telephone: (002) 315 807

Australian Film Television and Radio School
Salamanca Arts Centre
77 Salamanca Place
Hobart TAS 7000
Telephone/Fax: (002) 238 703

Locations Tasmania
64 Princes Street
Sandy Bay TAS 7005
Telephone: (002) 243 578; Fax: (002) 248 211)

GLOSSARY OF FILMSPEAK

A & B rolls	an expression for the processed camera original when it is negative matched and made ready for printing. The shots are with chequered/board black spacing. You can have as many rolls as required.
above the line	budget allocations for the major creative elements: writer, story rights, producer, director and major cast in the film.
academy framing	*see* **aspect ratio**
academy leader	*aka* **projection leader**; **SMPTE universal leader**; a numbered strip of film on the front of each reel of film. It assists with synchronisation of reel to reel projection. It syncs sound and vision when they are not married on the film. It is also used for focussing. *See also* **leader**
account executive	the liaison person between the advertising agency and their client. He or she would manage the business of several clients, e.g., retail store, manufacturer.
accrued expenses	incurred but not yet paid.
accrued revenue	income earned but not yet received.
action	1) command given by director for the pre-planned performance to begin, given after film and sound are running synchronously; 2) the description of the elements seen in any take.
action loops	sections of film printed for dubbing. The short section is looped and run continuously through a projector with an equal length of sound film until a satisfactory sound recording is achieved.
action props	props intended for specific use in a film.
action vehicles	vehicles used for filming. Implies vehicles for stunts and movement rather than parked cars in the background.
actionable	liable to a lawsuit
actor	*see* **artist**
actors' agents	*aka* **theatrical agents**; agents who represent cast. They promote and negotiate contracts for them. They usually charge 10 per cent of the artist's fee for this service.

actors' cross plot	*see* **cross plot**
actor's time sheet	*see* **second assistant's daily report**
adaptation	a screenplay which has been adapted from another source, e.g., short story, poem, song, novel.
Ado	*see* **digital effects generator**
advertising	paid promotion in newspapers, radio and TV spots, billboards, etc.
aerials	shooting executed from a fixed or rotary wing aircraft. It may be shots of areas from above or air-to-air photography of aircraft in flight.
AFC	Australian Film Commission
agency producer	the executive in an advertising agency who oversees the production of commercials.
aka	also known as
album	a long-playing sound recording offered for sale.
ambient sound	*see* **atmosphere**
anamorphic lens	*aka* **squeeze lens**; an optical lens which squeezes the image onto standard film. By projecting the film using a similar lens, the image is widened again on the screen. Cinemascope, Panavision etc., are the result.
ancillary markets	1) any market outside the principal one the film was designed for;
	2) syndication, non-theatrical, video, pay TV – everything except theatrical;
	3) the Acting Awards define ancillary rights differently in each Award.
ancillary rights	the following rights in relation to the script and the film. These rights form part of the underlying rights: – to write and present a stage play – to make a film about the production of the film – to write and publish a book based on the script – to make soundtrack records – to use the film's title – to use the characters, etc. in the script and the film.
animal wrangler	*see* **wrangler**

305

animation	the impression of continuous movement by inanimate drawings. Still illustrations are photographed frame by frame. When screened one gets the impression of continuous movement.
answer print	*aka* **approval print, trial print, balanced print, first print**; first print from original negative. It is used to access the success of the grading and as a check to the negative matching. It also provides the first opportunity to hear the optical sound track.
antagonist	the individual or opponent who attempts to prevent the protagonist from succeeding.
apple box	*aka* **riser**; a sturdy box with one side open, used to raise the height of actors or objects.
approval print	*see* **answer print**
archival footage	*see* **stock shot**
armourer	a member of the art department in charge of supply and supervision of all weaponry; a person suitably licensed to handle guns, swords, etc.
arrangement	the adaptation of a musical score for particular instruments or voices
arranger	*aka* **orchestrator**; the person who prepares, rewrites and adapts written music for a different presentation. Arrangers usually work from a composer's draft and vary the work to best effect.
art house	limited exhibition through theatre which normally run specialised, high quality, foreign or non-mainstream films.
art department administrator	*aka* **art department co-ordinator**; the manager of the art department. He/she controls expenditure and organises people and resources.
art director	where no production designer is employed, the art director is the head of the department representing design, construction, wardrobe, make-up, special FX, etc. Otherwise he/she is the second in charge of the art department. *See also* **production designer**
artist	*aka* **actor**; performer, double, crowd, extra, stand-in or stunt person engaged for visual or oral performance.
artistic work	the material form of the creator's intention, e.g., photographs, model of set, sculpture, drawing, script.

artist's release form   an agreement which is signed by people who appear in the film who are not already contracted to do so. It is a release giving permission for the producer to use a person's image and voice. Releases are obtained on location every day as required.

art work   *see* **graphics**

aspect ratio   the width of the screen ratio in relationship to its height. The standard ratio is 1.33:1 (called **academy framing**). The 35 mm and 16 mm frame is in that proportion. Super 16 is 1.66:1. Cinemas in Australia, UK and US like to screen films in the ratio of 1.85:1 generally. During projection they crop the top and bottom of the standard ratio.

assembly cut   the mostly mechanical compilation of print takes in script order.

assignment of rights   the act of a copyright owner assigning defined rights in a work under certain conditions. It's always wise to put the contract in writing.

associate producer   1) a title given to a person who has made a major contribution to the production. It could be a financier, production manager, writer, post-production supervisor, actor, etc.

2) second-in-charge of the production. The person who takes part of the producer responsibility both creatively and administratively.

Aston   *see* **character generator**

ATAEA   Australian Theatrical & Amusement Employees Association

atmosphere   *aka* **buzz track**; **ambient sound**; sound recording of ambient noise, e.g., the background which gives a sound mix depth and reality.

audience research   research carried out generally about audience taste and desires. It also refers to special screenings where test audiences are asked to react to a particular film. It is part of a marketing campaign.

audio restripe   *aka* **restripe**; transferring a new sound tack to a videotape. The image is unaltered but the sound track is changed.

audio tape   sound tape

audit   an independent examination of accounting records to verify accuracy.

audition   *see* **screen test**

Australian Film Industry Trust Fund	to qualify for tax deductions under the Film Investment Incentives, amounts contributed to the production of a qualifying Australian film are required to be held in a film account, administered by the Commonwealth Public Account, pending their expenditure in the production of the film.
A-wind	a term to describe the positioning of emulsion or sound base on a piece of film. If you hold a piece of film head upwards with the sprockets on the right, then the emulsion or sound base will be on the side facing you. *See also* **B-wind**
back lot	generally a permanent set or sets used for exterior shooting, e.g., a streetscape, in the proximity of a studio complex.
backup schedule	*see* **wet weather cover**
bad debts insurance	a normal business insurance to soften the blow if clients or sponsors don't pay you.
balanced print	*see* **answer print**
bank loan	a loan which attracts interest and must be repaid.
bankable star	*aka* **heavyweight name; box office star; marquee star;** an actor who by agreeing to appear in a film can increase its potential revenue. Pre-sales or production money can be more easily obtained with such an actor.
base office liaison	a person who remains in the base office, usually a capital city. When crews are on location, a base office liaison person can ease communications, speed up rushes, etc.
basic negotiated fee	*aka* **BNF**; an artist's basic negotiated fee is the minimum payment specific in the Award plus a personal margin. Payment of this amount entitles the producer to Australian theatrical rights.
below the line	cast and crew budgeted costs. It also includes technical and other elements needed to make a film. It's all the budgeted costs except above the line and indirect costs.
best boy/best girl	*aka* **second electrics**; second in charge of the lighting department under the supervision of the gaffer.
billing	the placement and prominence of names and titles on the film. Billing refers particularly to opening credits. Actors, producers, directors, etc., negotiate for particular order of appearance, lettering and time on screen.
biog	*see* **curriculum vitae**

blacking out	*aka* **blacks**; using black drapes to black out light during filming. Most commonly used during daylight hours to create an interior night scene (**day for night**). Blacks can also be used for a limited night shooting during the day.
blockbuster	*see* **hit**
blue sky	the potential for a feature film to make more money than is already guaranteed by pre-sale of distribution agreement.
bomb	a film which is a financial disaster.
bonus	an extra payment over and above that which is contracted. Usually paid to film crew members in gratitude if a project is made for less than its budget.
boom operator	the person who positions the microphone during a take for the optimum sound quality. Supervised by the sound recordist.
boom swinger	*see* **boom operator**
box office gross	*aka* **box office receipts**; the money paid by the general public for admission to the theatre.
box office receipts	*see* **box office gross**
box office star	*see* **bankable star**
breakdown sheet	*aka* **script breakdown**; a form on which various details of a scene are noted. Elements such as brief description of scene, length, cast involved, special requirements, etc. The breakdown sheet is one of the steps to creating the shooting schedule.
breakout picture	*see* **sleeper**
brokerage	a negotiated percentage paid to a person who raises production finance.
bromides	*see* **graphics**
brown paper bag	a bribe
Brylawski Cleary & Komen	the American law firm based in Washington, DC, which specialises in searching titles. Their report will contain recommendations.
budget	*aka* **production budget**; an estimate of total production cost based on many individual calculations.
budget summary	*see* **top sheet**

309

buyout

a reassignment to the producer by a development investor (including state and federal funding agencies) of its interest in a project on repayment of the development investment and payment of any agreed premium or interest. These agencies will acquire an interest in the copyright of the script and underlying work as a security interest during development.

buzz

see **word-of-mouth**

buzz track

see **atmosphere**

B-wind

see **A-wind**: the opposite situation applies

cable television

1) transmission of television broadcast for home receiving by cable rather than by broadcast air waves;

2) a subscriber TV system which provides programming, for a set monthly payment, not available on free television. *See also* **pay television**

call

a directive to cast and crew to report for work at a specific time and place.

call sheet

a written notice of future intent. Issued daily, it details the next day's shoot. It contains such information as call time, scenes to be filmed and other specific details.

camera operator

the person who, under the supervision of the director of photography, operates the camera. He/she will be responsible for the exact framing of each shot, focus, etc.

camera original

see **unexposed film stock**

camera report

see **camera sheet**

camera sheet

aka **dope sheet**; **camera report**; a list of takes recorded by the camera department. Laboratories will print the takes circled.

camera speed

the speed at which film passes through the camera. For the cinema it is usually 24 frames per second and for television 25 frames per second. Camera speed can be varied for fast or slow motion.

campaign

1) the marketing plan which combines research, publicity and advertising to maximise returns;

2) the advertising strategy designed to promote a product or service. It may include print advertising, TV commercial, radio, etc.

capital gains tax   tax paid on the increased value of capital items when sold or transferred.

caption   *aka* **subtitle**; title, descriptive text or translation placed between shots or superimposed on them.

carnet   a licence by a foreign government usually through their customs department to import equipment etc. for a shoot. Cash deposits are sometimes required. It is a temporary licence only and what comes in must go out.

carpenter   *aka* **chippy**; part the construction crew. Supervised by the construction manager.

cash book   a written record of cash received and paid out.

cash float   *see* **float**

cash flow   a prediction of monetary requirements usually divided into weeks. A time-based plan for the expenditure of the budget,

cast   1) *verb*: to select artists;

2) *noun*: generic word for all the people who appear on screen.

casting consultancy   a business which acts as adviser, casting director and negotiator for film producers. Casting consultancies are free from bias or influence from individual artists and can act in the best interests of the producer.

casting cover   *see* **film producer's indemnity**

casting director   *aka* **casting consultant**; the person who organises the casting function. He/she will arrange interviews and auditions, sometimes negotiate fees. The casting director will work closely with producer and director.

censorship rating   *aka* **cinema classification**; **rating**; the classification of films, TV programs and videos indicating their suitability for particular audiences. Conditions and public taste vary from country to country.

certification   obtaining a certificate from the Department of Communications and the Arts (DCA) that a film is a 'qualifying Australian film'. Certification by DCA is a pre-condition to securing funding from the FFC. Prior to commencement of production, DCA will issue a provisional certificate under Division 10BA of the *Income Tax Assessment Act*. DCA issues certificates for eligible films that are either to be made wholly or substantially in Australia, with significant Australian content, or are official co-

311

productions made under a treaty or similar arrangement and which are 'eligible' films, i.e., features, mini-series and documentaries. After a film is finished a producer must apply to DCA for a final certificate.

chain of title	the set of documentation that establishes the producer's ownership of the copyright in the script (and novel or stage play, if relevant) which entitles the producer to make and market the film. The chain of title documents will typically include scriptwriters' agreements, development agreements with funding agencies, and options or rights assignments.
character	the scripted role played by an actor.
character generator	*aka* **Chyron** (brand); **Aston** (brand); electronic machinery that produces lettering for use as identification, titles, captions, etc.
chart of accounts	that group of accounting records which makes up all the accounts.
cherry picker	a crane mounted on a truck. It is designed to reach street lights, etc. It has been borrowed by the film industry as a lighting tower or camera platform and sometimes even a crane for the art department.
chippy	*see* **carpenter**
choreographer	*aka* **dance director**; the person who creates the dance and movement and who supervises rehearsal and shoot. The film director decides on camera angle, etc.
Chyron	*see* **character generator**
cinema	a useful word to avoid confusion with the use of 'theatre'.
cinema classification	*see* **censorship rating**
cinema film	*see* **feature film**
cinematographer	*see* **director of photography**
circled take	*see* **print take**
clapper board	*see* **slate**
clapper/loader	*aka* **clapper boy/girl**; the person in the camera department who operated the slate or clapper for sync sound. He/she also loads and unloads magazines of film. Supervised by the director of photography.
clap sticks	*see* **slate**

312

clear spacing	*see* **junk spacing**
client	the person who is directly in contact with or who is the liaison between advertising agency or sponsor and the producer. Clients commission advertising agencies who in turn commission production companies to make commercials.
co-feature	*see* **double billing**
colour original	*see* **processed original**
combined print	*see* **composite print**
combo engagement	*see* **double billing**
commerical breaks	pre-planned breaks in the television program. Television stations advise producers of the number and placement of commercial breaks. Segments are designed to work in with them.
common law	the unwritten law based on custom or court decision.
company	*see* **public company; proprietary company**
company tax	tax payable on the profits of companies.
completion guarantee	*aka* **completion bond**; the guarantee to the investors that the film will be completed as per the script and by a certain date. Bonding companies charge approximately 6 per cent of budget and will provide funding to finish the film under most circumstances if required.
completion guarantee rebate	a rebate of the fee paid for the completion guarantee. The percentage of rebate is negotiated in pre-production. After the guarantor is released from the contract the rebate is sent to the producer. Disposal of the money is also predetermined and the producer usually receives a percentage.
composer	the person who writes an original score specifically for the film.
composite optical print	a married print which contains both image and optical sound track on the same piece of film.
composite print	aka **married print; combined print**; a film which contains both image and sound on one print.
concept	*aka* **idea; premise**; a one-page teaser which is designed to attract interest.
conforming	*see* **negative matching**
construction manager	*aka* **construction foreman**; the person in charge of the construction crew. Under the supervision of the production designer.

313

contact work print	*see* **cutting copy**
contingency	a percentage of budget, usually 10 per cent, added on to the end of a budget. It allows for unforeseen expenses and costs.
continuity	*aka* **script person**; **script supervisor**; **continuity clerk**; a crew member whose job is to notate every aspect of a take so that it conforms to the final edited sequence. Continuity will record camera angle, length, cast action, exact dialogue etc., so that takes designed to be cut on either side will match.
continuity sheet	a record of detailed information for each take in a film, e.g. dialogue, camera angle, etc.
contract	an agreement between two or more parties which is enforceable at law. A contract may be written or verbal.
contra deal	any arrangement which benefits the film production and the person or company offering it. Usually the producer offers a credit or product placement in the film in exchange for goods or services offered free or at a discount. Cash is not normally involved.
coproducer	it could mean what it implies or it could mean anything. It seems to be between the credit of **line producer** and **producer**. It may mean shared producer responsibility.
coproduction	two production entities sharing creative control and financial contributions to make one film.
coproduction treaties	government-to-government agreements which benefit both. production entities. They offer each party government subsidies and benefits as though the film were made entirely in either country.
copyright	the statutory protection under law to the owner of a work. The *Copyright Act* defines it as an 'exclusive right to do certain acts relating to dramatic, literary, musical and artistic works, sound recordings, television or sound broadcasts, cinematograph films and published editions'. Those acts include reproduction, publication, performance, broadcasting, transmitting or adapting the relevant work.
copyright owner	the author of the work is usually the copyright owner. Where a person makes a film pursuant to an agreement that person is, unless there is an agreement to the contrary, the owner of the copyright.

corporate video	programs produced on video tape for sponsors or clients.
cost report	an analysis of expenditure to date and cost to complete the film. Usually compiled weekly, it monitors cost and compares it to the production budget top sheet.
costume designer	under the creative and administrative guidance of the production designer, he or she will design, adapt, hire or purchase off the rack suitable clothing for the actors.
creative accounting	when the box office dollar makes its way cautiously back to the investors it has to pass through a nasty part of tinsel town. Not only do exhibitors and distributors have their way legally with the box office dollar, but creative accounting leaves it a shadow of its former self. Eight cents will probably make it home.
creative director	the executive in an advertising agency who designs and executes the whole campaign. He or she will use the various media to promote and sell products.
credit line	*see* **line of credit**
credits	*aka* **screen credits**; **titles**; a list of cast, crew and any contributors to the production. Credits generally appear at the beginning and end of a film.
cross-collateralisation	the laying off of risk by the distributor when he/she has guaranteed an advance to the producer. The distributor may want rights to cinema, television and video in specific territories before agreeing to a cash advance or even a cinema release. Losses in one market are balanced against profits in another.
cross plot	a cast and shooting day plan designed for easy reference. A performer's scheduled days will be noted against the days of work.
crowd	*see* **extra**
curriculum vitae	*aka* **biog**; **CV**; **resumé**; synopsis of a person's career, academic history and other relevant information.
cutting copy	*aka* **contact work print**; **cutting print**; **work print**; a positive print of the film used solely for the editing process.
CV	*see* **curriculum vitae**
DA	*see* **distribution advance**
dailies	*see* **rushes**

315

daily artist's voucher a clearance by the assistant director that an artist has performed work and can be released and paid. It is also a release by the artist to the production company for their appearance in the film.

daily progress report *aka* **production report**; **production progress report**; a detailed record of a day's shooting. It lists elements like hours of work, accidents, equipment usage, etc.

dance director *see* **choreographer**

DAT digital audio tape

date release the official opening date for a film at the cinema. The major opening. Previews, etc., are not regarded as the main opening.

day for night (D/N) shooting in daylight in such a way as to simulate night. Filters and stopped down lenses are used.

daybill its purpose is the same as a poster. The art work is similar. It is half the size of a cut-down-the-middle poster. *See also* **poster**

DCA the Department of Communications and the Arts: the federal government department with responsibility for film, including the FFC. DCA issues provisional and final certificates for film and television projects.

deal an agreement between two or more parties.

dealer's licence a permit to deal in securities, usually related to raising money from the general public.

debt financing the loan of money for film production. The bank or lending body will charge interest and demand the eventual return of money lent.

defamation to unlawfully damage the reputation of another. You have two actions:
 – *slander*: spoken defamation;
 – *libel*: written defamation.

deferment *aka* **deferral**; a fee or part of a fee owed to individuals or companies payable from revenue generated from sales of the film. Usually paid before profit distribution.

delivery date the release print's delivery date; the date on which the producer hands over the film to the distributor.

delivery items

tangible requirements supplied by the producer to the distributor so that the exhibitors and publisists can get the film to its audience, e.g., dupe neg, publicity stills, trailer, press kit.

demo memo

any written record of a contract and terms. It is the brief notes used to draw up legal contracts.

depreciation

wear and tear and out-of-dateness of a capital item. The taxation department allows a percentage of purchase price per year as a deduction.

development

the period of time it takes to get a film funded and into production. Acquiring various rights, writing the screenplay, raising the budget money, etc.

DG

distribution guarantee

dialogue

voice-over, soliloquy or exchange with other characters.

dialogue coach

a person who prepares actors in rehearsal. Useful for children or accent perfection. The dialogue coach will work to the film director's requirements.

dialogue tracks

the reels of sound tracks which contain sprocketed sound film and junk spacing used in the sound mix.

digital effects generator

aka **Mirage** (brand); **Ado** (brand); video computer-generated effects, usually made during the on-line process.

digital sound

a sound system which uses a series of numbers to produce sound. It eliminates problems such as tape hiss.

digital U-matic cassette

a $1/2$" video cassette used for pulse code modulation sound recording.

direct film

see **non-camera film**

director

the person who turns the written word of the screenplay into a moving picture. They say things like 'action' and 'cut'. The director's role is normally carried into editing.

director of photography

aka **DOP; lighting cameraman/camerawoman; cinematographer;** the person who is in charge of the camera department, lighting and grips departments. Also the person who artistically works to achieve a style and composition to suit the film being made. He/she works closely with the director.

director's cut

the fine cut version of the film as approved by the director

disclaimer	1) a statement which clearly informs the reader that a document is not an invitation to invest or an offer to the public. It serves to underline the fact that the document is not a prospectus; 2) a clause which protects the filmmaker from legal action.
disc music	*see* **library music**
discounting	raising a loan secured against a distribution agreement or pre-sale contract.
distribution advance	*aka* **DA**; an amount paid by a distributor to a producer in advance of and on account of the producer's share of revenues from the exploitation of the distribution rights granted to the distributor. The advance is generally recoupable, subject to negotiation of a more favourable split, from all revenues after payment of commissions and costs of marketing.
distribution expenses	*aka* **distribution fees**; the costs of making advertising and publicity materials, trailers, advertisements, press, TV etc., prints of the film, censorship fees, captioning, freight and insurance, etc.
distribution	a sum of money negotiated between distributor and producer to be paid on specific dates, usually on delivery of the first release print. This pre-sale may be subject to distribution fees and expenses.
distributor	the wholesaler of the film. Distributors contract with exhibitors to release films for negotiated prices and percentages of profit. Distributors arrange advertising campaigns, print requirements, etc.
distributor's gross	depending on the contract with the producer, it is the money received by the distributor from various sources, generally money from the various exhibitors, TV sales and possibly merchandising. The meaning of the word varies with each situation. *See also* **gross receipts**
docu-drama	a program which is all dramatised. The whole film is scripted and played by actors. It is based on a true event or person and is often shot in a documentary style.
Dolby	a patented noise-reduction system.
domestic market	the home market
dope sheet	*see* **camera sheet**

double *aka* **stunt double**; an actor who replaces another where a shot is dangerous or the set-up allows the substitution. The double is photographed so that he/she is not recognisable as a double.

double billing *aka* **co-feature**; **combo engagement**; **double feature;** two or more feature films playing at the same theatre at the same session for the one admission price.

double head screening *aka* **double system projection**; during the post-production process the image and sound components are separated for ease of editing. Screenings before the completion of production are therefore arranged by using an editing machine or projector which will lock the two elements together synchronously.

draft *see* **first, second, third draft**

dramatic work the written form of the creator's intention, e.g. film script, play choreography in the written form.

dramatised documentary a program which has fully dramatised segments in it but is not totally dramatised like a **docu-drama**.

dresser a person who assists cast to put on and take off costumes. Under the supervision of the wardrobe department.

dub 1) to make a copy from a video tape;

2) to revoice an actor;

3) to create the sound track during post-production;

4) to change a film's language to another by the use of actors' voices. *See also* **postsynch**

dubbing copy *see* **slash dupe**

dubbing editor *aka* **sound editor**; **track layer**; **sound cutter**; the person who edits sound to the film during post-production. For instance, dialogue may need to be post-synched or revoiced, sound effects created, music made available for the final mix.

dupe *aka* **duplicate**; make a copy of a film.

edge numberer the person who writes numbers by hand or operated the machine which prints consecutive edge numbers on the sound and image of the rushes. He/she is part of the editing department. Edge numbering can also be a lab service.

editor *aka* **film editor**; the person who creatively chooses the filmed material to best suit the script. In post-production the editor works with the director and producer to achieve the highest artistic standards.

EDL   edit decision list

effects   *see* **FX**

elbow   *see* **rissole**

electrician   *aka* **sparks**; **juicer**; crew member who sets, adjusts and strikes lights. Supervised by the gaffer.

elements   those ingredients which make the film proposal attractive to investors, e.g., a box office star, a bankable director, etc.

end credits   *see* **end titles**

end slate   *aka* **tail slate**; **upside-down slate**; the slate used at the end of a take to assist with sync. It displayed upside down. Sometimes it is difficult to slate the start of a take and so the end slate solves that problem.

end titles   *aka* **end credits**; a list of people and facilities involved in the film's production, which is shown at the end of the film.

English-speaking territories   those geographic areas which do not need foreign or dubbed versions of the film, e.g., US, UK.

entertainment lawyer   a lawyer who specialises in the entertainment industry. They can be rather entertaining as well.

episode   a part of a whole work; a segment of a mini-series, series or serial. An episode will stand on its own but is designed to be part of an overall concept.

equity finance   investment in the film's production in exchange for a percentage of the ownership of the film. Investors contribute money in expectation of returns and profit.

errors & omissions insurance   *aka* **motion picture producer's liability**; an insurance cover to indemnify the production company against suits brought in respect of libel, slander, defamation, plagiarism, breach of copyright, invasion of privacy or theft of rights.

executive in charge of production   a title which implies closeness to the **executive producer** level. The title you have when everyone else has taken all the other titles.

executive producer   usually the person who has arranged finance for the film. The title is also used for star's agents, people who find pre-sales – anyone really.

exhibition   showing a feature film in the cinema; the act of selling sessions to the public.

exhibitor   the person who retails films to the general public; the point of sale merchant.

expendables   items which are used up during production, e.g., lamps for lighting, gaffer tape, etc.

exploitation   1) a marketing ploy to promote a specific aspect of a film by using gimmicks, e.g., stunts, parades, anything, to bring the film to the public attention;

2) the maximisation of returns from a film.

exploitation film   a feature film whose plot is salacious or violent; subjects include rock'n'roll, horror, bikies, teen sex comedies.

exposed film   *aka* **exposed stock**; **undeveloped film**; film which has been exposed to light through a camera but has not been processed at a laboratory.

expression of interest   better than a 'no'; an unwitten verbal indication of interest in a film. Don't try to cash it.

extended treatment   *see* **treatment**

extra   *aka* **crowd, supernumerary**; **walk-on extra**; an artist who appears in the background or with a group of other cast in a crowd; a non-speaking role except as part of a group.

extra expense   an insurance which provides adequate financial compensation of increased costs incurred due to loss or damage to facilities, equipment or art department items.

F64   a very bright person

FACTS   Federation of Australian Commercial Television Stations

feature article   a reasonably wordy newspaper or magazine report of the film; usually with one or two still photographs.

feature film   *aka* **cinema film**; **theatrical film**; **motion picture**; **movie**; a film of approximately 90 minutes, designed principally for screening to the public in a cinema. There is no restriction on subject matter.

FFC	Film Finance Corporation
film clip	a short piece of the finished film given to a TV program as part of the campaign. Film clips are run with interviews and critics' comments.
film editor	*see* **editor**
Film Exemption Scheme	an alternative system which allows a simpler form of prospectus to be issued for raising money from the public.
film producer's indemnity	*aka* **cast cover**; **FPI**; an insurance which provides adequate financial compensation for increased costs due to death, injury or illness of nominated personnel. Normally the director and leading cast are insured.
film rental	*aka* **gross film rental**; it usually means monies received by the distributor from the exhibitor. The exhibitor would have retained house nut and his/her share of profits. The term is defined differently from contract to contract.
film rights	the rights which the owner of copyright in a film possesses, e.g., the right to reproduce, broadcast in public and to sell or otherwise deal with those rights.
film to tape	*see* **film to video transfer**
film to video transfer	*aka* **film to tape**; **telecine transfer**; a transfer from film to video format.
film vault	storage place for the film's essential elements. Vaults allow authorised access as required. Films, tapes and paperwork are stored for safety.
Final Certificate	confirmation by Department of Communications and the Arts that a film on completion is still an eligible film for tax concessions under the provisions of the *Income Tax Assessment Act* and that investors can benefit by it.
final cut	the locked off edit of the image, after all approvals have been sought from producer, distributor, etc.
fine cut	the completed edit of the image of the film; the last stage before **final cut**.
final draft	*aka* **shooting script**; the last draft of the screenplay approved by those who are contracted to do so. The draft of the script which becomes the blueprint for the final budget and shooting schedule. A film script may have any number of drafts.

fine grain stock	aspecial intermediate film stock used to make internegs or interpositives.
final mix	the combination of various sound tracks balanced for best effect. Dialogue, atmospheres, sound effects, music, etc., are mixed together onto one track.
first answer print	*see* **answer print**
first assistant director	the person who organises the crew to the best advantage for filming. They say things like 'quiet please' and 'turn over'. He/she will act as floor manager or stage manager and efficiently draw together the necessary elements for shooting. First assistant directors usually design and control the shooting schedule and generally liaise between the production office and the set.
first draft	the first full script written from the treatment and other source material. It contains all the dialogue, characters, locations and full plot and resolution.
first print	*see* **answer print**
fix it in the mix	*see* **we'll fix it in the mix**
float	an advance of cash given to various crew members to allow them to make purchases or other cash transactions.
flyer	*see* **handbill**
focus puller	the person who works closely with the camera operator to achieve maximum effect during the shooting. He/she will adjust focus and aperture during the shoot and attend to various technical requirements of the camera.
foley	postsynch effects which simulate those made by human beings, e.g., dancing, fighting, breathing. It is normally produced by screening the section of film and recording the effect as it is made.
format	the width of video tape, e.g. $\frac{1}{2}$", 1".
four-walling	a method of distribution in which a film is released without profit share mechanisms by exhibitors. A negotiated price for the cinema is set and all other costs, e.g., prints and advertising, are met by the producer or distributor.
FPI	*see* **film producer's indemnity**
FPS	frames per second

free television	the broadcast of a program over the television system which does not require the viewer to pay any fee.
fringe benefits tax	a tax payable by employers on the value of non-wage benefits given to employees.
FX	short for 'effects':

1) sound FX – the sound component which is neither music nor dialogue, e.g., wind, door slam, breaking glass;

2) special FX – visual set-ups for the camera; they may be explosions, trick devices, floods, etc.

gaffer	the chief electrician. Under the supervision of the director of photography, he/she will arrange lighting as required.
gaffer tape	any strong adhesive tape which will hold something in place for the length of the shot. A couple of strips will stick a small person to the ceiling, temporarily.
gag	*see* **stunt**
gauge	the width of film, e.g., 16 mm, 35 mm, 70 mm
generator	*aka* **genny**, **Jenny**; a mobile power source used on location.
generator operator	the person in charge of operating the generator
genny	*see* **generator**
genre	a way of describing or grouping films, e.g. westerns, comedies, animated films.
glitch	a minor technical malfunction.
gofer	*see* **unit runner**
goose	1) increase – e.g., goose up the sound, light;

2) camera truck;

3) a foolish or silly person;

4) an unexpected jab in the buttocks.

grading	the laboratory process of improving the prints available from the processed original negative. The grader adjusts the colour and intensity of the film.
grant	money donated for production or marketing which does not have to be repaid.

graphics	*aka* **art work**; **bromides**; materials made for filming titles, supers, etc.
gratuity	a gift, tip or bribe money or goods given to someone for services, etc., to the production.
grease pencil	a writing implement designed for use on non-paper surfaces. The grease pencil allows the editor to mark the film with cues and information.
green mail	claim of plagiarism made to the production company after the release of the film. Financially small claims are usually paid even though the case may seem very dubious.
Green Room	any area set aside for the artists' use; a waiting area where they can relax before being called on set.
grip	the grip works with the **key grip**.
gross film rental	*see* **film rental**
gross receipts	all revenue from sales of a film, including receipts from exploitation of ancillary and other underlying rights, any claims relating to the film and its underlying rights, export marketing grants, export expansion schemes, statutory licences under the *Copyright Act* and interest on the returns account. *See also* **distributor's gross**
group tax	a method of paying tax instalment deductions for wages. At the end of every month the accountant will send a cheque to the taxation department for the total tax collected from cast and crews' wages, under the PAYE system.
guarantee	promise or assurance that whatever is contracted will occur.
hair stylist	*see* **hairdresser**
hairdresser	a crew member who specialises in styling, cutting and tinting the hair of the artists. Wigs are also styled by the hairdresser. He/she is part of the art department.
hair in the gate	*aka* **rabbit (hare) in the gate**; the discovery that a hair, dirt or emulsion filings are in the gate of the camera. The take is usually redone.
handbill	*aka* **herald**; **flyer**; a one- or two-sheet promotion for the film. Usually about A4 size, it is designed to be picked up and removed by potential audiences.
handle	a summary of the commercial elements in the property which will be used for promotion, publicity and advertising.

325

hard top a theatre with a roof; an area which can be darkened and is fitted with a projection system; the alternative to a drive-in theatre.

heads of department people in charge of various departments in the crew, e.g., director of photography, production designer.

Heavens Gate bum the physical and mental condition which sets in after several hours of watching a feature film which seems to have no plot.

heavyweight name *see* **bankable star**

herald *see* **handbill**

hit *aka* **blockbuster**; a huge success. You know when you have one because people you don't know and don't want to know, wave to you and smile. You come into fashion for a short time.

hit song a musical work which makes lots of money and everybody is terribly pleased.

holiday pay an extra payment to employees based on salary or wages. Based on four weeks annual leave, it is $1/12$th of the employee's wage.

hook the premise which triggers the plot.

house nut *aka* **theatre nut**; a negotiated price for the cinema per week without allowing for potential box office gross. It is calculated by estimating the costs for staff wages, cleaning, office supplies, insurance, depreciation, taxes etc.

hyphenate a filmmaker who fulfils more than one function, e.g. producer-director, actor-writer.

ID identification

idea *see* **concept**

illness & injury insurance a sort of paid sick leave for independent contractors. A policy will guarantee a payment if you become ill or incapacitated through work.

income averaging provisions in the *Income Tax Assessment Act* allow for some people in the film industry to spread their income over several financial years. This allows for a more equitable system as income can be very high in one year and very low in the next. Tax is reduced overall.

income projection a forward prediction of returns and profit based on educated guesses. Projections are made to a time scale.

in development	a nice way of saying that you are doing your best and that good times are just around the corner; the period between concept and pre-production.
independent	1) a product not under contract to a studio or large production house;
	2) a cinema which is not part of a major chain.
indirect costs	the financial and legal costs in a budget. It also includes overheads.
interactive video	any video machine which allows the viewer to make decisions on content during the program. A system by which viewers can direct the plot or request more detailed information, e.g., video games, surveys, how-to-do-it programs.
interdupe	*see* **internegative**
interface	the joining up of various computers so that information can pass between them.
internegative	*aka* **interneg**; **interdupe**; a duplicate negative made from an interpositive. It is used to make multiple prints of the film.
interpositive	a positive print made on fine grain stock from the exposed camera original.
interview	the preliminary casting step. An actor will be asked to attend an interview with director and casting consultant for a discussion before a screen test. Not everyone interviewed will be called back for a screen test.
in the can	1) the end of principal photography;
	2) a shot or sequence complete.
in turnaround	*see* **turnaround**
invasion of privacy	infringement by intrusion. Citizens have a right to seclusion and filmmakers have a right to film subjects in the public interest. A fine balance is generally maintained.
investors' representative	the person or company who is empowered to act on behalf of the film's various investors. Duties are defined in the production deed.
invoice	a written list of goods which were delivered to you, stating price and quantities.

Jenny   *see* **generator**

JEST   the Joint Entertainment Superannuation Trust provides a fund for actors and musicians. Production companies pay 3 per cent of actors and musicians' salaries into the fund at the request of the employee. Production companies cannot refuse.

joint venture   a commercial combination in common by way of a contract for the mutual benefit of the parties.

journal   an accounting day book which records all transactions prior to posting the ledger.

journeyman   a person who has learned their craft but has not, as yet, perfected it, e.g., a director who directs well but does not demonstrate flair or brilliance.

Judas pre-sale   the false pre-sale. A pre-sale consisting of two contracts: one document, for investors to see, with a standard pre-sale, the other document, for no one to see, a full release from the pre-sale signed by the producer. The people arranging these pre-sales are killing our industry.

juicer   *see* **electrician**

junket   a way of generating publicity. Members of the press are given an all-expenses paid trip, often on location, in the hope that they will write a favourable report or feature article. Expenses are generally generous.

junk spacing   *aka* **spacing**; 16 mm or 35 mm film stock which has fulfilled its original purpose and is now used to space out the various sound recordings for mixing.

key grip   the chief grip. Under the supervision of the director of photography, he/she will arrange for cranes, dollies, etc., to be in place and operating. The key grip is in charge of anything that holds the camera in place for a shot.

Kine   *aka* **tape to video transfer;** video tape to film transfer.

kiss you out the door   the response of 99 per cent of Hollywood when you seek their interest in your film. Executives in the US film business like to hedge their bets by not committing. They will rarely say 'yes' and never 'no'. You will be charmed and encouraged a lot.

laboratory access letter permission by the production company for another company, usually the distributor, to make prints, etc., from materials held in the laboratory.

lateral thinking	a way of thinking pioneered by Edward de Bono. Problem-solving by the unconventional use of other apparently unrelated ideas. It is the opposite of vertical thinking, which is problem-solving by conventional means.
lay-up	the act of placing sound recordings on tracks or multi-track synchronously together in preparation for the mix.
leader	extra film joined on to the front and end of a film to protect it and to assist in lacing it up on a projector. *See also* **academy leader**
leading characters	principal people in the plot.
ledger	an accounting record of final entry which lists all the accounts.
legs	1) the staying power of a film. After the initial few weeks at the cinema, films which continue strongly are said to have legs';
	2) a camera tripod.
letter of credit	a non-revocable promise of credit in the future.
letter of intent	a written statement by the completion guarantor that he/she intends to provide coverage subject to certain conditions being satisfied.
libel	*see* **defamation**
library footage	*see* **stock shot**
library music	*aka* **disc music**; **mood music**; music made available for non-exclusive use. For set licence fees, producers can use such music in their films.
lightingcameraman/ camerawoman	*see* **director of photography**
line of credit	*aka* **credit line**; an arrangement with a lending institution whereby the producer or financier can borrow up to a specific amount of money. Terms and conditions are negotiated before-hand. The producer draws the money as required like an overdraft facility.
line producer	the person who takes responsibility for the production of the film. Line producers are generally employed just before pre-production and complete their work at the answer print stage.
listed company	*see* **public company**

329

literary work	the written form of the creator's intention, e.g., magazines, novels, newspaper stories, lyrics.
living allowance	*see* **travelling allowance**
loading	an extra payment added on for purchase of rights, special skills, etc.
location	any area, interior or exterior, which is used for filming. Any place which is not specifically designed for filming. An area which is not a sound stage or permanent street set (back lot).
location agreement	the contract between the production company and the owner of the land on which the film is to be shot. Agreements usually state money, time and special conditions and may require council's and tenant's permission as well.
location manager	a person who finds suitable locations for filming. After approval by producer, director, he/she negotiates fees and dates for filming.
location survey	having done the recce and found the perfect locations, it is time to show them to heads of departments and other interested people. A location survey will iron out problems and is a valuable part of the pre-production.
log	a cross-reference in writing which notes edge numbers to time code.
logo	a trademark or symbol.
looping	a short section of film is joined at both ends. An equal length of sound film is also looped. By running these synchronously, you can record and erase each attempt until the post-synch is perfect.
loudhailer	a portable megaphone with a built-in amplifier.
lyricist	a person who writes words for songs.
machinist	a person who makes, repairs, etc., costumes. A sewer who works in the wardrobe department.
made-for-TV movie	a film produced specifically for television broadcast, trying to look like a feature film.
magnetic tape	an iron oxide coating. Sound can be recorded and reproduced from it.
main title	*see* **title**

main unit	the principal film crew. The term is used to differentiate it from the second unit.
mainstream	a film released by a major distribution chain in the expectation of substantial audiences.
majors	MGM/UA, 20th Century Fox, Columbia, Warner Bros, Paramount, Universal, Disney
make-up artist	the person who is expert in applying creams, greasepaint, etc., to the actors to achieve the desired effect. He/she is in the art department.
M&E	*aka* **music & effects track**; a final mix track without dialogue or voice over. It is used as a base for foreign versions of the film.
marine & aviation	an insurance policy which provides compensation for loss of
insurance	or damage to boats and aircraft – normally specific items on specific days.
market	a place where buyers and sellers come together, e.g., MIPTV, American Film Market.
marquee value	a promotional asset. The use of box office stars to attract an audience.
married print	*see* **composite print**
master	a vague term which applies to both film and video tape. The original of the duplicating material.
MCU	medium close up
MEAA	Media, Entertainment & Arts Alliance
mechanical rights	the right to reproduce a musical work in a material form, e.g., making a recording of music for incorporation into a film's sound track.
merchandising	selling goods which are promoted by a film in release. In return the sale and promotion of those goods will publicise the film and increase revenue. Most common forms of merchandising are books and sound recordings. Others are toys, t-shirts, drinking mugs, posters, etc. *See also* **spin-off**
mini-majors	Orion, TriStar, Embassy
mini-series	programs made specifically for television in thirteen or fewer episodes or parts. The episodes have an interlinking relationship which may be narrative, thematic or by format.

331

Mirage	*see* **digital effects**
mix	the combination of various sounds onto one balanced sound track.
mixer	*aka* **sound mixer**; the person who blends the various sound tracks to produce a balanced professional sound mix.
money insurance	an insurance cover to provide compensation for the loss of cash or negotiable instruments.
monitor	high quality television screen
mono	single source sound
mood music	*see* **library music**
moral rights	the right of a copyright owner to accreditation. It also embraces the right to preservation and protection of the creator's original intention.
motion pictures	*see* **feature film**
motion picture producer's liability	*see* **errors & omissions insurance**
Motion Picture Production Awards	the industrial award which applies to most film crew members. It sets out minimum rates of pay, annual leave and working conditions, etc.
motor vehicle comprehensive insurance	an insurance policy which provides compensation for personal or property damage caused by motor vehicle.
movement order	written instructions for cast and crew explaining personnel allocated to vehicles or flights etc., and times of departure.
movie	*see* **feature film**
movie of the week	*aka* **MOW**; a US network program slot. It refers to the movie either specially made for the purpose or a film which is premiering on US network. It is screened in a prime time spot.
MOW	*see* **movie of the week**
multi risks	an insurance which provides adequate financial compensation for loss of or damage to:
	1) props, sets and wardrobe;
	2) camera, lighting and electrical equipment.

multi-track	the recording of more than one sound track onto one tape. Most common is the use of 2" magnetic tape for 24 tracks.
mug	boofhead, cretin, drongo, turkey
music & effects	*see* **M&E**
musical work	the written form of the creator's intention, e.g. music scores, sheet music.
music cue sheets	a complete list of music used in the film. It lists source and publishers etc.
music publisher	a musician's agent, promoting both the musician and his/her work.
mute	*aka* **silent**; a film negative or positive without sound. It is implied that a sound track exists.
negative breakdown	the act of cutting processed original into individual shots and labelling them. This is in preparation of negative matching.
negative conforming	*see* **negative matching**
negative cost	the cost of producing the film. If all is well this is the budgeted cost.
negative cutting	*see* **negative matching**
negative filing	the process which follows negative breakdown. To file individual shots in labelled cans ready for the negative matching stage.
negative film risks	an insurance which provides adequate financial compensation for increased costs incurred due to loss of or damage to the negative, and includes the risks of faulty stock, camera and processing.
negative matching	*aka* **conforming**; **negative conforming**; **negative cutting**; process of cutting original negative to match the cutting copy. An interpositive is then printed from the conformed negative.
negative pick-up	an agreement with the production company and a US studio, which agrees to pay an agreed sum of money on delivery of the release print. This agreement can be discounted at a bank to provide budget funding.
net profit	one of the most important words in your vocabulary. Unfortunately the term means nothing unless it is clearly defined. The method of calculating net profit in the distributor agreement can mean the difference between profit to your investors and you, or loss. Speak at length with your lawyer.

333

network sale
a television sale which involves a fee which gives the network rights to televise the film on a variety of individual stations. Rights would cover a territory or country. Number of runs, etc., would be negotiated.

NG
no good. Generally refers to takes of a shot which for technical or artistic reasons are not useable. Such takes are not printed onto work print by the laboratory.

night for day
shooting at night but lighting a scene as if it were day.

non-camera film
aka **direct film**; a film made without using a camera. This is achieved by exposing film to light under controlled conditions. Film can be scratched, tinted or drawn on.

non-deductibles
budget items which do not qualify for the Division 10BA tax deductions, e.g., underwriting, some legal fees, brokerage, finance and marketing charges, formation of the production company. They are sums which the Australian Tax Office considers are not expended directly on the production of the film. They range from 10 per cent to 20 per cent of total budget.

non theatrical
the secondary distribution market, e.g., schools, libraries, film, clubs, the Forces, airlines, ships.

notices
critical response to a film released in the press and on television.

novelisation
a novel which is based on the plot and characters of finished films, or based on the screenplay.

NTSC
National Television System Committee – 565 lines. A television broadcast standard used in the USA. Devised in the 1950s by the Committee, NTSC2 has been developed since. By the late 1960s it had been adopted by Canada and Japan. It is subject to colour variations and is known as 'never the same colour twice'. *See also* **PAL**

number board
see **slate**

offer document
a short form prospectus specially designed for the film industry under the Film Exemption Scheme.

offer to the public
to invite the general public to subscribe money.

off-line editing
an editing suite designed with two or more video tape recorders interlinked to allow transfers between them. It is a low cost system for editing prior to the on-line process.

offshore production
a film shot partly or fully in Australia using some local cast and mostly local crew. A film fully funded outside Australia

which takes advantage of lower production costs here. A film with overseas creative control usually, but this may vary film to film.

one sheeter	*see* **poster**
on-line	the process which conforms video images to match the edited version. Master videos are made with all titles and effects required. The standard is 1" video.
on-running series	*aka* **open-end series**; a television series which has the potential to continue forever. The concept may allow as many new stories as writers can dream up, e.g. 'A Country Practice', 'Rafferty's Rules'.
open-end series	*see* **on-running series**
optical effects	*see* **opticals**
opticals	*aka* **optical effects**; changes to the image of a film made in the laboratory. Common opticals are fades, dissolves, wipes.
optical sound track	*aka* **optical track**; sound track reproduced on photographic film. Sound can be reproduced by electronic conversion through an amplifier.
optical track	*see* **optical sound track**
option	the purchase of time to develop a property. Producers take out options on any written work for a specific time and fee. This allows them exclusive right to develop and hopefully finance the film. The fee is generally small but non-refundable.
orchestrator	*see* **arranger**
original negative	*see* **processed original**
original screenplay	a screenplay which is not based on any other work. The writer is entitled to a 'written by' credit.
outline	approximately three to ten pages – an expanded synopsis. Outlines show the initial shape and structure, and leading characters.
outright sale	a set price is paid by a distributor for the right to exhibit a film in a particular territory for a specific period. No profit percentages are paid.
overage	in production, a budget over-run. In distribution, the revenue paid by a distributor to a producer in excess of a distribution or guarantee.

335

overhead	A budget item which allows sufficient funds to continue servicing the film after the answer print stage. Producers continue to spend time and money on films to maximise profits for up to 10 years.
overseas travel insurance	an insurance policy which provides compensation for injury to or death of employees during filming assignments overseas.
P&A	expenditure on release prints and advertising – the launch costs of a cinema release.
packaging	the combination of bankable creative elements, e.g., director, writer, star, to induce investment or pre-sale. Theatrical agents in the USA are involved in this area.
PAL	phase alteration line – 625 lines. A television broadcast standard. A modification of the **NTSC** system developed in Germany in 1963. It solves the principal weakness of NTSC. The standard in countries such as Australia, UK and most of Western Europe.
pari passu	a term used to describe investor recoupment. Investors are paid in equal proportion to contributed funds. In most cases deferments and profits are distributed after full recoupment of the budget.
participation	a percentage of the film's net profit. It is negotiated at contract stage, usually paid to producer, director, writer and leading actors.
partnership	a legal document which contains the partnership agreement. Most partnership agreements are contained in a deed, although they may be less formally made.
pay cable	*see* **pay television**
pay or play	a clause in a contract – usually of a star or bankable director – which compels the production company to compensate the person if the deal does not proceed. Cut-off dates and payments are an essential part of the clause. It gives the production company exclusive rights for the time stated.
pay per view	current release feature films made available on television for a fee, e.g. hotels charge their guests approximately $6 per viewing if they watch any one of a choice of films.
PAYE	it stands for 'pay as you earn' and is a method of tax collection. The employer collects the income tax due each payday from the employee's pay, and sends it to the Taxation Department at the end of every month as group tax.

payroll	the listing of cast and crew to be paid, usually weekly, with the gross and net amounts noted.
payroll tax	a tax which varies from state to state but is approximately 6 per cent with a minimum threshold. It is based on the total payroll.
pay television	*aka* **subscription television**; **pay cable**; television services supported by viewers directly. Includes subscription TV, pay cable, e.g., 'Home Box Office', 'Showtime'. *See also* **cable television**
per diems	daily allowances paid to cast and crew to cover the cost of meals and laundry. The fee cannot be less than those listed in the applicable awards.
performance rights	the right to perform in public, broadcast or transmit over a diffusion service, any recording of a musical work.
performer	an artist who is featured generally in a speaking role. It does not include extras, doubles and stand-ins.
personal accident & disability insurance	an insurance cover which is additional to normal requirements, e.g., for hazardous situations, unscheduled flights.
pick-up	1) a scene or shot or sound recording which is made without using the main unit. It may be made during the shoot or in post-production; 2) the decision by a TV network to proceed with a project, usually based on a pilot; 3) to re-shoot a part of a shot.
picture stock	*see* **unexposed film stock**
pilot	a television program made in the hope of a network sale. Pilots are made as tangible evidence of program possibilities. They are used to sell a series or serial concept.
piracy	the unauthorised use of copyrighted material.
plagiarism	the act of passing off someone else's work as one's own.
platform release	a marketing strategy where a film is released initially on a limited number of screens then goes wider as press and word-of-mouth builds.
play back	any pre-recorded dialogue or music played back while shooting takes place. Usually musical sequences are shot this way with the performers miming.

points a percentage of profit in a film. It is a percentage of the producer's profit.

polish minor adjustments to the screenplay by the writer.

poster *aka* **one sheeter**; a single sheet promotion for a film. It is designed to attract audiences and usually has colourful artwork, a quick description of content and various credits. It is normally displayed in theatre foyers. *See also* **day bill**

postponement deferring a cast call to a later time or date. Various penalties apply – *see* the relevant award.

post-production the period of time after the end of principal photography up to the acceptance of the answer print.

post-production script *aka* **release script**; a detailed description of the final film on paper. It notes such details as shot description, camera angle, length, dialogue, music, etc.

post-production supervisor the person who oversees the whole of the post-production schedule. He/she supervises the technical aspects and monitors expenditure.

postsynch *aka* **postsynchronisation**; the technique of recording sound, e.g., dialogue, effects, to the projected image after shooting has taken place. *See also* **dub**

postsynch effects sound effects simulated and recorded after the shoot. Crew or cast synchronise created effects to a projected image.

precursor *aka* **prequel**; the history or events which occurred before a film's storyline. *Wish You Were Here* is the precursor to *Personal Services*.

pre-light before shooting a sequence and the full crew's arrival, it is helpful to pre-set lights. This practice saves valuable time during the shoot. It is particularly useful for sound stage shooting.

premise *see* **concept**

premix the early stages of the final mix. Where there are many sound tracks it is normal practice to mix various tracks together, e.g., the effects track, atmosphere, etc., before the final mix.

pre-production the period of time before the first day of principal photography. Pre-production starts when heads of department commence full-time work, e.g., production manager, production designer, etc.

338 **prequel** *see* **precursor**

pre-sale

a sale of rights in a film secured by the production company before completion of production. A pre-sale may be 'cashflowed' entirely or partly into the production and/or paid entirely or partly on delivery.

press agent

see **publicist**

press cuttings

a collection of printed matter for newspapers and magazines about the film.

press kit

a package of promotional materials given to the press to encourage them to publicise the film. Press kits contain synopses, still photos, biogs, press releases and sometimes scenes from the film on video.

press release

an announcement in writing by the publicist regarding some aspect of the film. Press releases usually have an embargo on them so that their release timing is to the best advantage of the film's promotion.

preview

a screening of the film to help promote it. Previews are arranged for press, the public, the cast and crew, etc.

principal photography

any shooting with the full crew. The period between pre-production and post-production.

principals

the main actors featured in the film.

print take

aka **circled take**; **selected take**; the best take selected from a shot.

private company

see **proprietary company**

private investor

the person or company who provides equity financing for a film project. They risk their investment but receive a share of profits if all goes well.

private sector participation

the FFC's current funding guidelines set out the indicative targets for this participation in different categories of the production slate supported by the FFC. Private sector participation is all funds contributed to a budget other than funds contributed as an equity investment by a state or federal body, e.g., the ABC.

processed original

aka **original negative**; **colour original negative**; the original film which has been exposed to light through a camera and has been processed in the lab.

producer

the person responsible for the film from concept to maximisation of revenue; the person in authority to make artistic and financial decisions; the entrepreneur who causes the film to be made. **339**

producer's cut	if the producer and director cannot agree on a version of the fine cut, then the producer can usually make changes to the director's cut. The existence of a producer's cut implies that a dispute has taken place.
producer's profit	the percentage split of profits to the producer. Investors and producers often split profits 50/50. The producer then shares points with director, writer, lead actors, etc.
producer's secretary	a person with secretarial skills who works principally with the producer.
product	what marketing people call your wonderful work of genius which has just taken you two years of sweat and nurturing to get to release print.
production accountant	the person responsible for accounting for monies spent from the budget. Supervised by the production manager.
production assistant	a person with limited experience who may be an assistant director or any capacity that you specify.
production board	*see* **strip board**
production budget	*see* **budget**
production company	the legal entity which is used for the making of the film.
production co-ordinator	arranges production requirements on a daily basis. A co-ordinator will be closely involved with detail from the schedule and call sheet. Supervised by the production manager.
production designer	*aka* **art director**; person in charge of the design department. He/she will provide creative guidance for the sets, props, wardrobe and overall design and style of the film. The production designer will also be responsible for the design budget.
production manager	*aka* **unit production manager**; second in charge of the production. Executive who supervises administrative, financial and technical details of the filming. Usually employed in pre-production, he/she usually leaves the production a few weeks after the end of shooting.
production office	the production manager's department. The place from where production manager, co-ordinator, accountant and others run the film.
production report	*see* **daily progress report**
production secretary	the secretary to the production office.

production stills   *see* **stills**

production supervisor   a qualified person who oversees several producers or production managers. It could be an upmarket title for a production manager.

product placement   giving various goods and advertising prominence in scenes. It is a form of promotion for specific goods and services. Production budgets get a boost – money, discounts or goods – for such considerations.

profit participation   a share in the net profits

project   one of those helpful words which allows you to write a sentence without using the word 'film' twice.

projection leader   *see* **academy leader**

promo reel   a short promotional version of the film. For a feature it is usually 6 to 10 minutes long. Generally the storyline is used to highlight the most commercial aspects of the film. Used to show distributors and other buyers.

promotion   anything which draws attention to the film and gets bums on seats. A sort of unpaid advertising, but it generally costs some money to arrange.

properties   *see* **props**

property   a literary, musical, dramatic or artistic work, e.g., short story, novel, composed music, library music, set design, costume design, still photograph. A script is a property.

property buyer   *aka* **props buyer**; a member of the art department who is responsible for finding, hiring, borrowing or purchasing props as required.

property master   *aka* **props master**; a member of the art department who is responsible for maintenance, storage and availability of props as required.

proprietary company   *aka* **private company**; a company in which there are restrictions on ownership and to which certain prohibitions apply with respect to requesting the public for money.

props   *aka* **properties**; any inanimate objects used in filming, e.g., cars, guns, cutlery, etc. They do not include wardrobe.

pro rata and pari passu   the expression relates to contributions to a budget and to recoupment of investments, and refers to the percentage of contribution or recoupment (*pro rata*) and contributions or

341

recoupment being made at the same time (*pari passu*) as another party.

prospectus   an authorised invitation for the general public to subscribe for securities in a corporation or proposed corporation. One or a number of films can be funded by use of a prospectus.

prosthetics   the addition of artificial parts of the body, usually human, e.g., artificial eyes, arms, etc.

protagonist   the main character, the hero or heroine, around whom the action takes place. Major opponent is the antagonist.

protection copy   *see* **safety copy**

Provisional Certificate   a document issued by Department of Communications and the Arts to certify that the film is eligible for tax consessions under the provisions of the *Income Tax Assessment Act*. The provisional certificate is based on information supplied to the department by the producer as to creative control and key production elements. *See also* **Final Certificate**

provisional tax   tax paid in advance on income anticipated to be earned in the next financial year. It is calculated by adding 10 per cent to income tax not subject to PAYE tax in the present year.

public company   *aka* **listed company**; any company other than a proprietary company.

public domain   works cease to be copyright after statutory periods of time. A work in the public domain means that anyone can use the work without fee or condition.

public holidays   New Years Day, Australia Day, Good Friday, Easter Saturday, Easter Monday, Anzac Day, Queen's Birthday, Christmas Day, Boxing Day, Labour Day – and additional state-declared public holidays.

public liability   an insurance policy which covers the production company from claims made against it by third parties for acts of negligence resulting in property damage or injury to or death of persons, other than employees of the production company.

publicist   *aka* **press agent**; the person, during the release of a film, who causes as much publicity and promotion as possible around the film.

publicity   all the free advertising that you and the publicist can arrange, beg for, or trick up.

publicity director　　person employed during the marketing stage to co-ordinate all the activities which help to get bums on seats.

pulse code modulation　　the PCM offers a superior sound system to the analog system. Sound levels are converted to a series of binary codes.

pyrotechnics　　explosions, fireworks, etc.

quality control person　　a person employed by a large production house to oversee the technical quality of all film and video tape product.

quit claim　　an agreement to give up interest in property, usually the release of rights and claims thereto.

rabbit in the gate　　*see* **hair in the gate**

rating　　*see* **television ratings**; **censorship ratings**

raw stock　　*see* **unexposed film stock**

readers' reports　　script assessments by professionals.

real estate　　*see* **real property**

real property　　*aka* **real estate**; an area of land including buildings, mineral rights, etc.

recap　　*see* **reprise**

recce　　the search for the perfect location.

recordist　　*see* **sound recordist**

recoupment　　repayment to investors from available returns.

release print　　*aka* **show print**; projection print ready for commercial screening.

release script　　*see* **post-production script**

remake　　a film which is made using the plot and characters or major elements from a previous film, e.g. *The Shiralee, A Town Like Alice.*

repeat fee　　a percentage payment made to performers when a program is televised more than once. Repeat fees can be prepaid.

reprise　　*aka* **recap**; a summary of the last movie or part of a mini-series placed at the front of a film. It informs and updates the audience on the story so far.

re-release　　the re-issue of a film after its original release, e.g., children's films re-run at Christmas time.

343

residual	*see* **secondary usage fee**
restripe	*see* **audio restripe**
resumé	*see* **curriculum vitae**
revisions	*aka* **script amendments**; partial rewrites of the script after issue of the final shooting script. The colour page order is blue, pink, yellow, green, goldenrod and white again.
revoice	replacement of an artist's voice with another actor's voice.
rewrite	significant changes to story, plot, character or setting.
right	a just claim or title, whether prescriptive, moral or legal.
riser	*see* **apple box**
rissole	*aka* **elbow**; to remove or take away something which is reasonably portable, e.g. 'rissole the C stand'. *See also* **strike**
round robin	1) the provision of pre-sales by over-inflating film budgets, e.g., budget to produce the film is really $2 m but a budget of $3 m is raised. $1 m can now be offered to investors as a pre-sale; 2) moving money from one account to another to the advantage of the person moving it.
royalty	the fee which is paid according to sales. It is a negotiated percentage, paid to the owner of copyright.
rushes	*aka* **dailies**; the first screening of a day's work. 'Okay' scenes are synchronised with location sound and screened before editing.
SPAA	Screen Producers' Association of Australia
safety code	a standardised code of behaviour relating to safety on film sets. Agreed to by SPAA, Actors Equity and ATAEA.
safety copy	*aka* **protection copy**; a copy made for protection from negative matched processed original. The laboratory will make an interpositive. From the magnetic final mix and M&E a magnetic copy is made.
safety officer	a person who oversees and controls the safety of the stunt personnel, e.g., makes the stunt as safe as possible, controls fire extinguishing equipment, etc. He/she cannot carry out other duties. The safety officer is overseen by the safety supervisor.
safety report	a written report compiled before principal photography by a

safety consultant. The report lists safety recommendations for each scene and location. Copies go to relevant members of crew, Actors Equity and ATAEA. The producer is ultimately responsible for safety.

safety supervisor a person who oversees and controls the safety for cast and crew, e.g., camera set-ups, dangerous locations, health hazards, stunts, etc. He/she cannot carry out other duties.

SAG rates the minimum rates of pay for performers in the USA. They have been agreed to by the Screen Actors Guild.

sales agent the person licensed by the producer to represent the film. He/she seeks to obtain the highest sale or best conditions possible for the film. They generally charge 10–20 per cent of the sale.

sales tax the tax added to the retail price of goods. Film attracts a tax of 20 per cent on specific budget items.

sales tax exemption items purchased for use in the production of the film do not attract sales tax. An exemption clause on order forms allows the production to purchase goods without paying sales tax.

SAP *see* **stunt action personnel**

scale award minimum. A situation where certain cast members have agreed to work for minimum payments or close to it. The balance of the fees can be deferred.

scene a part of the script with its own scene number. It is not necessarily a whole sequence. A scene usually occurs in the same place and time frame. Each scene will have its own identity. It adds a piece of information about character or plot.

scene by scene breakdown *see* **treatment**

scenic artist the person who paints or tints photographs and murals which are used as backgrounds for filming.

schedule 1) production schedule – time frame for the whole film from concept to market;

2) shooting schedule;

3) post-production schedule.

score 1) written music for voice and instruments;

2) the recorded music track for a film.

scratch print	*see* **slash dupe**
screenplay	*aka* **script**; the complete written form of a dramatic film. It contains dialogue, characters, etc., sufficient for the reader to fully understand the writer's intent.
screen test	*aka* **audition**; an audition conducted with the actor directed to play a few scenes from the script. Usually recorded on $^1/_2$" video tape.
script	*see* **screenplay**
script amendments	*see* **revisions**
script breakdown	*see* **breakdown sheet**
script person/supervisor	*see* **continuity**
script editor	the person who provides support and assistance to the writer. They keep an objective eye on the script, looking, in particular, at structure, character development, character motivation and theme. They act as the audience and provide an overview on the script as it develops.
Secam	a television broadcast standard. Developed in France and adopted by the USSR and Middle Eastern countries. It is a radical departure from **NTSC**.
second assistant director	under the supervision of the first assistant director, the second looks after the cast. He/she also occasionally takes charge of the set and organises the next day's call sheet. Second assistants tend also to be liaison between the set and the production office.
second assistant's daily report	*aka* **actor's time sheet**; a daily record of start and finish times for actors. Details like meal breaks and overtime are noted.
second camera	the addition of another camera to the main unit. Sometimes it is advantageous to film a scene from two angles at once, e.g., stunts, complicated action, long dialogue scene, etc.
second draft	the second version of the screenplay following the first draft. This version should reflect the producer's and director's and script editor's notes. It usually runs close to the desired length. The second draft stage is a way of defining payments for the writer.
second electrics	*see* **best boy**
second unit	an additional and separate film crew to the main unit. A second unit director, camera person and assistant, and assistant director

will occasionally be employed to film sequences which do not require the services of the full shooting crew. It saves time and money.

secondary usage fee *aka* **residual**; a percentage payment made to a performer or crew member as detailed in his/her contract. The fee is payable when a sale is made of the film outside its primary purpose, e.g., a feature film sold to video may pay an extra fee to performers.

seed money development funding

segment a part of the plot between commercial breaks.

selected take *see* **print take**

sequel a film which continues the narrative set in the previous film; the follow-on story.

sequence a series of scenes which relate strongly to form a group. They may be related by location, character or idea. A sequence should be able to stand alone and make sense within its context.

serial a dramatic story, each episode of which is predetermined by the previous episodes and leads on to the next episode. Episodes must be shown consecutively.

series a film which belongs to a group of other films by commonality of theme, character, genre, etc. Each film will stand alone and events will be satisfactorily resolved within each episode.

set the interior or exterior location where the film is being shot

set decorator using the production designer's concept, he/she chooses props, wall coverings, etc.

set dresser the person who carries out the production designer's and set decorator's instructions.

set-up a camera, sound and lighting position to allow a shot or shots to be filmed.

shooting ratio the ratio of film exposed through the camera to film actually used in the final cut of the film. For drama productions this ranges from 10:1 to 15:1. Documentary shooting can require ratios of 20:1 or more.

shooting schedule the written representation of the strip board with other information added, e.g., special notes for wardrobe, special effects, clearer description of the scheme.

347

shooting script	*see* **final draft**
short	*aka* **theatrical short**; films of less than 30 minutes on any subject, e.g., travelogue, drama. The term usually refers to material screened in the first half of a cinema presentation.
short film	a film of less than 50 minutes.
shot	any number of takes from a particular set-up.
shot under protest	*aka* **SUP**; a crew member who feels that his/her advice has not been heeded will request that the slate show 'SUP'. Confucius says, 'Producer who disregards this sign of discontent will live to rue the day'.
show print	*see* **release print**
silent	*see* **mute**
slander	*see* **defamation**
slash dupe	*aka* **dubbing copy**; **scratch print**; a print taken from the cutting copy or matched original negative for use in the sound mix.
slate	*aka* **clapper board**; **clap sticks**; **number board**:
	1) clapper board used to synchronise rushes and identify shots; it is seen at the front or end of every take;
	2) production slate, or slate of projects: a producer's or production house's productions planned, in production, or in release;
	3) the continuous numbering system which differentiates shots.
sleeper	*aka* **breakout picture**; a film that becomes a box office hit when no one expected it to.
sole trader	a person carrying on business on their own, that is, not in partnership or as a company.
sound cutter/editor	*see* **dubbing editor**
sound mixer	*see* **mixer**
sound recordist	*aka* **recordist**; crew member responsible for the recording of sound during the shooting period.
sound report	*see* **sound sheet**
sound sheet	*aka* **sound report**; **sound loc**; a report from the sound recordist listing sound takes and relevant information.

sound track	1) in merchandising, the separate sale of the music used in a film;
	2) the magnetic or optical recording of the mix for a film. It is striped on the side of a release print.
sound transfer	to make a copy of any sound recording.
SPAA	Screen Producers' Association of Australia
spacing	*see* **junk spacing**
sparks	*see* **electrician**
special	*aka* **special event**; a television broadcast which doesn't fit into a station's weekly programming. A one-off program which can't be marketed as a movie.
special effects	*aka* **special FX**; the wide variety of tricks and illusions used in making films.
special effects co-ordinator	person who works with the director to realise the special effects requirements of the script. They will design and maintain special FX and supervise staff.
special effects make-up	any make-up out of the ordinary, e.g., blood, bruises, prosthesis, etc.
special event	*see* **special**
speed	the command given by the sound recordist which confirms that the sound recording is running synchronously with the camera.
spin-off	1) a film inspired by another; a second film made as the result of the success of the first;
	2) in merchandising, the saleable items which increase revenue and assist with publicity and promotion. *See also* **merchandising**
sponsor	1) the person or company who pays for the production of the film; sponsored films are ones which are tailored for a specific purpose;
	2) the person or company pays a premium to the TV station for advertising time and to be billed as the sponsor of a particular program. ('This program is proudly sponsored by...')
spot FX	predominant effects which are essential for the sound mix, e.g.,

349

door slams, gun shots. Spot FX require exact synchronisation.

splice to join two lengths of film together.

squeeze lens *see* **anamorphic lens**

STA the Superannuation Trust of Australia provides a fund for technicians. Production companies pay 3 per cent of the technician's salary into the Fund at the request of the technician. Production companies cannot refuse.

standby props the person on set who provides the props for each take as required.

stand-in an artist who replaces another for the purposes of rehearsal or technical requirements. Such an artist would approximate the stature and height of the artist for whom they are standing in.

star system the use of well-known actors' names to market and promote films.

step development the funding of a film with set cut-off stages. At the completion of each stage, e.g., first draft, final draft, etc., the funding body can decide not to proceed if it wish.

stereo/stereophonic sound soundtrack which is reproduced on two or more speakers. It increases the effect of three-dimensional sound.

stills *aka* **production stills**; still photographs taken during production to assist with the film's promotion. Both colour and black and white are usually shot.

stock shot *aka* **stock footage**; **archival footage**; **library footage**; film taken from another source. Libraries license the use of shots from other films. Used extensively for the establishment of background shots. A series can shoot their own stock shots for use in various episodes, e.g., exterior of commonly used building, etc.

storyboard a set of sketches which represent the director's intention with regard to camera angle, lens size and content of shot. There is no formula or 'best' way. They are a tool designed before the shoot to assist director, production designer and director of photography, etc.

storyline approximately ten to fifteen pages for a feature film. An extended outline. A more detailed explanation of plot dynamics. The characters should be clearly defined and the resolution satisfactorily worked out.

story treatment	*see* **treatment**
strip board	*aka* **production board**; a portable frame designed to hold thin cardboard strips approximately 40 mm long. Each scene in the script is noted by the use of brief description, symbols and numbers. Each strip contains information such as scene number, day or night, characters required, brief description etc. Strips are assembled in shooting day order. Strip boards speed the process of scheduling.
strike	1) to remove or disassemble a set; 2) to rissole a prop.
studio	1) a major or mini-major; 2) a complex where sound stages, back lots and offices are to be found; 3) in television, the studio is the place where programs are taped; 4) term sometimes used for sound stage.
studio deal	a contract with a US studio which usually is structured around a step development deal. The studio pays well but normally holds all creative control and decision-making powers.
study guide	a pack of materials which may include text, posters, photographs, for the further understanding of a film. Study guides are an aid to teachers and students in that they promote discussion and further investigation of the film, what it means and associated areas of interest.
stunt	*aka* **gag**; a potentially dangerous act which requires the supervision or advice of the stunt co-ordinator or safety supervisor. Stunts are generally performed by specially qualified stunt personnel.
stunt actionpersonnel	*aka* **SAP**; trainee stunt personnel who must always be supervised by a stunt co-ordinator. They can provide background simple stunt action. An action extra.
stunt co-ordinator	a co-ordinator assists the director in realising the screenplay. Co-ordinators advise and design stunts, as well as directing stunt personnel.
stunt double	*see* **double**

stunt loading	a negotiated add-on fee for stunt personnel calculated by assessment of the risk factor in a stunt.
stunt performer	an experienced stunt person who can perform stunts as required.
stunt personnel	the industry recognises three gradings:
	1) stunt co-ordinator;
	2) stunt performer;
	3) stunt action personnel (SAP).
subordination	a subordinated investment is one in which one investor recoups on more favourable terms than the others. A 'fully' subordinated investment is one where the favoured investor recoups in priority to any others.
subscription television	*see* **pay television**
subtitle	*see* **caption**
suit	prosecution of claim in law.
SUP	*see* **shot under protest**
superannuation	an amount of money set aside in anticipation of retirement. A provision of further income after paying work ends.
supernumerary	*see* **extra**
Super-16	a method of achieving wide screen format on 16 mm film. A wide gate is fitted to the 16 mm camera to expose the area normally used for the sound track. The quality of 35 mm blow-ups is enhanced by this method.
supervising editor	where several film editors are employed on the one series, then a supervising editor may be employed. He/she would liaise and administer the editing process. He/she would ensure that editors were cutting the programs to a common theme and style.
SVHS	Super VHS
synchronisation	*aka* **sync**; the marrying of sound and image.
synchronisation licence	the right to incorporate a sound recording in the soundtrack of a film
syndication	sale of TV program in the USA to syndicates of independent television stations or individual stations. A sale outside of a US network.

synopsis	a one to three page proposal with brief notes about the plot and main characters.
T&A	anatomical attributes requested by some distributors. Tits and arse.
tail slate	*see* **end slate**
take	a version of a shot. The director will shoot more than one take until he/she is satisfied artistically and technically. A piece of film between camera stops.
talent	the word is still used by some people who make commercials but it is thought to be derogatory. The terms actors, cast or artists are preferred.
tape to film	*see* **Kine**
tax advantage	any financial arrangement which minimises taxation.
tax stamps	a method of paying tax instalment deductions from wages to the Taxation Department. Tax stamps are purchased at the end of every month to the value of the tax deduction.
teaser trailer	*aka* **trailer**; a promotional advertisement designed to be screened in advance of a film's opening date. Usually one to one and a half minutes long.
technicians' agents	an answering service for technicians. A flat monthly fee is charged for all crew listed. The service maintains a diary, informs employers of availability and makes bookings.
telecine	*see* **film to video transfer**
teledrama	a dramatised program specially written and produced for television.
telefeature	*see* **telemovie**
telemovie	*aka* **telefeature**; **telefilm**; **telepix**; a film made specially for television broadcast. Usually approximately 90 minutes long to fit a 2-hour slot with commercials.
teleplay	1) a play written for live theatre which is made into a television program; 2) any program made for TV which is less than 50 minutes.
television ratings	the compilation of a sample of TV viewer preferences extended to show a pattern.

353

television spots	commercials made to promote the film
territory	1) a geographic area, e.g., North America, Australasia. Used for distribution contracts;
	2) also used in 'English-speaking territories', etc.
textless background	where graphics or captions appear, a duplicate of the shot is printed without wording. Normally a requirement for foreign language versions of the film.
theatre	*see* **cinema**
theatre circuit	a chain of theatres owned or controlled by one organisation.
theatre nut	*see* **house nut**
theatrical agents	*see* **actors' agents**
theatrical film	*see* **feature film**
theatrical short	*see* **short**
theatrical trailer	*aka* **trailer**; a promotional tool designed for screening in the cinema to advertise a film which is either coming soon or is in release. It is usually 90 seconds to 3 minutes in length and uses the persuasive style of TV advertisements.
third assistant director	under the supervision of the first assistant director, the third assists the first in any way required.
third draft	a film can have any number of drafts but this is usually merchandising.
tie-in	any commercial enterprise that is connected to a film, usually merchandising.
time code	an electronic time-numbering system on video tapes. The time code can be made visible on the tape by making a special tape transfer.
title	the name of the film. 'Working title' implies that there may be a change to the title in the future.
titles	*see* **credits**
tool allowance	a hire fee for tools supplied by crew.
top sheet	*aka* **budget summary**; the budget summary showing totals for budget categories and total budget cost.
track	1) magnetic sound track synchronised to image, used for the mix;

354

2) a preset path for the dolly.

track layer   *see* **dubbing editor**

trades   *aka* **trade paper/magazine; trade publication**; publications which specialise in the film, TV or video industries, e.g., *Variety, Hollywood Reporter, Encore.*

trade union   *see* **union**

trailer   *see* **teaser trailer; theatrical trailer**

transport manager   crew member in charge of the vehicles. Also purchase, hire and disposal of vehicles. A transport manager would also oversee maintenance and service of vehicles.

travelling allowance   *aka* **living allowance**; a daily allowance paid to cast and crew to cover the cost of accommodation, meals and laundry. The fee paid cannot be less than those listed in the applicable awards and amendments.

travel time   the time expended for a cast or crew member to get from his/her permanent or temporary residence to the location or the production office.

treatment   *aka* **story treatment; scene by scene breakdown; extended treatment**; a full narrative description of the storyline, characters, motivations, etc. Information should be sufficient for a writer to take it to first draft stage.

trust   a legal arrangement for the holding and management of property by one party (called the trustee) for the benefit of another (the beneficiary) or for special purposes.

trial print   *see* **answer print**

trust deed   a legal document which appoints trustees and defines their power.

twinning   domestically oriented projects from separate countries are packaged together to benefit from the individual government assistance offered in each country.

turnaround   *aka* **in turnaround**:

1) a contract clause which allows the writer or producer to take a partially developed property elsewhere at the end of a development stage. This prevents those who funded development initially, from stalling because of their lack of interest;

2) also a property available for further development.

355

U-matic	a ¹/₂" video cassette
underlying rights	the bundle of rights in the copyright of the script (and any novel or stage play on which it is based) acquired by the producer and which includes the right to make and distribute a film or films based on the script, ancillary rights, the right to make a sequel, spin-off or remake and the right to incorporate the relevant music in the soundtrack of the film.
underwriter	a person or company who guarantees the part or full funding of a prospectus or offer document. Underwriting guarantees investors that the film which they have chosen will go into production.
underwriting	a contractual obligation to provide a specified amount by way of investment to meet some or all of the budgeted cost of a film in the event that third party investors cannot be found to contribute that amount.
undeveloped film	*see* **exposed film**
unexposed film stock	*aka* **camera original**; **raw stock**; **picture stock**; film which is in your possession but has not been passed through a camera and exposed to light.
union	*aka* **trade union**; **trades union**; an association of employees who join together for mutual benefit. Unions are registered to represent different groups of people within the film industry.
union representative	*aka* **union rep**; a person elected to express the point of view of the group and to act as liaison for the union. Sometimes cast and crew elect union representatives on a particular film shoot.
unit manager	the person who arranges for the smooth operation of the day's shoot on location. Some of his/her duties are organising parking, traffic control, local liaison at the time of the shoot.
unit production manager	*see* **production manager**
unit publicist	the publicist working on the film during the production period.
unit runner	*aka* **gofer**; a person attached to the production office who goes between the office and set with messages, equipment, etc. A specialised courier.
unscheduled flights	any flight not made available to the general public. Special insurance cover is generally required for cast and crew.
upside-down slate	*see* **end slate**

356

US networks	NBC, CBS, ABC
VCR	videocassette recorder
vertical integration	the reduction of film investment risk by owning or controlling the means of production, distribution and exhibition. Companies control a substantial number of films and spread the risk.
video clip	*aka* **video music clip**; a program made to synchronise with an already made sound track or song.
voice over	narration; any spoken dialogue off screen.
walkie-talkie	a two-way communication device. It allows crew members to communicate stylishly.
walk-on extra	*see* **extra**
wardrobe assistant	assists the wardrobe supervisor.
wardrobe designer	person who chooses or designs the costumes.
wardrobe standby	crew member who is on set to look after wardrobe requirements for each take.
wardrobe supervisor	the wardrobe department's manager. Carries out wardrobe designer's intentions. Also oversees wardrobe staff and administration.
watch your back	it's a bit like 'fore' on the golf course. It means 'you appear to be in some kind of danger, and I have warned you'.
weather check	a predetermined method for contacting cast and crew prior to the start of the shot. This allows last minute changes of location, due to the weather, to be made as efficiently as possible.
weather cover	*see* **wet weather cover**
weather insurance	an insurance policy which provides compensation for loss of filming time due to weather conditions.
we'll fix it in the mix	heard on film sets. It means we'll settle for what we've got and nothing can fix it in post-production.
wet weather cover	*aka* **weather cover**; **back up schedule**; a contingency plan to overcome hold-ups to the shoot. Weather can interrupt filming and so interior scenes are often substituted so that time is not lost. Cast and sets may need to be on stand-by.
wide screen	the projection of the screen image in an aspect ratio greater than 1.85:1. Anamorphic lenses or several projectors may be

used to achieve this. Wider gauge film prints are also used, e.g., 70 mm, Imax.

wide effects sounds recorded for use in the mix. They are recorded non-synchronously.

window the time between a film's release in one medium and its release in another. There is usually a time gap between cinema, television and video releases.

withholding tax a tax paid in one country on an amount remitted from that country to a second country. Applicable to revenue from all sales and calculated on the amount remitted at a standard percentage which varies from country to country and from time to time.

word-of-mouth *aka* **buzz**; thought to be the most valuable publicity for a film – if it's favourable. Word-of-mouth is the reaction expressed by audiences to their friends and colleagues after seeing your wonderful film.

work an artistic creation in material form, e.g., sculpture, film script, novel, music score.

workers' compensation a compulsory insurance cover, which is different in every state of Australia, which provides employees with compensation due to injury or death while working for the production company.

work print *see* **cutting copy**

wrangler an animal handler, sometimes of horses.

wrap 1) the termination of principal photography;

2) the end of a shooting day.

BIBLIOGRAPHY

KEY READING AND REFERENCE SOURCES

Production budgeting and film management, 1995, 2nd ed, Australian Film Commission (AFC)/ Australian Film, Television & Radio School (AFTRS), Sydney.

Actors Equity awards, rate sheets, information manual, as updated, Media and Arts Alliance, Sydney.

Encore directory, Reed Publications, Sydney. Annual

The production book, PB Publishing, Sydney. Annual

Australasian casting directory, Ruse, Havern, NSW. 2 vols. Annual

INTRODUCTION TO FILM MAKING AND THE FILM BUSINESS

Australian film industry: an overview [information sheet], 1994, AFC, Sydney.

Eberts, J and Ilott, T, 1990, *My indecision is final: the rise and fall of Goldcrest Films,* Faber & Faber, London.

Get the picture: essential data on Australian film, television and video, AFC, Sydney. Biennial

Goldman, W, 1983, *Adventures in the screen trade: a personal view of Hollywood and screenwriting*, Warner Books, New York.

Molloy, S and Burgan, B, 1994, *The economics of film and television in Australia*, AFC, Sydney.

Murray, S, ed, 1994, *Australian cinema*, Allen & Unwin, Sydney.

Reid, Mary Anne, 1993, *Long shots to favourites: Australian cinema successes in the 1990s*, AFC, Sydney.

Report of the Moving Pictures Inquiry, 1992, Standing Committee on Environment, Recreation and the Arts, Canberra.

Seger, L and Whetmore, E J, 1994, *From script to screen: the collaborative art of filmmaking*, Holt, New York.

Shand, J and Wellington, T, 1988, *Don't shoot the best boy!: the film crew at work*, Currency Press, Sydney.

Ward, E and Silver, A, 1983, *The film director's team*, Arco, New York.

Wiese, M, 1984, *The independent film and videomakers guide*, 4th ed, The Author, Westport, Connecticut.

PRODUCING

Bronfield, S, 1984, *How to produce a film*, Englewood Cliffs, Prentice-Hall, New Jersey.

Broughton, I, ed, 1986, *Producers on producing: the making of film and television*, McFarland, Jefferson, NC.

Co-productions: A hypothetical exercise in dealmaking, 1 videocassette (VHS) (85 min) sd.col, 1993, AFTRS, Sydney.

Cruthers, J, ed, 1988, *Case studies in independent production*, AFTRS/AFC, Sydney.

Delivery items: a guide for film and video producers, 1989, AFC, Sydney.

Garvy, H, 1985, *Before you shoot: a guide to low budget film production*, Shire Press, Santa Cruz, Ca.

Harcourt, A and others, 1986, *The independent producer: film and television*, Faber & Faber, London.

Harmon, R, 1988, *Film producing: low budget films that sell*, Samuel French, Hollywood.

Houghton, B, 1992, *What a producer does: the art of moviemaking (not the business)*, Silman-James, Los Angeles.

Lazarus, P N, 1992, *The movie producer: a handbook for producing*, St Martin's Press, New York.

Maddox, G, 1992, Independent film and television producers: who's making what and how they're surviving: a report for the Australian Film Commission, [AFC], Sydney.

Schmidt, R, 1988, *Feature filmmaking at used-car prices*, Penguin, New York.

Watson, J, ed, 1990, *Co-production Europe/IPPA, Broadcast, Technicolour*, International Thomson Business Pubs, London.

Producing For Television

Breyer, R and Moller, P, 1984, *Making television programs: a professional approach*, Longman, New York.

Burrows, T D and others, 1989, *Television production: disciplines and techniques*, 4th ed, W C Brown, Dubuque.

Hilliard, R L ed, 1989, *Television station operations and management*, Focal Press, Boston.

Millerson, G, 1990, *The technique of television production*, 12th ed, Focal Press, London.

Lindheim, R D and Blum, R A, 1991, *Inside television producing*, Focal Press, Boston.

Establishing A Business

English, J W, 1992, *How to organise and operate a small business in Australia*, 5th ed, Allen & Unwin, Sydney.

Smart tactics: a directory of business programs for the cultural industries, 1994, Department of Communications and the Arts, Canberra.

Financing

Cones, John W, 1992, *Film finance and distribution: a dictionary of terms*, Silman-James, Los Angeles.

Funding guidelines, 1993, AFC, Sydney.

Levison, L, 1994, *Filmmakers and financing: business plans for independents*, Focal Press, Boston.

Molloy, S and Burgan, B, 1994, *The economics of film and television in Australia*, AFC, Sydney.

Wiese, M, 1991, *Film and video financing*, The Author, Studio City, Ca.

COMMERCIALS

Baldwin, H, 1989, *How to create effective TV commercials,* 2nd ed, NTC Business Books, Lincolnwood, Ill.

Kinkead, J P, 1990, *The biggest commercial in the world!* 1 videocassette (VHS) (30 min) sd, col, Television in Business, United Kingdom.

Schihl, R J, 1992, *Television commercial processes and procedures*, Focal Press, Boston.

Smythe, Mervyn and Associates, 1994, *TV and cinema advertising production in Australia and New Zealand*, AFC, Sydney.

ANIMATION

Culhane, S, 1988, *Animation: from script to screen*, St Martin's Press, New York.

CORPORATE VIDEO

DiZazzo, R, 1990, *Corporate television: a producer's handbook*, Focal Press, Boston.

DOCUMENTARIES

Croton, G, 1986, *From script to screen: documentaries*, BBC Television Training, Borehamwood, Herefordshire.

Marketing documentary programs internationally [information sheet], 1994, AFC, Sydney.

Rosenthal, Alan, 1990, *Writing, directing and producing documentary films*, Carbondale, Southern Illinois University Press, Ill.

LAW AND COPYRIGHT

Armstrong, M, Blakeney, M and Watterson, R, 1988, *Media law in Australia*, 2nd ed, Oxford University Press, Melbourne, 1988.

Australian Conciliation and Arbitration Commission, 1988, *Theatrical Employees Motion Picture Production Award*, as updated.

Barron, M and Cooper, J, 1990, *Australian arts and entertainment law practice manual, Volume 1: film and television*, The Authors, Sydney.

Film and copyright (Australian Copyright Council Bulletin No. 71), 1992, Australian Copyright Council, Sydney.

361

Sayers-Jones, L, 1992, *Law brief: the Australian film and television industry in the nineties: a film lawyer's guide for non-lawyers*, Trade News, Sydney.

Simpson, S and Seeger, C, 1994, *Music business*, Warner/Chappel Music.

BUDGETING

Production budgeting and film management, 1994, AFC/AFTRS, Sydney.

Cruthers, J, ed, 1986, *Preparing budgets: an approach to budgeting for short and low budget feature film on 16mm*, 2nd ed, AFTRS/AFC, Melbourne.

PRODUCTION MANAGEMENT

Bernstein, S, 1994, *Film production*, 2nd ed, Focal Press, Oxford.

Cleve, B, 1994, *Film production management*, Butterworth-Heinemann, Boston.

Gates, R, 1992, *Production management for film and video*, Focal Press, Oxford.

Jarvis, P A, 1993, *Production handbook: a guide to the pitfalls of program making*, Focal Press, Oxford.

Maier, R G, 1994, *Location scouting and management handbook: television, film and still photography*, Focal Press, Boston.

Production budgeting and film management, 1994, AFC/AFTRS, Sydney.

Schihl, R J, 1992, *Studio drama processes and procedures*, Focal Press, Boston.

Singleton, R S, 1994, *Film scheduling, or, how long will it take to shoot your movie*, Lone Eagle, Beverly Hills, Ca.

MARKETING AND DISTRIBUTION

Australian distributors: a list of theatrical, non-theatrical and video distributors [information sheet], 1994, AFC, Sydney.

Field, S, 1989, *Selling a screenplay: the screenwriter's guide to Hollywood*, Delacorte, New York.

International agents for Australian feature films [information sheet], 1994, AFC, Sydney.*International agents for Australian TV programs* [information sheet], AFC, Sydney.

International film and television markets: a guide to AFC marketing [information sheet], 1994, AFC, Sydney.

Mallone, Tony, 1991, *Film distribution down under: a handbook*, Redcarp, Leura.

Marketing short films internationally [information sheet], 1994, AFC, Sydney.

Pham, A and Watson, N, 1993, *The filmmarketing handbook: a practical guide to marketing strategies for independent films*, Media Business School, London.

Rosen, D, 1989, *Off Hollywood: the making and marketing of American independent films*, Grove, New York.

Sherman, E, 1990, *Selling your film: a guide to the contemporary marketplace*, Acrobat, Los Angeles.

Stott, J, 1990, *Marketing and Distribution*, AFTRS/AFC, Sydney.

Wiese, M, 1989, *Film and video marketing*, The Author, Studio City, California.

MULTIMEDIA

Callas, Peter, ed, 1993, *International guide for electronic media art distribution*, AFC, Sydney.

Cardillo, Ben, 1993, *Interactive multimedia: an introduction*, Film Australia, Sydney.

Commerce in content: building Australia's international future in interactive multimedia markets, 1994, Department of Industry, Science and Technology, Canberra.

The Filmmaker and Multimedia: the selected conference papers, October 1993, AFC, Sydney.

Harley, R, ed, 1993, *New media technologies*, AFTRS/AFC, Sydney.

Hayward, P and Wollen, T, eds, 1993, *Future visions: new technologies of the screen*, BFI Pubs, Arts Council of Great Britain, London.

POST-PRODUCTION AND EDITING

Browne, S E, 1993, *Videotape editing: a postproduction primer*, 2nd ed, Focal Press, Oxford.

Dancyger, K, 1993, *The technique of film and video editing*, Focal Press, Boston.

Dmytryk, E, 1984, *On film editing: an introduction to the art of film construction*, Focal Press, Boston.

Murch, Walter, 1992, *In the blink of an eye: a perspective on film editing*, AFTRS, Sydney.

NON-LINEAR EDITING

Ohanian, T A, 1992, *Digital nonlinear editing: new approaches to editing film and video*, Focal Press, Boston.

Sudderman, M, 1994,' Cut to the chase', in *Filmmaker* Vol.3, No.1.

PERIODICALS

Australian:

Cinema Papers

Encore

Media International Australia (formerly *Media Information Australia*)

Multimedia Digest

International:

The Business

Filmmaker

Moving Pictures

Screen Digest

Screen International

Television Business International

TV World

Variety

CONTRIBUTORS

BEN CARDILLO

A graduate of the Australian Film, Television and Radio School in 1979, Ben Cardillo has worked in the Australian film and television industry as a writer, producer and director for more than sixteen years. During that time he has produced hundreds of hours of television, including live, interactive satellite broadcasts. He has also produced and directed many documentaries, television commercials and corporate videos.

His first encounter with personal computers was in 1982, when he undertook a TAFE course *Computers and Programming in Basic*. This course cured him permanently of the desire to write computer programs. However, it did confirm his belief that computers were going to change forever the way we would live, work and play. He has maintained his interest in personal computer technology ever since.

Ben's first opportunity to combine his interest in PCs with film making occurred in 1990 when Film Australia commissioned its first interactive multimedia production, *Roads to Xanadu*, a Level 3 interactive videodisc. He went on to become Film Australia's specialist producer responsible for interactive multimedia and new technologies.

Ben is currently Head of New Media at the ABC in Sydney.

PENNY CARL

Moneypenny Services is a company that was formed by Penny Carl in 1980 to provide a specialist accounting and financial management service for the film and television industry. Before 1980, Penny had more than eight years experience with theatrical and film productions, and so over the last fifteen years has combined this experience together with her formal accounting qualifications (ACANZ) to develop a comprehensive computer program for the industry.

The Moneypenny System, practised by the current staff of 18, who are attached to individual productions as the on-site accountants, provides maximum control and information for the management team as well as taking into account the requirements of current legislation.

In 1989 Penny sold Moneypenny Services to Jane Corden who continues the efficient accounting and budget management service which Penny established. After four years as Head of Business Affairs at the Australian Film, Television and Radio School, Penny was appointed General Manager of the Woollahra Municipal Council in Sydney.

IAN COLLIE

Ian Collie is the Director of the Arts Law Centre of Australia, a position he has held since February 1993.

Prior to the Arts Law Centre, Ian worked as a solicitor in the areas of product liability, medical negligence and general practice. He also worked in the New South Wales Law Reform Commission on the subject of reproductive technology and the law.

JOHN DANIELL

John's experience in the Australian film industry covers 50 years. He was a war correspondent cameraman at the end of the Second World War covering the surrender of the Japanese, and later in the Korean war. After working as a TV news cameraman at Cinesound in the early days of black and white television, he moved into production management. This led to a position as studio manager, followed by a period as general manager of a production house (Ajax Films) that specialised in cinema and TV commercial production, as well as features and TV programs financed from overseas. In the 1970s, John was for seven years Director of Projects at the Australian Film Commission, after which he became General Manager of Hoyts Edgley and was involved with three feature films during the days of 10BA.

In 1989, after four years as Executive Director of the (then) Screen Production Association of Australia, John returned to the arena of commercials production as a freelance film consultant and as the part-time Executive Director of the Commercial Film Production Association. In 1990 John was appointed a Member of the Order of Australia (AM) for his services to the film production industry.

SANDRA GROSS

Sandra Gross is Associate Producer at the Yoram Gross Film Studios in Sydney, handling the business side of the company. A skilled negotiator, Sandra travels the world meeting agents and distributors, and negotiating merchandising contracts. Her successes include record-breaking sales of her films to American buyers.

Born in 1946, Sandra studied graphic design at the Tel Aviv School of Art in Israel. Later she joined the Yoram Gross Film Studios, then the largest animation studio in Israel, as an artist. When the studio moved to Australia in the late 1960s, Sandra and Yoram expanded the company into a major film production house.

Sandra and Yoram have two children: Guy, a composer, and Karen, an artist.

FRANK HEIMANS

Filmography:

1991-95: Producer/Director/Writer/Editor of *Australian Biography*, a series of half-hour television profiles on the lives of notable Australians being produced by Film Australia and screened by SBS.

1990: Producer/Director/Writer/Editor of *Australia Dances*, 86 mins, a celebration of the renaissance of Australian dance. Screened on ABC-TV, Australia, Finalist, American Film & TV Festival, 1991; selected by *Video Danse* Competition, France, 1990.

1989: Co-Producer/Director/Editor of *In Moral Panic*, 1-hr, the first Australian television documentary to take an international perspective on punishment. Screened on ABC-TV, 1989. Finalist, International Film & TV Festival of New York, 1990.

1988: Producer/Writer/Director of *Margaret Mead and Samoa*, 55-min television program on the controversy about Margaret Mead's field work in the 1920s. Pre-sold to the ABC (Australian Broadcasting Corporation) and the Discovery Channel in the USA for screening during 1988.

1987: Co-Producer/Director/Editor of *The Sword and the Flower*, 52-min television program for the series *Warriors* for SBS-TV, Australia. A film about Australians, formerly at war with Japan, who have built bridges of understanding between the two nations.

1986: Co-Producer/Director/Editor of *Paradise Camp*, 56-min TV program about Theresienstadt, the bizarre showcamp established by the Nazis in Czechoslovakia during the Second World War for prominent Jewish artists, musicians and intellectuals. Screened on SBS-TV in Australia 1986. Gold Award, International Film & TV Festival of New York, 1986; selected by Festival dei Popoli, Florence, Italy, 1986; selected by Cork Film Festival, 1987.

1986: Producer/Director of *The Occult Experience*, 95-min film examining shamanism, witchcraft, and demon exorcism in the Western world. Screened on the TEN network in Australia, 1985. Bronze Award, International Film & TV Festival of New York, 1985.

Other films by Frank Heimans include: *Where Death Wears a Smile, Class of '39, Cave of Dreams, The Eleven Powers, Shadow Sister, The Living Goddess, The Elusive Geisha* and *What Have You Done With My Country.*

TOM JEFFREY

Tom Jeffrey's career in the Australian film and television production industry has spanned a period of over 35 years.

Tom first worked for fourteen years with the Australian Broadcasting Commission. During his last three years there, he was producer/director of successful film drama productions including *Pastures Of The Blue Crane*, and episodes of *Delta* and *Dynasty*.

He also worked twice in the United Kingdom and in 1965 was under contract as a film director to BBC Television.

In 1972 Tom turned to independent motion picture production. His credits include *The Removalists, The Odd Angry Shot, Weekend Of Shadows, The Best Of Friends, Fighting Back* and *Going Sane*. He was variously producer, director and writer.

In 1985, Tom took up television production again and over the following four years produced a number of successful programs including *Tarflowers*, a children's TV drama for the acclaimed *Winners* anthology series; *Stock Squad*, a movie of the week for the Channel 9 Network; and *Five Times Dizzy*, the multi-award winning children's drama mini-series.

Tom was appointed Head of Training at the Australian Film, Television and Radio School in 1989, and completed his contract in December 1993.

Throughout his career, Tom has been one of the strongest advocates for the Australian film and television production industry, having been involved at all levels with a wide range of industry organisations for more than 30 years.

He was President of the Producers and Directors Guild of Australia in 1972 and 1973. In 1972 he was consultant to the committee which advised the federal government on the establishment of the Australian Film and Television School. In 1974 he was appointed first a Member, then Chairman, of the Film, Radio and Television Board of the Australia Council. From 1976 until 1981 he was Chairman of the (then) Australian Film and Television School. During 1983 Tom was a member of the NSW government's Commission of Inquiry into the Distribution and Exhibition of Cinematograph Films. In the early 1980s Tom was Convener of the Film Industry Standing Committee, and also served as a Board Member of the Australian Children's Television Foundation. He is currently Chair of Arts Training NSW.

In 1981, Tom was appointed a Member of the Order of Australia (AM) for his services to the Australian film and television industry.

GINNY LOWNDES

Ginny Lowndes has worked as the writer, script editor, script consultant and assessor for the Australian Children's Television Foundation in Melbourne for eighteen months on over two hundred projects.

She worked in the same capacity for the Australian Film Theatre, and her adaptation of a stage play now entitled *Hold Onto Your Hats* went into pre-production as a feature film, at the end of 1986-7. The film, *A Single Life*, which Ginny worked on as a script editor/story consultant has been sold worldwide and was nominated for an AFI award.

Ginny worked as the writer, script editor and story editor on the Logie and Penguin Award winning serial, *Neighbours*, for the Grundy Organisation from 1985 to 1987 (Channels 7 & 10).

She has over 70 hours of television writing credits, an estimated 200 or more hours of story editing credits, and over 200 hours of script editing credits for a variety of productions. Ginny has also worked for *A Country Practice* as a script editor and story consultant.

Ginny's fiction, mainly short stories, has been extensively published and her work has been represented in magazines such as *Playboy, Woman's Day, Nation Review* etc. In 1980, she was awarded the Billy Blue/John Clemenger Short Story Award for *The Mother's Day Special*. Her short stories are included in the following collections: *The Hilton Hotel Collection, Stories of Her Life* and *The Bedside Blue*. Her technical book, *Writing for Television*, is published by Allen & Unwin.

Ginny Lowndes also has credits in radio, theatre, record production and preparing media study guides such as *Bodyline, Fire in the Stone* etc. She also lectures from time to time in film and television.

HAL MCELROY

Hal McElroy is one of Australia's most prolific and commercially successful film and television producers. With his brother, Jim, he made his debut producing Peter Weir's first film, *The Cars That Ate Paris*. This film was the first Australian film to gain international recognition at the Cannes Film Festival in 1974.

Hal produced Peter's next two films, *Picnic at Hanging Rock* and *The Last Wave*, which both became huge critical and box office hits. Following this auspicious start to his producing career, Hal has moved regularly from cinema to television projects, arranging projects with World Vision, CBS, Home Box Office and Turner Network Television.

In 1992 Hal set up a joint venture with Southern Star Entertainment, and in 1994 he released a very successful feature film, *The Sum of Us*, starring Jack Thompson (*Breaker Morant*) and Russell Crowe (*Romper Stomper*), based on David Stevens highly successful Off Broadway gay themed comedy. It won Best Screenplay Adaptation at the AFI and Best Actor (Jack Thompson), Best Support (John Polson) and again Best Adapted Screenplay at the Film Critics Circle of Australia Awards. It was released in North America by the Samuel Goldwyn Company in March 1995.

In the same year, Hal created and acted as Executive Producer for the Seven Network's weekly police drama series, *Blue Heelers*. It became the Number One drama on Australian television in 1994, and winner of The People's Choice Award and the Houston Film Festival.

Hal (in partnership with Concept TV) created another rating winner for the Seven Network, *Amazing*. This is a late afternoon educational strip game show for kids involving computer games, with 130 episodes produced and another 65 to be produced in 1995.

The always busy Hal continues as Executive Producer of *Blue Heelers,* and by the end of 1995 will have nearly 100 episodes completed. Hal has four TV series in development, a television movie package, two mini-series and a feature film.

NEIL McEWIN

Neil McEwin has spent the last 25 years in the insurance industry, the past eighteen years of which he has specialised solely in film and television insurance. He was chief executive of Cinesure until eight years ago when he formed Film Insurance Underwriting Agencies Pty Ltd where he is the Managing Director.

SUSIE MAIZELS

Susie Maizels owns and operates a freelance casting consultancy called Maizels & Associates Pty Ltd. Established in 1975, the consultancy has grown with the industry. It not only casts for Australia nationally but also for the UK, USA, New Zealand and South-east Asia.

Maizels and Associates has been involved in total casting for films, television series and programs, TV commercials, many of which have won awards both in Australia and overseas, and still photography.

Some of the films and television cast are:

TV series and telemovies: *The Last Outlaw, The Love Boat Down Under, Chase Through The Night, Butterfly Island, The Anzacs, The Dismissal, The Harp in the South, The Australian Break, Willessee's Australians, Fire, The Heroes 1 & 2, The River Kings, Poor Man's Orange.*

Films: *Mad Max 1 & 2, Man from Snowy River 1 & 2, Killing of Angel Street, We of the Never Never, The Wild Duck, Playing Beattie Bow, Shame, BMX Bandits, Fortress, Annie's Coming Out, On Our Selection, Bliss, Tudawali.*

369

DAMIEN PARER

Damien Parer is the Manager, Film Development for the South Australian Film Corporation. He plays a pro-active role in the film and video community, seeking out writers, producers and directors and encouraging creative and commercial film and video production. He administers funds for script development, production investment, short and experimental film funding, training and professional development, and cultural organisation funding. Parer manages the operations, annual budget and staff of the Film Development Office.

Damien started his career in the Australian film and television industry in 1965. He joined the Australian Broadcasting Corporation as an Assistant Film Editor, where he worked on such programs as *This Day Tonight, Sportsview, Signpost* and *Weekend Magazine.*

Damien then moved into commercial television as a film editor, working for Channel 9 and Channel 10 in Sydney. He edited *Newsbeat*, TV trailers, and was the Art Director on *Great Temptation.* As a props man he worked on episodes of *Spyforce, Evil Touch* and *Riptide*, and on the feature films, *Sunstruck* and *Don Quixote.*

In 1973 Damien became production manager at Film Australia and worked on a large number of projects including *The Fifth Facade, Travellin' Round* and *When Will The Birds Return, Shadow Dance, Hector & Millie Save Uncle Tom, Maybe Tomorrow, Viewpoint on Adelaide, Viewpoint on Perth, Chorus & Principals on Stage Please*, and the series *Asian Insight*, which took him throughout the Orient. He was Production Manager on dramas such as *No Roses for Michael* and three telefeatures – *A Good Thing Going, Cass* and *Say You Want Me.*

As Producer for the Tasmanian Film Corporation he completed the following programs: *Harry Butler's Tasmania, Land Use and Abuse, The Australian Littering Quest, Habits for Health and Happiness, Life Be In It, Hydatid Control, Mining and our Environment, Glimpses, Workskill Australia, The Automated Mariner, New Land New Life, Impressions of a Colony, Making It* and *Convention Tasmania*, as well as audio-visuals, corporate documentaries and many national commercials.

Damien produced *Slippery Slide*, a teleplay directed by Donald Crombie, starring John Waters and Simon Burke, which was telecast throughout Australia by the Nine Network; *Round the Bend*, a 50-minute drama for television starring Shane Porteous, Penny Downie and Olivia Brown; the telemovie, *Matthew and Son*, a 90-minute drama starring Paul Cronin, Paula Duncan and Darius Perkins for Network Ten; Production Supervisor of *Winners*, eight hours of drama for Network Ten and the Australian Children's Television Foundation which was distributed by ITC Entertainment. He was Co-Producer of the feature film *Dead End Drive-in*, a futuristic action adventure directed by Brian Trenchard-Smith; and Producer of two martial arts feature films – *Day of the Panther* and *Strike of the Panther* - starring John Stanton and Rowena Wallace. Parer also produced the feature film, *Shame*, directed by Steve Jodrell and starring Deborra-Lee Furness, Tony Barry and Simone Buchanan. *Shame* has won a certificate of merit from the Chicago International Film Festival and Deborra-Lee Furness has won Best Actress from the Seattle International Film Festival. *Shame* won the Australian Film Critics Circle Award for Best Screenplay and Best Actress.

He produced a four-hour mini-series for the South Australian Film Corporation, *Grim Pickings*, starring Lorraine Bayly, Max Cullen, Liddy Clark and Catherine Wilkin. The program won Best Adaptation of a Mini-Series from the Australian Writers' Guild.

Damien also produced the feature film, *Father,* starring Max Von Sydow, Carol Drinkwater, Julia Blake (Best Supporting Actress). Australian Film Critics Circle Award for Best Actress of 1990 went to Carol Drinkwater.

Damien was Head of Production for Barron Films Ltd, one of Australia's most consistent and successful producers of quality feature films and television drama. Barron Films has financed and produced various programs including *Shame, Fran, Father, A Waltz Through the Hills, Windrider, Bush Christmas* and *Haydaze.*

In 1991 he produced a mini-series, *Tracks of Glory*, which was shot in Adelaide and Winnipeg. It stars Phil Morris, Cameron Daddo, Robert Vaughn, Nicholas Eadie, Renee Jones, Janet MacLachlan and Joan Sydney, and was directed by Marcus Cole. It has been sold to the US Syndicator Action Media, Paragon International and the Seven Network. *Tracks of Glory* won Logies for most popular mini-series and most popular actor in a mini-series (Cameron Daddo).

Damien also produced *Rough Diamonds,* a feature film starring Jason Donovan, Angie Milliken and Peter Phelps. The romantic comedy is written and directed by Donald Crombie.

Damien has designed and conducted fifteen film and television courses for the Australian Film, Television and Radio School and Film Queensland. His course on pitching and packaging programs is now part of the full time program at the AFTRS.

He edited the first edition of this handbook for producers, *Film Business*, which is now used extensively as a text in Australian universities. He was also Publications Co-ordinator on a Tasmanian Calendar, a promotional booklet, *Hobart and Antarctica,* and an instructional manual, *Planning and Starting a Small Business.*

Damien has worked in the Marketing Branch of the Australian Film Commission. He has attended the American Film Market in Los Angeles and MIP-TV and MIPCOM in Cannes. He has travelled overseas regularly on pre-selling trips to London, New York, Los Angeles, Toronto and Cannes. He represented the Australian Children's Television Foundation selling their series at two markets in Australia.

STEPHEN PEACH

Stephen Peach is a partner of the media, technology and communications law firm, Gilbert & Tobin. He specialises in the area of intellectual property, particularly copyright. He was the author of two substantial submissions to the Copyright Convergence Group on behalf of the Australian record industry and the film industry and many of the recommendations contained in those submissions were subsequently taken up by the Group. He also advises heavily in the areas of licensing, distribution and litigation in both the record industry and the film industry.

KERRY REGAN

Kerry has edited many corporate documentaries, short films, rock clips and commercials. In particular he was the post-production supervisor and editor on: *The Migrant Experience* (documentary series); *A Fortunate Life* (mini-series); *The Great Bookie Robbery* (mini-series);

Butterfly Island (TV Series); *Shame* (feature); *Day of the Panther* (feature); *Strike of the Panther* (feature); *Tudawali* (telefeature); *Spit McPhee* (mini-series); *Willessee's Australians* (mini-series).

LYNDON SAYER-JONES

Graduating at the University of Sydney with Bachelor of Arts and Bachelor of Law degrees, Lyndon commenced practice in Sydney as a solicitor in 1979 in a medium-sized commercial practice with some theatrical work. In early 1984 he became the Corporate Lawyer for the New South Wales Film Corporation. When that organisation was replaced in 1988 by the New South Wales Film and Television Office, Lyndon was appointed Director. He later started his own practice, specialising in entertainment law. He now practices as Lyndon Sayer-Jones & Associates in Sydney.

Lyndon is a well-recognised figure in the Australian film and television industry and has given numerous seminars and written many articles for trade publications.

STEPHEN F SMITH

With over 25 years in the film and television industry, Stephen started his career as a film editor and documentary filmmaker. He arrived in Sydney from the US in the early 1970s where he worked for Network Ten. He returned to the States in 1976 to work as a documentary producer for the CBS affiliate, KPIX, San Francisco. While in San Francisco, Stephen became interested in new technology as it related to the film and television industry. He later became involved in the development of the first computer graphics system for the broadcast industry and managed a post-production facility.

After eight years in San Francisco, Stephen moved back to Sydney to take up a one-year contract with the ABC. In 1985, continuing his interest in technology, he started The Video Paint Brush Company, Sydney. VPB was Australia's first computer graphics design company utilising 3D computer animation, Paintbox graphics, live action and digital compositing with the first Harry system.

In 1992, Stephen with Frame, Set and Match as partners, formed Frameworks and introduced the first digital non-linear editing system to Australia. In three short years Frameworks has grown from 1 Avid to currently 5 Avids, making it the largest and most experienced non-linear facility in Australia. The majority of projects going through Frameworks are 'long form', with numerous documentaries, television series and feature films to their credit.

MARK TURNBULL

Mark Turnbull has worked as a freelance assistant director since 1974. Prior to that he graduated with a Bachelor of Economics degree from La Trobe University. On occasion he has directed and produced. Each project had its own challenges: *Stir*'s brutal prison riot and burning jail, *Star Struck*'s dancing and musical comedy. Locations as diverse as Kakadu in Australia's Northern Territory to New York City for *Croc I and II*, and from productions on the scale of *Burke and Wills* to the intimacy of *High Tide*. His latest credits are as Associate Producer and First Assistant Director on *The Piano*, and First Assistant Director on *Little Women*.

BOB TURNBULL

Bob commenced his career in film and video production in 1958 at HSV-7 as a stagehand/cameraman, moving to ATN-7 in 1962. In 1965 he became a foundation staff member at Channel 10 and established the first videotape commercial production unit. As senior producer/director he directed everything from commercials through news to outside broadcasts and light entertainment.

In 1970 Bob became a partner in Clapperboard Film Productions in Brisbane and in 1975, he became Producer at Maher Shannon Advertising. Two years later he became General Manager of VTC Victoria and then, in 1979, Executive Producer at Fortune Advertising; from 1984, he worked for four years as a freelance producer and director.

In 1988 Bob became Proprietor and Managing Director of Image East, a position he still holds. He was elected President of ITVA in 1988 and has served as a judge on the international panel for global ITVA Awards; in 1993 Australian delegate to the ITVA International Forum.

INDEX

383